Issue | 136

RADICAL *Review*
HISTORY

Revolutionary Positions: Gender and Sexuality in Cuba and Beyond
Issue Editors: Michelle Chase and Isabella Cosse
(with Melina Pappademos and Heidi Tinsman)

REFLECTIONS

Revolutionary Positions

Sexuality and Gender in Cuba and Beyond

Michelle Chase and Isabella Cosse

This issue's publication coincides roughly with the sixtieth anniversary of the Cuban Revolution. Now, as sixty years ago, we find ourselves in a dramatic time for Cuba. The revolutionary generation is fading and the promises of socialism seem to have failed. The market reforms that began in the 1990s have gradually deepened, contributing to the resurgence of gendered and racialized inequalities. The recent decline of the so-called Pink Tide in Latin America and the rise of a more aggressive foreign policy in the United States have put the revolutionary government on the defensive. The utopian promises of the revolution's early years now routinely evoke either nostalgia or disdain. And yet Cuba still provokes heated global debates.

Ever since the revolutionary victory more than a half-century ago, those debates have often centered on Cuba's attempts to reform gender and sexuality. Utopian ideals of the "New Man," emancipated women, and revolutionary love have inspired intense curiosity and scrutiny on an international scale. This widespread influence has long been recognized. And yet the extant scholarship on the global impact of the Cuban Revolution still focuses mainly on diplomatic relations, Cold War military conflicts, or the Cuban-inspired rise of Latin America's armed revolutionary Left.[1] Meanwhile, recent scholarship exploring Cuba's halting transformations of gender, sexuality, or the family has often employed a national framework.[2] The global reverberations of Cuba's transformative aspirations for gender, sexuality, and the family have yet to be fully explored in the literature.[3]

Radical History Review
Issue 136 (January 2020)   DOI 10.1215/01636545-7857211
© 2020 by MARHO: The Radical Historians' Organization, Inc.

This issue of *Radical History Review* centers the sexual and gendered dimensions of Cuba's 1959 revolution—topics now being explored in new historiography on Cuba—but pushes the analysis toward a global scale. The issue asks how these aspects of the revolution were interpreted, debated, appropriated, and reimagined globally. We weave together heretofore-unconnected scholarly and analytical threads to arrive at a new assessment of the Cuban Revolution's complex transnational legacies regarding gender and sexuality. In so doing, the issue yields several fresh insights about the Cuban Revolution, the New Left, and the utopian and transformative spirit of the sixties.

First, the essays here illuminate the range of "revolutionary positions" that Cuba prompted, and which we refer to in the issue's title. Scholarship on the Cuban Revolution's global influence has most often focused on Cuba's direct military interventions or on the New Left's romance with armed insurgency, which Cuba encouraged. Yet this issue views revolutionary positions on gender, sexuality, and family as equally influential, serving as touchstones and central arenas of struggle that helped define the new sensibilities of the Global Left over the course of the next few decades. In line with other recent scholarship, the issue brings "public" debates about revolution, socialism, and decolonization into the same scholarly frame as ostensibly "private" questions of gender and sexuality. Doing so reveals that the debates over gender and sexuality in Latin America, which we often assume emerged first in the Global North, were in fact deployed simultaneously in the Global South, albeit with their own inflections. It also reveals that gender, sexuality, and family were central to Cuba's internationalist politics, not peripheral to them. The issue therefore insists on the centrality of questions of gender and sexuality to the internationalism and global politics of the period.

Second, the issue offers nuanced analyses of the cultural, subjective, and affective dimensions of the revolution and its outward impact. The Cuban Revolution inaugurated new political and military strategies, but also new styles and sensibilities, as embodied by the bearded and fatigue-clad leadership. It nurtured the promise of a New Left, capable of shaking off the rigidity of the Old Left, and was in tune with the dawning global youth rebellion. Focusing on the lived experiences and practices of revolutionary and leftist actors in this period takes us beyond their more programmatic manifestos and communiqués, giving us deeper insight into how the New Left was lived.

Third, by adopting a transnational perspective, this issue seeks to problematize common perceptions of Cuba as static and isolated—an island both literally and metaphorically. Scholarly accounts of Cuba's international relations frequently reduce the country to a mere victim of US aggression or client state of the Soviet Union.[4] Yet the image of revolutionary Cuba that emerges here is of a dynamic country that waged its own diplomacy and influence through cultural forms such as journalism, cinema, music, or poster art; through military and diplomatic missions to other countries in the throes of revolution; and through relationships with other revolutionary leaders. Cuban revolutionaries sought global allies and influence, especially in the Western Hemisphere and Africa, and the connections Cuba prompted involved the circulation of people as well as ideas. Recovering these transnational debates over gender and sexuality—and the concrete effects these had on people's lives—contributes to a fuller historic accounting of the Cuban Revolution's transnational impact and legacy.

Finally, this issue rejects depictions of the revolutionary Left as monolithic. Exploring the conversations and tensions that took place on the Left remind us that the Cuban Revolution's influence was never static or impervious to outside pressure. Among the most important tensions of the period were the revolutionary Left's infamous *machismo* and homophobia and the trenchant critiques these generated. No less important were the different ideas expressed by leaders and others about what revolutionary forms of love, marriage, and family might look like. The Left was also in dialogue with its opponents, responding to conservative forces' rejection and manipulation of the Left's perceived moral transgressions. These tensions and conflicts, which cut across the political landscape, demonstrate that gender and sexuality became crucial terrains of struggle during the Cold War—in the Global South as well as in the Global North.

The issue covers the history of an era with important implications for current political struggles. We contribute to understanding the period in several ways. First, attending to the truly global impact of the Cuban Revolution helps us transcend the limits of area studies, illuminating parallels and connections between Latin American revolutionary movements and decolonization efforts elsewhere in the same period. As discussed above, the Cuban Revolution formed part of a broader landscape of struggles of Third World and anticolonial movements that challenged racial and imperial exploitation. Second, seeing the era's transformative aspirations for gender and sexuality from the perspective of the Cuban Revolution and the debates it generated contributes to histories of the Left, focusing on its relation with the global sexual revolution. This issue argues that personal politics, identity politics, and the politics of gender and sexuality also formed part of revolutionary and leftist projects in the 1960s and beyond, albeit as an arena of conflict. Third, the essays in this issue offer fine-grained sociocultural and political histories that embrace a global scale. This more transnational and interconnected approach to the history of the Left in the Cold War offers new insights, particularly concerning the areas of gender and sexuality.

The issue takes up the challenge of reassessing the history of the Cuban Revolution's outward impact with the conviction that we can learn from this history only by considering its full complexity. The authors included here represent a new generation of scholars who make strenuous attempts to transcend the polarized approaches that often characterized studies of Cuba in the past. This enables them to explore new directions, providing more nuanced analyses. Thus this new wave of scholarship forms part of the first truly post–Cold War historiography on the Cuban Revolution and its global impact. Finally, hoping to contribute to ongoing conversations that extend beyond the US academy, this issue includes scholarly visions from the Global South, including Cuba, in an attempt to decentralize as well as globalize histories of the Cuban Revolution.

The first group of essays, "Internationalism and Solidarity," captures the full range and complexity of Cuba's transnational engagements, decentering standard approaches to Cuban international relations that focus on the United States or the Soviet Union. The essays here offer some of the first social and cultural histories of Cuba's engagement with the Global South or subaltern actors of the north—from military interventions in Angola to civilian internationalism in Nicaragua to public support for the black freedom struggle in the United States—and the ways that gender inflected each of these experiments. These essays demonstrate unequivocally that women took active part in internationalist work; that internationalist campaigns had ramifications for family formation; and that gender, race, and family figured prominently in the symbolism of internationalist campaigns.

Sarah J. Seidman's "Angela Davis in Cuba as Symbol and Subject" provides an in-depth exploration of the encounters between the Cuban Revolution and Angela Davis in the late 1960s and early 1970s. For Davis, the Cuban Revolution provided a powerful example of a socialist state attempting to eradicate long-standing racial and gender inequalities. For Cuba, Davis's status as an African American woman, an anti-imperialist activist, a victim of US governmental repression, and a card-carrying member of the US Communist Party all made her a fitting subject for an intense campaign of support. Seidman shows how Cuba's state propaganda contributed to Davis's growing status as a global icon, challenging US government depictions of her as a dangerous subversive, and how Davis, as a woman, enjoyed certain platforms within Cuba not afforded to the many black radical men who also visited the island. While the encounter between black radicals and the Cuban state has often been told as a story of mutual disillusionment, by focusing on Davis, Seidman shows how the African American freedom struggle and the Cuban Revolution occasionally reinforced one another on a transnational stage.

Lorraine Bayard de Volo's article, "Tactical *Negrificación* and White Femininity: Race, Gender, and Internationalism in Cuba's Angolan Mission," takes an intersectional approach to Cuba's internationalist efforts in Angola in the late 1970s and 1980s, interrogating the racial and gender politics of the campaign's public justification. She finds that the Cuban state selectively employed certain discursive tropes, moving beyond a long-standing "raceless" nationalism to emphasize Cuba's historic African ancestry and its character as a "Latin-African" nation. Yet women—while highlighted in contemporaneous domestic defense campaigns—figured little in the state's discourse on Angola. And when women did figure, they often were depicted as light-skinned. Thus the Angolan campaign involved strategic "blackening" and whitened femininity.

The final article in this section, Emily Snyder's "Internationalizing the Revolutionary Family: Love and Politics in Cuba and Nicaragua, 1979–1990," provides one of the first social histories of Cuba's attempts to support the Nicaraguan Revolution of 1979–90. Snyder explores the way Cuban state discourse promoted ideals of a self-sacrificing internationalist who could transcend ties of love and family obligations. She contrasts this with the messy realities of internationalist practice, which often resulted in divorces, "mixed" Cuban-Nicaraguan marriages, or Cuban children left with grandparents. Snyder argues that these transnational family formations show how Cubans and Nicaraguans created alternative understandings of solidarity and internationalism on the ground.

The section "New Men, New Women" interrogates the way Cuba's idealized constructions of revolutionary subjectivity, gender relations, and sexuality were interpreted transnationally on both the Left and the Right. As these essays show, local actors forged their own creative interpretations of what the Cuban Revolution meant, from the anticommunist movement in Chile to the margins of the Mexican Left. Cuba's example and influence allowed some New Left activists to imagine simultaneously ending capitalism, colonialism, gender inequality, and heteronormativity. It also fueled the mobilization of anticommunist actors, who saw in Cuba an apocalyptic vision of the destruction of the family and femininity. Thus the Cuban Revolution became an essential factor in the formation of political subjectivities in the 1960s and 1970s, especially in the Western Hemisphere.

Robert Franco's article "Transgressing Che: Irina Layevska Echeverría Gaitán, Disability Politics, and Transgendering the New Man in Mexico, 1964–2001" takes a biographical approach, exploring how one Mexican transgender and disability rights activist pushed Che's concept of the "New Man" far beyond its original conceptualization. Echeverría Gaitán viewed the New Man as an aspirational but gender-neutral identity that could encompass and give meaning to sexual minorities and those with disabilities. In contradistinction to recent scholarship on Cuba, which emphasizes the more restrictive and disciplinary aspects of the New Man, Franco's exploration of the concept in a transnational frame stresses its plasticity and sustained potential for human liberation.

Chelsea Schields's "Insurgent Intimacies: Sex, Socialism, and Black Power in the Dutch Atlantic" de-centers the Global North in our understanding of the history of sexual liberation. She shows that in the late 1960s and early 1970s radical youth in the Dutch Antilles drew on contemporary movements, including the Cuban Revolution and the black freedom struggle in the United States, to simultaneously demand sexual revolution, racial equality, and decolonization. In a surprising counterpoint to the revolutionary masculinity embraced by New Left militants elsewhere, Schields contends that Antilleans pioneered an intersectional interpretation of sexual revolution.

This section concludes with Marcelo Casals's essay, "'Chilean! Is This How You Want to See Your Daughter?' The Cuban Revolution and Representations of Gender and Family during Chile's 1964 Anti-Communist 'Campaign of Terror.'" Casals offers an important intervention by examining the interplay between Left and Right in the 1960s, and the important role that Cuban women's perceived politicization and militarization played in the elaboration of the anticommunist imaginary in Chile and beyond.

The sections "Cultural Diplomacy and Mass Media" and Curated Spaces examine film, music, and the media as important spaces in which meanings were attributed to the Cuban Revolution. As the essays here show, Cuban leaders, cultural figures, and cultural institutions consciously operated on a transnational stage, informing global audiences about the transformations to gender and sexuality purportedly taking place within Cuba during the Cold War and beyond. Against the still-common tendency in scholarship and popular discourse to assume that Cuba's greatest influence on the Global New Left were the turn to arms and dissemination of "foco" theory, the works in this section suggest Cuba's more complex legacy in contributing to the sensibility and subjectivity of the New Left.

The "Cultural Diplomacy and Mass Media" section begins with Ximena Espeche's essay, "Between Emotion and Calculation: Press Coverage of Operation Truth (1959)," on the mass media and the Cuban Revolution. The author focuses on Operation Truth, an early intervention in the international media carried out by the revolutionary leadership in the context of the trials and executions of members of the prerevolutionary security forces. Espeche offers a new perspective on this campaign, reconstructing the positions of both Latin American and US journalists. She explores subtle differences between them, including the way they constructed ideas of gender and ethnicity in relation to emotion and reason. The essay decenters the US media in our understanding of the symbolic battles that began as early as January 1959 and illuminates the complex interplay between the revolutionary leadership's projections and journalists' responses.

Aviva Chomsky's essay, "Rewriting Gender in the New Revolutionary Song: Cuba's Nueva Trova and Beyond," explores the way Cuban Nueva Trova composers challenged gender conventions in their lyrics and their visions of love, sexuality, and gender relations. Cuban singer-songwriters Silvio Rodríguez and Pablo Milanés were perhaps Cuba's most important global ambassadors, especially in Latin America, at a time when military dictatorships tortured, disappeared, and killed thousands, and when the Nicaraguan Revolution opened a new wave of optimism for the Global Left. Chomsky agues that Cuban Nueva Trova represented a renovation of politics and sensibilities in this period, and opens a window onto the subjectivities of new generations of youth in the 1980s and 1990s.

Paula Halperin's article, "Between Politics and Desire: *Fresa y Chocolate*, Homosexuality, and Democratization in 1990s Brazil," analyzes the reception of the famous Cuban film *Fresa y Chocolate (Strawberry and Chocolate)* in Brazil. The film received wide recognition for heralding a more accepting stance toward homosexuals, who had been routinely persecuted in revolutionary Cuba. Yet, as Halperin shows, Brazilian critics largely avoided the issue of sexuality, instead using the film as a prism through which to debate Brazil's own legacies of authoritarianism and its transition to a neoliberal economy.

In the Curated Spaces section, Lani Hanna traces the origin and circulation of a repertoire of visual images for the Global New Left as it imagined national liberation and internationalist solidarity. She focuses on the posters produced in the aftermath of the Tricontinental Conference in 1966, a high-water mark for Cuban solidarity with the decolonizing world and the nonaligned movement. Moving beyond masculinist or exclusively military imaginings, Hanna highlights women as central actors in this visual panorama, and family roots and generational linkages as central concepts in global struggles for socialism and self-determination.

The Interviews section presents different individual visions of Cuba interlaced with questions of gender, sexuality, and women's history, and how these interacted with the transnational circulation of people and ideas. The first two interviews recover two distinct accounts of a shared experience. Elizabeth Quay Hutchison interviews Margaret Randall (one of the most emblematic US intellectuals of the 1960s), who lived in Cuba from 1969 to 1980, while Isabella Cosse interviews Randall's son, Gregory Randall, who moved to Cuba with his family as a child. Margaret Randall reflects, from her own experiences, on the Cuban Revolution's policies toward women and the evolving role of feminism in her analysis. Gregory Randall shows the way these transitions impacted his own life experience and those of other youths. He offers detailed memories about daily life and the visions of his mother, his fathers (he recognizes that he had more than one), and his generation. These are the insightful reflections of an individual who found himself among the "children of the revolution," in the most direct and metaphorical senses of the term. Michelle Chase interviews two young Cuban scholars, Ailynn Torres Santana and Diosnara Ortega González, about their forthcoming book of oral histories with Cuban women, *Mujeres en Revolución*. They reflect on the significance of women's history, feminism, and oral history within Cuba's intellectual traditions. The interview also serves to illustrate the various ways in which feminism has challenged and renovated historiographical production within Cuba.

The issue closes with Jennifer L. Lambe's essay, "Historicizing Sexuality in the Cuban Revolution: The Spectral 'Before.'" Lambe provides a lucid rumination on the way scholarly understandings of sexuality in revolutionary Cuba are shaped by assumptions about Cuba's historical periodization. She suggests that scholars question the extent to which 1959 was a historical watershed, remaining attentive to continuities as well as breaks, and that they employ a *longue durée* analysis to more fully understand questions of sexuality and sexual practice in Cuban history. This long historical perspective provides a fitting closure to the issue by probing the various ways in which we make sense of Cuba's present through its past.

Michelle Chase is assistant professor of history at Pace University. She is the author of *Revolution within the Revolution: Women and Gender Politics in Cuba, 1952–1962* (2015). Her current research explores the transnational influence of the Cuban Revolution.

Isabella Cosse is a researcher at the Consejo Nacional de Investigaciones Científicas y Técnicas (CONICET) and the Universidad de Buenos Aires. She is the author of multiple books, including *Estigmas de nacimiento: Peronismo y orden familiar* (2006), *Pareja, sexualidad y familia en los anos sesenta* (2010), and *Mafalda: A Social and Political History of Latin America's Global Comic* (2019). The Spanish version of *Mafalda* received LASA's Iberoamericano Book Award.

Notes

We would like to thank Melina Pappademos and Heidi Tinsman for the strong support and guidance they offered during the preparation of this issue. We would also like to thank *Radical History Review*'s managing editor, Thomas Harbison.

1. An influential study of Cuba's impact on the Latin American Left was Castañeda, *Utopia Unarmed*. Recent notable publications include Brands, *Latin America's Cold War*; Brown, *Cuba's Revolution World*; Gleijeses, *Conflicting Missions* and *Visions of Freedom*; Harmer, *Allende's Chile and the Inter-American Cold War*; Keller, *Mexico's Cold War*; and Marchesi, *Latin America's Radical Left*. There is also a significant body of scholarship on Cuba's impact within global intellectual and cultural circles during the Cold War, including Franco, *The Decline and Fall of the Lettered City*; Gilman, *Entre la pluma y el fusil*; Markarian, *Uruguay, 1968*; Rojas, *Fighting Over Fidel*; and Iber, *Neither Peace nor Freedom*. The Cuban Revolution is considered a watershed in Latin American history, particularly for the emergence of the New Left, and it would be impossible to cite all of the relevant literature here.

2. See especially Guerra, "Gender Policing"; Hamilton, *Sexual Revolutions*; Hynson, "'Count, Capture, and Reeducate,'" and *Laboring for the State*; Serra, *The "New Man" in Cuba;* and Sierra Madero, "El trabajo os hará hombres." Pioneering studies of the history of homosexuality in modern Cuba include Bejel, *Gay Cuban Nation* and Lumsden, *Machos, Maricones, and Gays*.

3. Partial exceptions include Gosse, *Where the Boys Are*; Gronbeck-Tedesco, *Cuba, The United States, and Cultures of the Transnational Left*; and Gorsuch, "'Cuba, My Love.'" Many studies focus on revolutionary subjectivity, the "New Man," and the figure of Che. See, for example, Mallon, "*Barbudos*, Warriors, and *Rotos*"; Tinsman, *Partners in Conflict*; Oberti, *Las revolucionarias*; and Carnovale, *Los combatientes*. On women's internationalist institutions and the relationships between the Global South and the socialist world, see Ghodsee, *Second World, Second Sex*.

4. The numerous publications on Bay of Pigs and the Missile Crisis, for example, often foreground either the United States or the Soviet Union as historical actors. For a criticism of this paradigm, see Leffey and Weldes, "Decolonizing the Cuban Missile Crisis."

References

Bejel, Emilio. *Gay Cuban Nation.* Chicago: University of Chicago Press, 2001.

Brands, Hal. *Latin America's Cold War.* Cambridge, MA: Harvard University Press, 2012.

Brown, Jonathan C. *Cuba's Revolution World.* Cambridge, MA: Harvard University Press, 2017.

Carnovale, Vera. *Los combatientes. Historia del PRT-ERP.* Buenos Aires: Siglo XXI, 2009.

Franco, Jean. *The Decline and Fall of the Lettered City: Latin America in the Cold War.* Cambridge, MA: Harvard University Press, 2009.

Ghodsee, Kristen. *Second World, Second Sex: Socialist Women's Activism and Global Solidarity During the Cold War.* Durham, NC: Duke University Press, 2019.

Gilman, Claudia. *Entre la pluma y el fusil: Debates y dilemas del escritor revolucionario en América Latina.* Buenos Aires: Siglo XXI, 2012.

Gleijeses, Piero. *Conflicting Missions: Havana, Washington, and Africa, 1959–1976.* Chapel Hill: University of North Carolina Press, 2011.

Gleijeses, Piero. *Visions of Freedom: Havana, Washington, Pretoria, and the Struggle for Southern Africa, 1976–1991.* Chapel Hill: University of North Carolina Press, 2013.

Gorsuch, Anne. "'Cuba, My Love': The Romance of Revolutionary Cuba in the Socialist Sixties." *American Historical Review,* no. 125 (2015): 497–526.

Gosse, Van. *Where the Boys Are: Cuba, Cold War America, and the Making of a New Left.* New York: Verso, 1993.

Gronbeck-Tedesco, John. *Cuba, The United States, and Cultures of the Transnational Left.* New York: Cambridge University Press, 2017.

Guerra, Lillian. "Gender Policing, Homosexuality, and the New Patriarchy of the Cuban Revolution, 1965–70." *Social History* 35, no. 3 (August 2010): 268–89.

Gutman, Jorge Castañeda. *Utopia Unarmed: The Latin American Left After the Cold War.* New York: Vintage Books, 1993.

Hamilton, Carrie. *Sexual Revolutions in Cuba: Passion, Politics, and Memory.* Chapel Hill: University of North Carolina Press, 2014.

Harmer, Tanya. *Allende's Chile and the Inter-American Cold War.* Chapel Hill: University of North Carolina Press, 2011.

Hynson, Rachel. "'Count, Capture, and Reeducate': The Campaign to Rehabilitate Cuba's Female Sex Workers, 1959–1966." *Journal of the History of Sexuality* 24, no. 1 (2015): 125–53.

Hynson, Rachel. *Laboring for the State: Women, Family, and Work in Revolutionary Cuba, 1959–1971.* New York: Cambridge University Press, 2020.

Iber, Patrick. *Neither Peace nor Freedom: The Cultural Cold War in Latin America.* Cambridge, MA: Harvard University Press, 2015.

Keller, Renata. *Mexico's Cold War: Cuba, the United States, and the Legacy of the Mexican Revolution.* New York: Cambridge University Press, 2017.

Leffey, Mark, and Jutta Weldes. "Decolonizing the Cuban Missile Crisis." *International Studies Quarterly,* no. 52 (2008): 555–77.

Lumsden, Ian. *Machos, Maricones, and Gays.* Philadelphia: Temple University Press, 2010.

Mallon, Florencia. "*Barbudos,* Warriors, and *Rotos*: The MIR, Masculinity, and Power in the Chilean Agrarian Reform, 1965–1974." In *Changing Men and Masculinities in Latin America,* edited by Matthew Gutmann, 179–215. Durham, NC: Duke University Press, 2003.

Marchesi, Aldo. *Latin America's Radical Left: Rebellion and Cold War in the Global 1960s.* New York: Cambridge University Press, 2017.

Markarian, Vania. *Uruguay, 1968: Student Activism from Global Counterculture to Molotov Cocktails*, translated by Laura Pérez Carrara. Oakland: University of California Press, 2017.

Oberti, Alejandra. *Las revolucionarias: Militancia, vida cotidiana y afectividad en los setenta.* Buenos Aires: Edhasa, 2015.

Rojas, Rafael. *Fighting Over Fidel: The New York Intellectuals and the Cuban Revolution.* Princeton, NJ: Princeton University Press, 2015.

Serra, Ana. *The "New Man" in Cuba: Culture and Identity in the Revolution*. Gainesville: University Press of Florida, 2007.

Sierra Madero, Abel. "'El trabajo os hará hombres': Masculinización nacional, trabajo forzado y control social en Cuba durante los años sesenta." *Cuban Studies*, no. 44 (2016): 309–49.

Tinsman, Heidi. *Partners in Conflict: The Politics of Gender, Sexuality, and Labor in the Chilean Agrarian Reform 1950–1973.* Durham, NC: Duke University Press, 2002.

Angela Davis in Cuba as Symbol and Subject

Sarah J. Seidman

When Angela Davis visited a childcare center in Havana in early October 1972, a young girl, mistaking the visitor's traveling companion and fellow US Communist Party member Kendra Alexander for Davis, proclaimed there were "two Angelas." There were in fact many Angelas at the Cuban daycare that morning, as the children greeted Davis holding placards of her visage.[1] The images of Davis were adapted from one of countless photographs taken of the activist-scholar after she was targeted by the US government in 1970 and in turn defended by socialist countries and leftist activists worldwide as a global symbol of repression and resistance. Yet the Cuban Revolution did embrace "two Angelas" in the late 1960s and early 1970s: the symbol and the person. More than other African American activists who encountered the Cuban Revolution in the 1960s and 1970s through visits or exile—major figures from the black liberation movement such as Robert F. Williams, Stokely Carmichael, Huey P. Newton, and others—Davis was exalted in Cuba both through her iconic image and her physical self.

In this essay, I explore how gender facilitated the encounters between Angela Y. Davis and the Cuban Revolution. Davis has written that her identity as a "black woman Communist" precipitated the US government's actions against her.[2] This identity in turn strengthened Davis's relationship with Cuba, where its socialist state, large black population, and purported egalitarianism toward women drew the scholar and activist several times beginning in 1969. Specifically, Davis's gender,

Radical History Review

Issue 136 (January 2020)   DOI 10.1215/01636545-7857227

operating in tandem with her socialism and blackness and membership in the American Communist Party (CPUSA), provided a stage not afforded the range of prominent, noncommunist, black male activists and intellectuals who allied with the Cuban Revolution in the 1960s and 1970s. The institutional platforms created by the Federación de Mujeres Cubanas (Federation of Cuban Women, or FMC) and the Partido Comunista de Cuba (Cuban Communist Party, or PCC) gave Davis officially sanctioned and highly visible platforms from which to speak and be seen. The visibility the Cuban state provided helped solidify Davis as a symbol of US repression, and her freedom a victory for international solidarity.

As part of the broader transnational and hemispheric turn in historical scholarship of the "long" 1960s, a growing number of works have examined connections between the US Left and Cuba after the triumph of the revolution of 1959. This ranges from the Beats' fascination with Castro and the multiracial Fair Play for Cuba Committee's work in the early 1960s, to the New Left Venceremos Brigade delegations that began in 1969 and the Cuban American Antonio Maceo Brigades that followed.[3] A few scholars have focused on questions of gender and sexuality.[4] More have centered race, suggesting that the Cuban revolutionary state's economic egalitarianism lessened racial disparities and Fidel Castro's pronouncements against racism inspired both African Americans and Afro-Cubans in support of the revolution, but that racial equality in Cuba ultimately remained unrealized and black nationalism repressed.[5] Yet studies focusing on African American and Cuban connections remain piecemeal, and no scholarship has thoroughly engaged with Angela Davis's encounters with Cuba.[6]

Davis was part of a broader network of African American activists who encountered the Cuban Revolution in the 1960s and 1970s.[7] Delegations from the Student Nonviolent Coordinating Committee (SNCC), the *Black Scholar* journal, and the Black Panther Party visited the island; Robert F. Williams, Eldridge Cleaver, and Huey P. Newton all lived there in political exile, while Stokely Carmichael enjoyed a standing offer to take refuge there. Some of these figures, and many others lesser known, grew disillusioned with Cuba; others lodged critiques but remained supportive of the revolutionary project. Most felt frustrated by their inability to publicly connect an affirmative blackness with support for the revolution. While many African American women traveled to Cuba or were inspired by the revolution in the 1960s and 1970s, Davis was the only woman in the pantheon of iconic figures of the black liberation movement who sought solidarity or refuge in Cuba.[8] And while African American radicals provided perhaps the most consistent solidarity with the Cuban Revolution of any community over several decades, no one else was treated in quite the way Davis was.

Davis has had a singular presence on the United States Left and in Cuba. She is singular and, yet, of course, multifaceted: in addition to being an African American woman and a one-time member of the CPUSA, Davis is an accomplished professional academic and public intellectual who spent sixteen months in jail after being accused and ultimately acquitted of murder. She is an historic figure who continues to have impact, a public persona who is not immune to objectification, yet is wary of her idolization and private about her personal life. Yet Davis's personal attributes—her education, cosmopolitanism, and appearance—attracted widespread interracial interest.[9] Her combined anti-imperialism, antiracism, and Marxist orientation appealed particularly to Cuban leaders as well as everyday Cubans. Taking an intersectional approach to understanding how Davis's identity and ideology were expressed in Cuba and interpreted by the Cuban state—and focusing on the role of gender within this mix—teaches us not only about Davis's unique positionality, but also about the complexities of transnational solidarity and the Cuban revolutionary project.

Becoming Angela Davis

Davis's upbringing laid the foundation for her activism: her dedication to racial justice, her membership in the CPUSA, and her advocacy of gender equality. Born to a politically engaged middle-class family in 1950s Birmingham, Alabama, family friends included black CPUSA members James Jackson and Esther Cooper Jackson and the family of Carole Robertson, who was killed in the 1964 bombing of the 16th Street Baptist Church. Intent on leaving the segregation and racial terrorism that gave the city the nickname "Bombingham," Davis finished high school at the progressive Elisabeth Irwin School in New York City, where she lived with a politically engaged family in Brooklyn and participated in the city's Marxist youth culture.[10]

The Cuban Revolution played an important role in Davis's burgeoning cosmopolitan internationalism. In 1962 Davis traveled abroad for the first time to Helsinki, Finland, for the Eighth World Festival for Youth and Students, where her interaction with a Cuban youth delegation had a lasting influence. Founded as an antifascist international friendship organization in 1945, the festivals brought youth from around the world to countries within the Soviet sphere. In Helsinki it was the Cubans, wearing pins of doves with machine guns and embodying the revolution's youthful exuberance—who took their delegation's conga line from the stage into the audience and then the street—that struck Davis as the festival's "most impressive event."[11] Davis later studied abroad in Paris during college at Brandeis University, a period in which she befriended immigrant women from Martinique, protested the afterlives of French colonialism in Algeria, and pursued graduate studies with Frankfurt School theorist Theodor Adorno in Germany. She attended the Dialectics of Liberation Conference in London in 1967, where she heard Stokely Carmichael speak about the Third World before he flew to Havana for the Organización Latinoamericana de Solidaridad (Organization of Latin American Solidarity, or OLAS) conference. These travels and interactions helped Davis form a global philosophy of liberation. "The new places, the new experiences I had expected to discover through travel turned out to be the same old places," she wrote in the early 1970s, "the same old experiences with a common message of struggle."[12] These formative experiences informed and were reinforced by decades of public life, from her transnational approach to scholarship and speaking engagements to her activism around Palestine and continued solidarity with Cuba.[13]

In addition to her internationalism and interest in socialism, gender drove Davis to find a political community that would ultimately lead her to Cuba. A longing to participate in the black liberation movement brought Davis back to the United States, where she resumed graduate studies with Herbert Marcuse at the University of California, San Diego, and became active on campus and in Los Angeles. Davis grew frustrated with the gender politics of groups like the largely autonomous West Coast branch of SNCC, as well as their resistance to Marxism and internal dissent. Men she encountered tended to "confuse their political activity with an assertion of their maleness."[14] In search of an intellectual and political collective, she joined the CPUSA in the summer of 1968.[15] In particular, the Party's new Che-Lumumba Club, affiliated with the Southern California chapter, beckoned. An all-black collective started by Charlene Mitchell and Franklin and Kendra Alexander the previous year, the club taught Marxist ideology and engaged with college students, workers, and community members in Los Angeles. The Che-Lumumba Club reflected the political flexibility of the California Communist Party under the leadership of women such as Mitchell and Dorothy Healy, in contrast to a more centralized, doctrinaire ideology in New York.[16] As Black Power came into ascendance and the CPUSA struggled to remain relevant, Mitchell, the Alexanders, and above all Davis offered ties between the Old Left and the New. These ties would prove crucial to connecting with the Cuban Revolution.

. . . . .

In the summer of 1969, Davis embarked on a transformative visit to Cuba. Traveling with a CPUSA delegation for the annual July 26th Cuban independence celebration, the group traversed the island and worked in coffee and sugarcane fields as part of the *gran zafra* (great harvest) campaign to cut ten million tons of sugarcane for the 1970 season as an economic and symbolic victory for the revolution. Davis participated in the official political and cultural activities common to visiting delegations in Cuba, getting to know the Cuban residents of a small town on the eastern end of the island where they lived and worked.[17] We "began to feel as if we had taken root in this small village in Oriente," she recalled. Despite not speaking Spanish, or perhaps because of this, she felt particularly accepted by Cuban children. Davis called the trip "a great climax in my life. Politically I felt infinitely more mature."[18] The energy of the Cuban Revolution—first encountered as a conga line through the Helsinki streets—and its defiance of the United States had a profound effect. "The Cubans' limitless revolutionary enthusiasm" left "a permanent mark" on her existence.[19]

Davis's 1969 visit came at an important moment for Cuba's relationship to the world. As the revolution completed a decade in power, some of its allies shifted. As it embarked on a period of cultural repression that came to be called the *quinquennio gris* (gray period) by 1971, it lost previous supporters in the global arena, particularly European intellectuals. Yet the same period witnessed the rise of new forms of solidarity: 1969 inaugurated the Venceremos Brigade (VB), interracial delegations of Americans who traveled to Cuba to work and tour the island. Members of the VB came to assist with the gran zafra. Although the harvest failed, the brigades and the model they established with the Cuban state have continued to this day. Davis recounted that Castro himself had explained the Cuban state's shift from "emphasizing armed struggle to mobilizing mass movements," and hosting delegations rather than exalting individuals.[20]

The late 1960s also reflected a new strategy regarding the Cuban leadership's search for African American allies. As the revolution's most experimental phase ended, the visible solidarity it had expressed with individuals in the black liberation movement also came to a close. But African Americans continued to look to Cuba's shores, and Cuban leaders embraced black communists, organized delegations, and a quieter hosting of subsequent exiles as part of the turn toward institutionalizing the revolution.[21] In an extraordinary statement Davis delivered privately to fellow CPUSA members after her visit in 1972, Davis claimed that Castro had told her that the government was increasingly interested in working with African American communists after previous encounters with black activists had soured.[22] Naming Robert F. Williams, Stokely Carmichael, and Eldridge Cleaver, Davis recalled Castro saying that when these figures "turned on Cuba and criticized the Cuban Revolution, criticized socialism," the Cuban state "felt that they had been in error by establishing such strong relationships with them at that time."[23] The Cuban government never spoke out publicly about these interactions, making this admission, as reported by Davis, quite unusual. Yet the summer of 1969 encapsulated this shift: as Cuban leadership sent the controversial Black Power movement figure Eldridge Cleaver off of the island on a plane bound for Algeria, it welcomed the Venceremos Brigade, Davis's delegation, and a separate delegation by black CPUSA leader Henry Winston.

Like many other black visitors in the CPUSA and other groups, Davis focused much of her attention on the racial politics of the revolution and its convergence with socialism. As one of three people of color on her delegation, she recounted the trio discussing it "incessantly." Davis lauded the revolutionary state for opposing segregation in Cuba upon their seizure of power in 1959—which occurred through laws such as land redistribution and free healthcare, and an anti-discrimination campaign announced by Fidel Castro.[24] Moreover, she emphasized the revolution's gains toward "the destruction of the material base of racism." Davis wrote of seeing black Cubans in the workforce in "factories, schools, hospitals and wherever else we went." She lingered in particular on a lesson from a sugarcane worker whose craft she admired. "The business of cutting cane was work not fit for human beings," she remembered him telling her, and would hopefully be eliminated in the future. With that she determined that poverty and underdevelopment were "nothing to be utopianized," even as the future of harvesting sugarcane in Cuba persisted. Davis never declared racist practices in Cuba over. But she wrote that she was "immensely impressed" by Cuba's efforts to eradicate racism, and convinced that "only under socialism could this fight against racism have been so successfully executed."[25]

Davis wrote less about women following her 1969 visit, but recognized the roles Cuban women played in the revolution and the challenges they faced. On one hand, she had long been impressed with the militancy of Cuban women, writing admiringly to the incarcerated activist and close friend George Jackson after her first trip to the island of "women patrolling the streets with rifles on their backs—defending the revolution." On the other, she alluded to sexism in Cuba, describing "young *compañeras* educating their husbands and lovers—demythologizing *machismo*."[26] Many white women who traveled to Cuba with the Venceremos Brigade struggled with feelings of alienation from Cuban women and their gender roles in society—which they perceived as objectifying.[27] But Davis, along with members of the Third World Women's Alliance, who also traveled with the Venceremos Brigade, wrote about Cuban women more from a vantage point of kinship than distance.[28] As the 1970s progressed, Davis increasingly viewed gender as a crucial variable for the Cuban revolutionary project.

Davis's initial trip to Cuba coincided with her catapult into the public sphere. Around the time of her visit in the summer of 1969, a student and FBI informant writing for the University of California, Los Angeles (UCLA) newspaper mentioned the Communist Party membership of a newly hired philosophy professor. The *San Francisco Examiner* picked up the article, naming Davis, and also publishing her home address and information related to a recent legal gun purchase.[29] The UCLA regents then sought to terminate Davis immediately, a decision she successfully appealed amid ongoing threats, but her teaching contract was not renewed. A year later, in August 1970, the state of California implicated Davis in the deaths of a judge, district attorney, and jurors taken hostage during courtroom proceedings against one of the three "Soledad Brothers" accused of killing a guard at a central California prison.[30] Davis was far from the courthouse that day, but authorities charged her with conspiracy, kidnapping, and murder. Proclaiming her innocence and questioning her ability to receive a fair trial, Davis went underground for two months before her apprehension in New York in October 1970.[31] She spent sixteen months in jail in New York and California and endured a highly publicized seven-month trial that at one point sought the death penalty. Ultimately, she was acquitted of all charges.

Davis's connection with Cuba helped solidify ideological sentiment and US government action against her. While the press did not report on her visit to the island during the summer of 1969, a lengthy article published in the *Los Angeles Times* while Davis was underground suggested a connection between her visit and her alleged role in the subsequent events in Marin County. Claiming "the pattern is clear," conservative columnist Georgie Anne Geyer and foreign correspondent Keyes Beech characterized Castro's Cuba as a "revolutionary factory for the processing and refining of American radicals for export back to the United States."[32] The media also repeatedly suggested that Davis had fled there, particularly when her sister Fania Davis was identified on a Canadian boat bound for the island with the Venceremos Brigade in the summer of 1970.[33] Fania Davis was still in Cuba when Angela Davis was captured.[34] While Davis wrote that she had considered the idea of fleeing there or elsewhere abroad and ruled it out, her connection to Cuba nevertheless helped cast her as a subversive enemy of the United States.

Icon of Repression

During the course of her imprisonment and trial, Davis became a contested symbol of persecution. The black liberation movement expressed widespread support for and identification with Davis. James Baldwin wrote in a letter to her in prison, "We must fight for your life as though it were our own—which it is," while the *Black Scholar* echoed in an editorial, "Her struggle is our struggle, and her victory shall be our victory."[35] Groups such as the Third World Women's Alliance and Harlem Black Women to Free Angela Davis rallied around Davis during her imprisonment and trial. White women also participated in the Free Angela Davis campaign, including Gloria Steinem, who served as national treasurer of Davis's defense fund, but Davis's case became a wedge issue in the burgeoning US women's movement. The recounting of Betty Friedan asking the Third World Women's Alliance to put down signs supporting Davis at the 1970 Women's Liberation Day March in New York spread far and wide. Third World Women's Alliance founder Frances Beale's experience of being told that "Angela Davis has nothing to do with women's liberation," and her response that Davis had "everything to do with the kind of liberation we're talking about," reflected the conflicts that defined the women's movement in the United States.[36]

Under the leadership of Fania Davis and fellow CPUSA member Franklin Alexander, the National United Committee to Free Angela Davis (NUCFAD) sustained a highly organized campaign that framed Davis's fight as part of a larger struggle of incarcerated and oppressed people in the United States and beyond.[37] A range of global solidarity groups, less divided by US debates, called for Davis's freedom.[38] Women across the globe mobilized for Davis through the Women's International Democratic Federation. Davis received particular support from Germany and France, where she had lived.[39] John Abt, a CPUSA member on Davis's legal team, found that, like African American communities in the United States, internationally "people everywhere not only identify with her but see her freedom struggle as indissolubly linked with their own aspirations."[40] Fania Davis emphasized, "It's up to the entire world to save her."[41]

Cuba played an integral role in the global campaign to free Davis. As it had done with other global solidarity campaigns, the Cuban state apparatus mobilized various sectors around her liberation. The Cuban press provided extensive, continuous coverage, often with visual elements. A government-led multiagency committee formed devoted to her release. Two songs, "Por Ángela," by the prominent Cuban songwriter Tania Castellanos, and "Canción para Ángela Davis," written by Pablo Milanés on a record by Milanés and Silvio Rodriguez (Cuba's two largest names in Nueva Trova), reflected her prevalence in popular culture. Advocates ranging from schoolchildren to government leaders spoke out in her defense.

Cuban women's initiatives spearheaded by the Federation of Cuban Women formed to proclaim Davis's innocence and free her from prison. A petition for Davis was a central component of the March 8, 1971, International Women's Day Conference in Havana, which brought together women from around the world. Elizabeth Catlett, the African American artist based in Mexico City who attended the conference, characterized the petition as a unifying gesture for disparate women, "one way of joining together in a common cause."[42] In June of that year the Federation of Cuban Women convened a meeting to form the Comité de Solidaridad con Angela Davis, or Solidarity Committee with Angela Davis, devoted to her release.[43] The woman chosen to lead the committee of representatives from a range of Cuban groups had long-standing ties to revolutionary leadership: Telma Bornot, of the ministry of armed forces, had participated in Castro's July 26th Movement and the founding of the FMC in Oriente Province. The committee denounced the incarceration of Davis to the international community, and sought to channel existing solidarity in Cuba.[44] FMC publications *Mujeres* and *Romances* published a stream of coverage of Davis's imprisonment and trial.[45]

Moreover, Cuba helped cement the image of Davis as a global signifier for repression and anti-US sentiment. The Cuban state's seasoned propaganda arm went into full effect, creating posters and pamphlets, including perhaps the best-known poster of Davis worldwide. Her photograph nearly always accompanied Cuban newspaper articles covering her case, while other publications featured original graphics. Catlett wrote in a letter to the scholar Bettina Aptheker, a longtime friend of Davis's who worked on her defense, that "her picture is seen in remote places" on the island, and that no one "had not heard of her struggle."[46] Davis acknowledged the effects of her support around the world. The movement abroad "exerted serious pressure on the government," she affirmed in her autobiography, and "stimulated the further growth of the mass movement at home."[47]

Figure 1. Alfredo Rostgaard, *Angela Davis*, OSPAAAL, 1970. Courtesy Lincoln Cushing / Docs Populi archive

Two black-and-white images from the United States and Cuba in 1970 illustrate how Davis became not just a symbol of repression, but also a visual icon. The first, a reprint of a somber photograph of her wearing round sunglasses, a dashiki, and her signature halo Afro, appeared alongside another photograph on the "Wanted" flyer for Davis issued that August by the FBI. The second image (fig. 1), a poster drawn by Cuban artist Alfredo Rostgaard folded and shipped internationally as part of the *Tricontinental* magazine created by the Organización de Solidaridad de los Pueblos de África, Asia, y América Latina (Organization of Solidarity with the Peoples of Africa, Asia, and Latin America, or OSPAAAL), also depicted Davis with round sunglasses and an Afro.[48] Yet Rostgaard's poster, perhaps created in response to the FBI flyer, depicted Davis with two sets of arms, one in handcuffs and the other raised above her head breaking her chains. A halo of light encircled these second arms, exaggerating her Afro and invoking religious icons. Both images, created respectively by US state and Cuban state-sanctioned organizations and widely circulated, helped not just to propagate but to craft Davis as an icon. Yet if the FBI flyer intended to facilitate her capture and imprisonment, Rostgaard's image, and a range of Cuban solidarity works, sought to set Davis free.

The most well-known image of Davis emerged from Cuba. More than Rostgaard's 1970 poster, Felix Beltrán's 1971 *Libertad Para Angela Davis* (Freedom for Angela Davis) helped make her image instantly recognizable around the world. As head of the propaganda department for the Cuban Communist Party, Beltrán was supplied with photographs of Davis and asked to create a poster. The poster he produced likely used a photograph taken at a New York press conference in 1969, which appeared on many of the New York Committee to Free Angela Davis's flyers.[49] Davis's profile appeared in stark outline with red skin and black hair against a deep blue background; the red and blue were intended, according to Beltrán, to invoke the American flag.[50] The rounded edges of her features reflected his approach to a pop art aesthetic. Beltrán had created other unused prototypes of Davis, and another poster he created from a *Newsweek* childhood photograph, declaring "ever since she was a girl she suffered discrimination," was used for International Children's Day.[51] But it was the blue, black, and red poster, originally printed in a small run in the thousands, that was reproduced in Cuba and elsewhere, and ended up in poster collections around the world. Variations of the image appeared on magazine covers, postcards, and billboards in Havana (fig. 2).[52] Beltrán's image became the most important image of Davis worldwide.

The proliferation of Davis's image in Cuban iconography far surpassed the visual presence of other African American radicals. Aside from Richard Nixon, no other living individual from the United States had a dedicated OSPAAAL poster.[53] While Cuban artists created several posters to express solidarity with the black liberation movement and groups such as the Black Panther Party, the only other person represented was George Jackson, in a 1971 poster by Raphael Morante, after he was killed in prison earlier that year. SNCC leader Stokely Carmichael's 1967 visit elicited a tremendous amount of press coverage featuring his photograph, but no posters.[54] Robert F. Williams's exile preceded the revolution's graphic apex, but his presence in Cuban discourse emerged through pronouncements or through cultural forms such as "Radio Free Dixie" created by Williams himself. Huey Newton, who appeared in graphic form in publications like the *Tricontinental* magazine and bulletin—referred to by Carmichael as a "bible in revolutionary circles"—never appeared on an official poster and received no Cuban press coverage during his exile on the island in the mid-1970s.[55]

Figure 2. Felix Beltrán's 1971 graphic of Angela Davis on a billboard in Havana, photograph by Rudy Suwara, 1971. Courtesy of the Tamiment Library, New York University

A postcard-writing campaign shows how Cubans further crafted a global iconography of liberation for Davis. Several countries sent mail to Davis in jail. France shipped postcards featuring a black-and-white photograph of a rose and the words "Angela Davis" on the front, with cursive prose printed on the back that left room only for a personalized signature. East German children created their own unique cards. The Cuban postcards featured a pink-and-black version of Beltrán's image of Davis, with the words *"Libertad para Angela Davison y sus hermanos de lucha,"* or "freedom for Angela Davis and her brothers in struggle" on the front, and personalized messages written or typed on the back. Several called Davis a sister and ally. Cecilia Silveira Cabrera explained that she used the familiar *"tú"* form of "you" because "we consider you a sister," while art school student Angelina D. Garcia invited Davis to Cuba upon her release so that they could "get to know you personally."[56] Among the global campaigns for Davis, Cuba's stands out as particularly engaged in a unified visual iconography as well as a consistent ideology—one that foregrounded gender.

The intersectional depiction of Davis in Cuban visual culture reflected her multifaceted identity as a radical black woman. Cuban solidarity discourse emphasized Davis's antiracist and anti-imperialist struggles: OSPAAAL declared that the charges against her were "against the entire black movement," while the magazine *Romances* later echoed that Davis had come to symbolize the African American freedom struggle and the fight against US imperialism.[57] Yet Davis's gender is also intrinsic to her representation in Cuban culture. Images of Davis routinely rendered her as regal, strong, determined, and feminine. A 1972 article in *Cuba* magazine cited Cuban posters of Davis as contributing to an artistic tradition of portraying women as integral to the Cuban Revolution.[58] Davis's representation defies easy categorization into fetishization or exaltation; Cuban images served not simply to lionize her or objectify her, but to exonerate her.

Cuban press coverage of Davis, however laudatory, took a specific interest in her appearance. One maudlin article in the *Granma* described her physique admiringly and at length. The author emphasized her tall and elegant stature, her light-skinned "bronze" coloring and, most of all, her "large" naturally styled hair, described as cascading over her temples and partially covering her long neck.[59] The FMC-run *Romances* ran a political article on Davis alongside the rare fashion spread of a young black Cuban model and performer.[60] The cover juxtaposed the two faces, Davis drawn in outline, and Mayda Limonta with processed hair styled in a way that referenced but did not fully promote the Afro. Media coverage of Davis in the United States also emphasized her physical appearance, commenting on her hair, her clothing, and her overall "glamorous revolutionary" aesthetic.[61]

While Davis's hair also elicited reactions and scrutiny in the United States, appearance in Cuba was more closely regulated by the state. Davis herself has critiqued the way history has depoliticized her struggle to render her "remembered as a hairdo," yet in Cuba, just as in the United States, the Afro attracted political as well as aesthetic interest.[62] Americans in Cuba in the late 1960s recounted receiving or witnessing hostility and discrimination toward the style's adherents.[63] Both countercultural long hair and overt symbols of blackness were discouraged on the island, and the Afro falls squarely into both subversive categories.[64] Davis's revolutionary credentials and Cuban institutional affiliations with women's groups and communists rather than disaffected Afro-Cubans, however, obfuscated public criticism of her hairstyle. In addition to remembering her because of it, some suggested that she made the style more acceptable.

Davis worried about becoming a symbol, yet she also acknowledged the power of her own image in determining her fate.[65] "The circulation of various photographic images of me," she later wrote, "played a major role in both the mobilization of public opinion against me and the development of the campaign that was ultimately responsible for my acquittal."[66] Upon her release, the Cuban Committee to Free Angela Davis admitted, "With [good] reason we feel like participants in this great triumph." The group reiterated its invitation to Davis to visit Cuba, given the "extraordinary admiration of our people."[67]

Davis, Gender, and Cuba

Davis's representation in Cuban visual culture as a heroic and symbolic figure continued to rise when she responded to the Cuban state's invitation to return to the island for a second visit following her acquittal in the fall of 1972. Davis and fellow black CPUSA members Kendra and Franklin Alexander traveled to the Soviet Union, the German Democratic Republic, Bulgaria, Czechoslovakia, Cuba, and Chile, six countries that had played large roles in the campaign to secure her freedom. In Cuba the three friends and comrades traveled the length of the island meeting with political and cultural leaders, encountering mobs of supporters at every turn. During a trip to Cuba's Isle of Youth, young student inhabitants "offered their young hearts to the beloved visitor" by flocking to Davis, prompting her to abandon her motorcade and lead a parade through the streets in the torrential rain.[68] Full-page spreads in the *Granma* and other publications chronicled her weeklong visit.[69] The Cuban state showered Davis with honors, including, in a solemn ceremony with President Osvaldo Dorticós and Fidel Castro, the *Orden Playa Girón* (Order of the Bay of Pigs)—the highest decoration bestowed by the Cuban government.[70] Publications called Davis "Our Angela" and repeatedly characterized her interactions with the Cuban people as an "indescribable phenomenon."

Figure 3. Davis at the Plaza de la Revolución with Osvaldo Dórticós, left, Fidel Castro, right, and others, 1972. From the photo collection held at the Tamiment Library, New York University, by permission of the Communist Party USA

Davis reciprocated Cuba's enthusiasm and support. Speaking to a crowd estimated at three-quarters of a million people in Havana's Plaza de la Revolución during the events surrounding the twelfth anniversary of the Comités de Defensa de la Revolución (Cuban Committees for the Defense of the Revolution, or CDRs), Davis stated that the reception upon her arrival in Cuba was the warmest and most enthusiastic of any place she had yet traveled.[71] On the dais with Castro (fig. 3), she described the Cuban Revolution as the "greatest inspiration" for the struggle for socialism and against racism and imperialism in the United States, and even referred to Cuba as her "true home."[72] Upon her departure, Davis thanked the Cuban people for receiving her with "such fervor."[73]

. . . . .

Davis's gender offered a particularly effective platform in Cuba from which to be seen. The FMC, the state-supported national women's organization active in Davis's solidarity campaign, hosted the CPUSA delegation of three. Further, the FMC provided an institutional structure for Davis not available to African American men in Cuba, as there was no male equivalent to the group and organizations based on race had been dissolved and banned in the early years of the revolution. The apparatus of gender provided Davis a stage for her to engage with Cuban audiences approved by the highest echelons of government.[74] Gender also continued to determine her representation in the Cuban press, in particular ways that both objectified and valorized. Davis's mobilization against the American criminal justice system, and her involvement in antiracist, anti-imperialist, and anticapitalist struggles qualified her as a feminized warrior in the existing framework of Cuban revolutionary culture.

Davis's vaunted reception in Cuba occurred in the context of long-standing veneration for the figure of the revolutionary woman warrior in Cuban society. The Cuban trope of militant heroines traces back to the nineteenth century, where *mambisas*, women fighters for Cuban independence, risked their lives and those of their family members to obtain freedom from Spain.[75] The mambisas enshrined as symbols in Cuban popular culture and nationalist discourse exuded bravery without sacrificing femininity. Their roles as mothers and sisters were emphasized, suggesting a willingness to risk their bodies, as well as their children and family, for a nationalist cause.[76] Black and white Cuban women had served as such symbols: Afro-Cuban Mariana Grajales Cuello reportedly sent ten of her eleven sons into battle against Spain, one of whom became the Cuban independence leader Antonio Maceo, and was immortalized as the mother of Cuban independence.[77]

Nearly one hundred years later, women played important roles in the Cuban Revolution's fight against Batista. A small group of women, including Celia Sánchez and Haydée Santamaría, joined Castro's group of rebels in the Sierra Maestra and were immortalized as fighters alongside the *barbudos*, or bearded rebels.[78] Many more women—an estimated 10 to 20 percent of members—joined urban underground networks in the late 1950s, where they strategized; printed and relayed messages; provided safe houses; and transported materials with minimal visibility.[79] Cuban women purposefully engaged the trope of maternalism in their fight against Batista, emphasizing their status as mothers, daughters, and wives of martyrs and insurgents.[80]

In the year after the revolution's victory, women mobilized in support of it, creating "Women's Revolutionary Brigades" and women's sections of the July 26th Movement, which provided a presence at rallies, organized other women at the grassroots level, and generated support for government initiatives.[81] While these individuals and groups have only just started to be recognized, archetypes of women warriors, such as prominent Cuban photographer Alberto Korda's 1960 image *Miliciana*, depicting a young woman wearing a beret and carrying a gun looking askance with a pensive yet determined gaze, remained visible in Cuban revolutionary culture.

The Federation of Cuban Women arose from the dismantling of these groups. While other organizations based on race, religion, or other markers of identity were prohibited after 1960, the state continued to view women as an interest group to be mobilized for the revolution. Founded that year upon the directive of Fidel Castro, the FMC was led for nearly five decades by Vilma Espín, who fought with the July 26th movement against Batista and married Raúl Castro. With nearly two million members and fourteen thousand employees in the mid-1970s, the organization played a major role in Cuban society. It provided job programs, educational opportunities, childcare, and women's health initiatives that sought to improve the conditions of women's lives.[82] It also followed a hierarchical structure and served to harness Cuban women to the mostly male-led Cuban revolutionary project.[83]

Like the grassroots groups that preceded them, as well as women's organizations in other socialist states, the FMC emphasized capitalism's exploitative practices against women rather than gender discrimination by men. It explicitly rejected a feminist approach to gender equality and left little room for dissent. Espín claimed, "We have never had a feminist movement."[84] She also asserted, "We hate the feminist movement in the United States," and called women who mobilized against men "absurd" and anything but revolutionary.[85] Women on the Venceremos Brigade recounted similar reactions from Cuban women in nonleadership positions.[86]

The FMC provided little space for public disagreement, or even slight variations of opinion, on this question before the mid-1970s. But recent scholarship has shown that Cuban women were not monolithic by examining black Cuban women in the cultural sphere, such as documentary filmmaker Sara Gómez, who highlighted challenges for women under the revolution in her largely obscured body of work.[87] The FMC did provide spaces for women to come together, as well as some opportunities for interactions with women such as Davis, Catlett, and others from around the world at conferences and events. Yet overall the FMC precluded the possibility of an openly grassroots women's activism.

The FMC was a logical group to host Davis. As a women's organization in a state apparatus without many women leaders, it made sense to arrange the visit of the highest-profile woman from the United States to visit Cuba since the revolution. Davis's own ambivalence about the US women's liberation movement made the question of feminism a moot point. Moreover, the FMC's position as an arm of the socialist state particularly influenced by the Old Left made it a fitting choice to host a woman affiliated with the CPUSA. Women were prominent members of the prerevolutionary communist organization, the Partido Socialista Popular (Popular Socialist Party, or PSP), where they had articulated a platform of gender equality, and after the revolution they reemerged to occupy prominent positions within the FMC.[88] Given that the PSP had not initially opposed Batista or supported Castro, July 26th members reacted to PSP involvement in the FMC and across the Castro government by 1960 with skepticism or sometimes disdain.[89] But the Old Left roots of many FMC members, and their familiarity with both organizing and centralized hierarchy, provided a fitting institutional base for Davis at the intersection of gender and communism—one uniquely accepted by the Cuban state.

Gender not only shaped the institutional reception of Davis in Cuba, but it also continued to shape her representation in public discourse. Depicted as both feminine and a fighter, the nature of the coverage of Davis differed from that of male visitors. An extensive spread in the *Granma* epitomizes this dual charge. In addition to the photograph of children at daycare holding placards of Davis's face mentioned at the beginning of this article, a second photograph showed Davis reaching into a crib and smiling at an infant, while a third showed her in a hard hat speaking to a large crowd of workers and students in the new Alamar housing complex. The journalist entitles Davis's visit to Cuba as "Entre la Arcilla y la Obra," or "Between Clay and Work."[90] Felix Pita Astudillo, who often covered the visits of American visitors to the island, compared Davis's engagement with children, the clay that could be shaped to lead Cuba's revolutionary future, with the hardness and necessary belligerence of Cuban workers—pillars already of Cuba's ongoing struggle. In addition to dwelling on Davis's interactions with children, Astudillo depicted Davis's visit as "indescribable" and "emotional," words seldom used to describe African American men visiting or living in Cuba.

Davis elaborated on her 1972 visit to Cuba at a CPUSA meeting upon her return. Like she did in 1969, Davis lauded Cuba's fight against racism, reporting, "We were extremely impressed by the way in which racism is being dealt with on a continual basis in Cuba."[91] But in the same meeting, an official, private gathering for party comrades that was recorded, Davis acknowledged that "there were substantial problems in the area of women" in Cuba.[92] She provided no comments about her own treatment on the island, nor about the FMC who hosted her visit. Yet Davis and

Kendra Alexander noted the absence of women in leadership positions in government and the Cuban Communist Party. She also emphasized a "deeply ingrained male supremacist" attitude on the island, and, relative to the Soviet Union and other countries they visited in 1972, a lack of awareness or intent about combating this supremacy. Davis recounted to ensuing laughter several discussions where their delegation raised the issue and found enthusiastic allies in Cuban women, along with polite men who "thanked us for the criticisms and suggestions."[93] Despite the humor she employed, Cuban gender relations troubled Davis.

Davis returned to Cuba in 1974 at a moment of reexamination of the roles of Cuban women. She came to attend the second congress of the FMC, which included nearly two thousand members and delegates from fifty-five international women's organizations.[94] Attendees broke into commissions on the topics of Cuban housewives, workers outside of the home, rural women, families, children living under socialism, and international solidarity. The conference anticipated the upcoming International Year of the Woman in 1975 and the UN Decade for Women from 1975 to 1985. Other Latin American women's organizations had a particular influence on Cuban women at these gatherings, creating a slightly larger opening for new conversations about feminism and gender equality.[95] The FMC Congress also occurred amid a series of significant domestic events heralding changes for women in Cuba, most of all the February 1975 passage of the Family Code, modeled on East Germany, which mandated equal housework and childcare responsibilities for Cuban husbands and wives. Although the Family Code did not usher in gender equality, its passage and the Congress heralded a more active role by the Cuban state and the FMC regarding women's rights.

While the FMC Congress suggested the possibility of change, Davis's presence confirmed her steadfast, special position in Cuban revolutionary culture. It also signaled Davis's increased attention to gender on the island. In her speech at the Congress, Davis reiterated her support for the Cuban Revolution and her belief that socialism lent itself to women's rights, declaring that "the example of Cuba has confirmed that there cannot be true emancipation for women without a socialist revolution," just as there couldn't be "socialist revolution without the participation and emancipation of the woman."[96] Conference leaders bestowed upon her the prestigious Ana Betancourt award, named for a Cuban fighter in the war of independence against Spain, and designated Davis as a conference President of Honor. Five years after her first visit to Cuba, she continued to be seen as a militant yet feminine ally; an enduring symbol of anti-imperialism, anticapitalism, antiracism, and women's rights.[97]

Conclusion

Angela Davis became more than a heroic woman in Cuba; she became a visually iconic revolutionary ideal. During her time on the island Davis emphasized her role not as an individual, but as part of a larger struggle and a symbol of what fruit grassroots movements could reap. When traveling with Communist Party delegations in 1969 and 1972, she accepted Cuban accolades in the name of the CPUSA, and claimed to speak not as an individual but in the name of "the other America."[98] The Cuban press echoed this designation in describing events such as Davis's reception at the Alamar housing construction site in familial and collective terms, where workers "received their sister in struggle as the most pure revolutionary ideal, as the representative of the other United States."[99] Like NUCFAD, she saw her role as a representative, not a cult of personality. This inescapably gendered position helped make Davis a lasting name, and face.

Did Cubans get to know Davis "personally," as Cuban student Angelina D. Garcia had requested on her postcard?[100] In addition to those she met on her first trip, some Cubans forged a connection with Davis through the campaign for her freedom and her subsequent presence in Cuban culture—youth in particular. Yet her 1972 visit was orchestrated under high-level auspices of the state. Cubans recall Davis's visit as occurring in an official capacity. Davis's multipronged identity and ideological affiliations provided her with accepted structures of credibility, security, and visibility on the island not often afforded to other black liberation activists, who had no corresponding organization to bolster their goals for the United States or international movement, nor to shape their reception in Cuba. The Cuban Revolution's embrace of Davis continued its pattern of solidarity with African American activists, but Davis's gender combined with her race and communist affiliation made her both an accepted individual and a beloved icon.

Davis also never openly criticized Cuba. The Cuban state extended refuge to African American activists for a range of reasons, including a shared opposition to US policies, Cold War pragmatism, and overlapping anti-imperialist, antiracist, and anticapitalist ideologies. Yet it would not be surprising, given the resources the Cuban government expended on black radicals on the island and the low tolerance for criticism of the revolution of any kind, for Cuban leadership to become wary of extending solidarity and refuge to African American activists who ultimately levied critiques. Undoubtedly Davis felt grateful to the revolutionary state and the Cuban people for supporting the campaign for her freedom, and for welcoming her repeatedly to the island. Her global philosophy of liberation may have prioritized US aggression toward Cuba over the revolution's shortcomings, or steered her toward a position of support for the radical vision of the Cuban struggle even if it had not come to pass. Further, her continued adherence to socialism precluded a denunciation of the Cuban Revolution along those grounds. But if socialism helped ensure Davis's relationship with Cuba, gender elevated it.

Furthermore, Davis's encounters with Cuba must be considered within the revolution's broader global politics. In the aftermath of the failed gran zafra sugarcane harvest that Davis witnessed in the summer of 1969, the revolutionary state turned increasingly to the Soviet Union for economic support and the apparatus of communism to structure Cuban society. These turns had ideological impact. Davis's communist affiliation rather than a perceived black nationalism made her attractive for Castro. But she also reflected a larger shift from the more experimental era that characterized the Cuban Revolution's first decade to the greater institutionalization of the 1970s, and became a transitional figure who was embraced as an individual but represented a centralized organization. Davis may have been different than those that came before her, but she also proved to be the last of the exalted icons from the United States.

Davis eventually dropped her CPUSA affiliation, although she remains an advocate of socialism. In the decades following her initial visit to Cuba, she wrote increasingly about women. Her seminal work *Women, Race, and Class* examined the racism and class divisions between US women from slavery into the twentieth century, while *Women, Culture, and Politics* incorporated women around the world.[101] In the short introduction to the 1988 edition of her autobiography, Davis wrote more about the women's liberation movement than in the first edition, expressing regret that "I was not able to also apply a measuring stick which manifested a more complex understanding of the dialectics of the personal and the political."[102] Studies of women's liberation have changed precipitously since 1988. Yet thinking through Davis's encounter with the Cuban Revolution in the 1960s and 1970s also benefits from a dialectic: one that positions Davis's political symbolism alongside her multifaceted personhood.

Sarah J. Seidman is the Puffin Foundation Curator of Social Activism at the Museum of the City of New York, where she curates *Activist New York* and other exhibitions. She holds a PhD in American studies and an MA in public humanities from Brown University, and is completing a book on the connections between the black liberation movement and the Cuban Revolution.

Notes

1. Astudillo, "Un día inolvidable con nuestra Angela."
2. Joe Walker, "Angela Davis," undated pamphlet, *Muhammed Speaks*, section 2, box 2, folder 18, Communist Party of the United States of America Records (old processing system), Tamiment Library and Robert F. Wagner Labor Archives, New York University (hereafter CPUSA Collection).
3. Gosse, *Where the Boys Are*; Elbaum, *Revolution in the Air*; Young, *Soul Power*; Tietchen, *The Cubalogues*; Gronbeck-Tedesco, *Cuba, the United States, and Cultures of the Transnational Left*; Rojas, *Fighting over Fidel*; and Latner, *Cuban Revolution in America*.
4. Lekus, "Queer Harvests"; and Tice, "The Politics of US Feminist Internationalism and Cuba."
5. Reitan, *The Rise and Decline of an Alliance*; de la Fuente, *A Nation for All*; Sawyer, *Racial Politics in Post-Revolutionary Cuba*; Seidman, "Tricontinental Routes of Solidarity"; and Benson, *Antiracism in Cuba*.
6. Davis donated her papers to the Schlesinger Library on the History of Women in America at Harvard University in 2018, which will be made available to researchers by 2020, paving the way for new research.

7. For more on this broader topic, see Seidman, "Venceremos Means We Shall Overcome."

8. For more on the later exiles of Assata Shakur and Nehanda Abiodun, see Latner, *Cuban Revolution in America*. Earlier visits by Sarah Wright, Jennifer Lawson, Alice Walker, and Elaine Brown have not been fully explored, nor has the exile of Mabel Williams, who was married to Robert F. Williams.

9. Gore and Aptheker, "Free Angela Davis."

10. Bhavnani and Davis, "Complexity, Activism, Optimism," 66.

11. Davis, *Angela Davis*, 123.

12. Davis, *Angela Davis*, 122, 125.

13. Regarding the controversy over the Birmingham Civil Rights Institute's rescinding of an award for Davis in early 2019, reportedly due to her support for the Palestinian Boycott, Divestment, and Sanctions movement, Davis told journalists she was glad the incident had led to a "conversation on internationalism." See Ramanathan, "Angela Davis is Beloved, Detested, Misunderstood."

14. Davis, *Angela Davis*, 161.

15. Davis, *Angela Davis*, 182.

16. Slutsky, *Gendering Radicalism*, 154.

17. Davis, *Angela Davis*, 209.

18. Davis, *Angela Davis*, 216.

19. Davis, *Angela Davis*, 203, 216.

20. "National Committee Meeting. Reports on Angela Davis Delegation to Cuba, Chile, USSR, GDR, etc.," October 17, 1972, box 62, disc 1–2, CD 93, Communist Party of the United States of America Audio Collection, Tamiment Library and Robert F. Wagner Labor Archives, New York University (hereafter CPUSA Audio Collection).

21. Mesa-Lago, *Cuba in the 1970s*.

22. "National Committee Meeting," CPUSA Audio Collection.

23. "National Committee Meeting," CPUSA Audio Collection. See also Robert F. Williams to Fidel Castro, The Black Power Movement Part 2: The Papers of Robert F. Williams, August 28, 1966, 25, reel 2 (microfilm); Cleaver, *Soul on Fire*, 108; and Carmichael and Thelwell, *Ready for Revolution*, 633–34.

24. Benson, *Antiracism in Cuba*, 6.

25. Davis, *Angela Davis*, 210.

26. Davis, *Angela Davis*, 371.

27. Tice, "The Politics of US Feminist Internationalism and Cuba," 8.

28. Tice, "The Politics of US Feminist Internationalism and Cuba," 5–6.

29. Divale, "FBI Student Spy"; Montgomery, "Maoist Prof Poses Problem for Regents."

30. Davis, *Angela Davis*, 6.

31. Charlton, "F.B.I. Seizes Angela Davis in Motel Here."

32. Geyer and Beech, "Parade of Radicals to Havana."

33. *Los Angeles Times*, "Alabama Press Search for Angela Davis"; *Chicago Defender*, "Says Angela's Sister Aboard Ship to Cuba."

34. Van Gelder, "The Radical Work of Healing."

35. Baldwin, "An Open Letter to My Sister"; and *Black Scholar*, "Angela Davis: Black Soldier," 1.

36. Springer, *Living for the Revolution*, 89.

37. "One Million People Sponsor Freedom for Angela Davis," box 4, folder 15, Angela Davis Legal Defense Collection, Schomburg Center for Research in Black Culture, New York Public Library.

38. Mitchell, *The Fight to Free Angela Davis*, 4–5. See also All India Students Congress, "Youth Accuses Imperialism"; and United Coalition for Angela Davis Day, "End Racism and Repression," section 2, box 2, folder 18, CPUSA Collection; and "Luckacs' Statement," box 4, folder 15, Angela Davis Legal Defense Collection.
39. Kaplan, *Dreaming in French*, 210–14.
40. Gore and Aptheker, "Free Angela Davis."
41. Gore and Aptheker, "Free Angela Davis."
42. Catlett to Aptheker, March 12, 1971, in Gore and Aptheker, "Free Angela Davis."
43. *Granma*, "Mensaje de la FMC al Comité de Solidaridad con Angela Davis."
44. *Granma*, "Constituyen Comite por la Libertad de Angela Davis."
45. *Mujeres*, "Declaración del Comite por la Libertad de Angela Davis"; and Casteñada, "¿Por qué Angela?," 70–71.
46. Catlett to Aptheker, in "Free Angela Davis."
47. Davis, *Angela Davis*, 398.
48. Carmichael and Thelwell, *Ready for Revolution*, 697.
49. The photograph was taken by F. Joseph Crawford at a September 9, 1969 press conference. See Marks, "Trailing Angela Davis."
50. Marks, "Trailing Angela Davis."
51. Marks, "Trailing Angela Davis."
52. See *Mujeres*, August 1971; and postcards to Angela Davis, box 138, folder 19, CPUSA Collection.
53. Frick, *The Tricontinental Solidarity Poster.*
54. *Granma*, "No Tenemos Otra Alternativa que Tomar las Armas," and "Entrevista Radio Habana Cuba a Stokely Carmichael."
55. Newton, "Cultura y Liberación," 100.
56. Garcia to Davis, box 138, folder 19, CPUSA Collection.
57. *Black Panther*, "OSPAAAL Supports the Afro-American People"; M. S., "Angela Davis," 15.
58. De Juan, "Cuba: La Mujer Pintada."
59. Astudillo, "No podría haber sido de otro modo, Angela." See also Ford, *Liberated Threads*; and Craig, *Ain't I a Beauty Queen?*
60. Casteñada, "¿Por Qué Angela?," 70–71; and Yara, "Imagen y colorido de Mayda," 24–25.
61. Nadelson, *Who Is Angela Davis?*, 22; and Petersen, "Movies: Angela Davis," 22.
62. Davis, "Afro Images," 37; and Kelley, "Nap Time," 339.
63. Randall, *To Change the World*, 55–56.
64. Kelley, "Nap Time," 339–52; and Mercer, *Welcome to the Jungle*, 97–128.
65. Davis, *Angela Davis*, xv–xvi.
66. Davis, "Afro Images," 39.
67. *Granma*, "Declarada Inocente Angela Davis"; and "Rieteran Invitación a Angela Davis."
68. *Granma*, "Desbordamiento popular en la Isla de la Juventud"; and Astudillo, "Angela Davis en la Isla de Juventud."
69. Rivero, "La otra Norteamerica."
70. Astudillo, "Recibe Angela Davis la orden 'Playa Giron.'"
71. Carrasco, "Ofrece Angela Davis conferencia de prensa."
72. Printed in the *Granma* as "verdadero patria," October 8, 1972.
73. Astudillo, "No Podría Haber Sido de Otro Modo, Angela"; and *Granma*, "Mensaje de Angela Davis al Pueblo de Cuba."

74. *Granma*, "Recibió Vilma Espín a Angela Davis."
75. Stoner, "Militant Heroines," 71–96.
76. Stoner, "Militant Heroines," 72.
77. Stoner, "Militant Heroines," 74–75.
78. Chase, "Women's Organizations," 440–58.
79. Chase, *Revolution within the Revolution*, 77, 97.
80. Chase, *Revolution within the Revolution*, 85–86.
81. Chase, *Revolution within the Revolution*, 117.
82. Chase, *Revolution within the Revolution*, 6, 39, 61.
83. Smith and Padula, *Sex and Revolution*, 32, 45, 50.
84. Molyneux, "State, Gender, and Institutional Change," 298.
85. Molyneux, "State, Gender, and Institutional Change," 299.
86. Tice, "The Politics of US Feminist Internationalism and Cuba," 9.
87. Benson, "Sara Gómez: *Afrocubana*."
88. Chase, *Revolution within the Revolution*, 108.
89. Chase, *Revolution within the Revolution*, 122–25.
90. Astudillo, "Un día inolvidable con nuestra Angela."
91. "National Committee Meeting," CPUSA Audio Collection.
92. "National Committee Meeting," CPUSA Audio Collection.
93. "National Committee Meeting," CPUSA Audio Collection.
94. Bhavnani and Davis, "Complexity, Activism, Optimism," 76–77; Carrasco, "Voy a tartar de poner en alto el legado de la orden 'Ana Betancourt.'"
95. Molyneux, "State, Gender, and Institutional Change," 298.
96. Carrasco, "Ofrece Angela Davis conferencia de prensa"; and Rojas, "Intervienen delegaciones de otros países."
97. Carrasco, "Llegó a Cuba la dirigente Comunista Angela Davis;" and Calderón, "Presidieron Fidel y Dorticós."
98. Davis, "Discurso Pronunciado por la Compañera Angela Davis."
99. Astudillo, "Un día inolvidable con nuestra Angela."
100. Garcia to Davis, box 138, folder 19, CPUSA Collection.
101. Davis, *Women, Race, and Class*; and Davis, *Women, Culture, and Politics*. See also Salem, "On Transnational Feminist Solidarity."
102. Davis, *Angela Davis*, viii.

References

Astudillo, Félix Pita. "Angela Davis en la Isla de Juventud: El verdadero 'Sueño Americano.'" *Granma*, October 4, 1972.
Astudillo, Félix Pita. "No podría haber sido de otro modo, Angela: Un inenarrable fenómeno de masas." *Granma*, October 8, 1972.
Astudillo, Félix Pita. "Recibe Angela Davis la orden 'Playa Giron,' la más alta condecoración instituida por el Gobierno Revolucionario de Cuba." *Granma*, October 5, 1972.
Astudillo, Félix Pita. "Un día inolvidable con nuestra Angela: Entre la arcilla y la obra." *Granma*, October 3, 1972.
Baldwin, James. "An Open Letter to My Sister, Miss Angela Davis." *New York Review of Books*, January 21, 1971.
Benson, Devyn Spence. *Antiracism in Cuba: The Unfinished Revolution*. Chapel Hill: University of North Carolina Press, 2016.

Benson, Devyn Spence. "Sara Gómez: *Afrocubana* (Afro-Cuban Women's) Activism After 1961." *Cuban Studies*, no. 46 (2018): 134–58.

Bhavnani, Kum-Kum, and Angela Davis, "Complexity, Activism, Optimism: An Interview with Angela Y. Davis." *Feminist Review*, no. 31 (1989): 66–81.

Black Panther. "OSPAAAL Supports the Afro-American People." November 28, 1970.

Black Scholar. "Angela Davis: Black Soldier." Vol. 2, no. 3 (1970): 1.

Calderón, Mirta Rodríguez. "Presidieron Fidel y Dorticós la Sesion Inaugural del II Congreso de la FMC." *Granma*, November 26, 1974.

Carmichael, Stokely, and Ekwueme Michael Thelwell. *Ready for Revolution: The Life and Struggles of Stokely Carmichael (Kwame Ture).* New York: Scribner, 2003.

Carrasco, Juana. "Llegó a Cuba la dirigente Comunista Angela Davis, invitada para el II Congreso." *Granma*, November 26, 1974.

Carrasco, Juana. "Ofrece Angela Davis conferencia de prensa." *Granma*, September 27, 1972.

Carrasco, Juana. "'Voy a tartar de poner en alto el legado de la orden 'Ana Betancourt' y lo que ello significa y el legado de la mujer Cubana y lo que ello significa.'" *Granma*, December 3, 1974.

Casteñada, Mireya. "¿Por qué Angela?" *Romances*, March 1971, 70–71.

Charlton, Linda. "F.B.I. Seizes Angela Davis in Motel Here." *New York Times*, October 14, 1970.

Chase, Michelle. "Women's Organizations and the Politics of Gender in Cuba's Urban Insurrection (1952–1958)." *Bulletin of Latin American Research* 29, no. 4 (2010): 440–58.

Chase, Michelle. *Revolution within the Revolution: Women and Gender Politics in Cuba, 1952–1962.* Chapel Hill: University of North Carolina Press, 2015.

Chicago Defender. "Says Angela's Sister Aboard Ship to Cuba." August 26, 1970.

Cleaver, Eldridge. *Soul on Fire.* Waco, TX: Word Books, 1978.

Craig, Maxine Leeds. *Ain't I a Beauty Queen? Black Women, Beauty, and the Politics of Race.* New York: Oxford University Press, 2002.

Davis, Angela Y. "Afro Images: Politics, Fashion, and Nostalgia." *Critical Inquiry* 21, no. 1 (1994): 37–45.

Davis, Angela Y. *Angela Davis—An Autobiography.* 1974; reprint, New York: International Publishers, 1988.

Davis, Angela Y. "Discurso Pronunciado por la Compañera Angela Davis." *Granma*, October 8, 1972.

Davis, Angela Y. *Women, Culture, and Politics.* New York: Random House, 1989.

Davis, Angela Y. *Women, Race, and Class.* New York: Random House, 1981.

de la Fuente, Alejandro. *A Nation for All: Race, Inequality, and Politics in Twentieth-Century Cuba.* Chapel Hill: University of North Carolina Press, 2001.

De Juan, Adelaida. "Cuba: La Mujer Pintada." *Cuba*, March 1972, 15–21.

Divale, William Tulio. "FBI Student Spy in CPUSA Answers Criticism." *UCLA Daily Bruin*, July 1, 1969.

Elbaum, Max. *Revolution in the Air: Sixties Radicals Turn to Lenin, Mao, and Che.* New York: Verso, 2002.

Ford, Tanisha C. *Liberated Threads: Black Women, Style, and the Global Politics of Soul.* Chapel Hill: University of North Carolina Press, 2015.

Frick, Richard. *The Tricontinental Solidarity Poster.* Bern, CH: Commedia-Verlag, 2003.

Geyer, Georgie Anne, and Keyes Beech. "Parade of Radicals to Havana: U.S. Bombers' Tactics Linked to Cuba Visits." *Los Angeles Times*, October 13, 1970.

Gore, Dayo, and Bettina Aptheker, eds. "Free Angela Davis, and All Political Prisoners! A Transnational Campaign for Liberation." *Women and Social Movements in the United States, 1600–2000* (editorial website). Alexander Street Press and State University of New York, Binghamton. womhist.alexanderstreet.com/freeangela/abstract.htm.

Gosse, Van. *Where the Boys Are: Cuba, Cold War America and the Making of a New Left*. New York: Verso, 1993.

Granma. "Constituyen comite por la libertad de Angela Davis." June 17, 1971.

Granma. "Declarada inocente Angela Davis; triunfo de la solidaridad internacional." June 5, 1972.

Granma. "Desbordamiento popular en la Isla de la Juventud durante la visita efectuada por Angela Davis." October 4, 1972.

Granma. "Entrevista Radio Habana Cuba a Stokely Carmichael." August 5, 1967.

Granma. "Mensaje de Angela Davis al Pueblo de Cuba minutos antes de partir rumbo a Chile." October 6, 1972.

Granma. "Mensaje de la FMC al Comité de Solidaridad con Angela Davis." December 9, 1970.

Granma. "No tenemos otra alternativa que tomar las armas, afirmó Stokely Carmichael." August 3, 1967.

Granma. "Recibió Vilma Espín a Angela Davis en la Federación de Mujeres Cubanas, y le entrego el carne que la acredita como miembro de la organización." September 28, 1972.

Granma. "Rieteran invitación a Angela Davis para que visite a Cuba." June 8, 1972.

Gronbeck-Tedesco, John. *Cuba, the United States, and Cultures of the Transnational Left, 1930–1975*. New York: Cambridge University Press, 2015.

Kaplan, Alice. *Dreaming in French: The Paris Years of Jacqueline Bouvier Kennedy, Susan Sontag, and Angela Davis*. Chicago: University of Chicago Press, 2012.

Kelley, Robin D. G. "Nap Time: Historicizing the Afro." *Fashion Theory* 1, no. 4 (1997): 339–51.

Latner, Teishan. *Cuban Revolution in America: Havana and the Making of a United States Left, 1968–1992*. Chapel Hill: University of North Carolina Press, 2018.

Lekus, Ian. "Queer Harvests: Homosexuality, the U.S. New Left, and the Venceremos Brigades to Cuba." In *Imagining Our Americas: Toward a Transnational Frame*, edited by Sandhya Shukla and Heidi Tinsman, 249–81. Durham, NC: Duke University Press, 2007.

Los Angeles Times. "Alabama Press Search for Angela Davis." August 18, 1970.

Marks, Ben. "Trailing Angela Davis, from FBI Flyers to 'Radical Chic' Art." *Collectors Weekly*, July 3, 2013.

Mercer, Kobena. *Welcome to the Jungle: New Positions in Black Cultural Studies*. New York: Routledge, 1994.

Mesa-Lago, Carmelo. *Cuba in the 1970s: Pragmatism and Institutionalization*, 2nd ed. Albuquerque: University of New Mexico Press, 1978.

Mitchell, Charlene. *The Fight to Free Angela Davis: Its Importance for the Working Class*. New York: New Outlook, 1972.

Molyneux, Maxine. "State, Gender, and Institutional Change: The Federación de Mujeres Cubanas." In *Hidden Histories of Gender and the State in Latin America*, edited by Elizabeth Dore and Maxine Molyneux, 291–321. Durham, NC: Duke University Press, 2000.

Montgomery, Ed. "Maoist Prof Poses Problem for Regents." *San Francisco Examiner*, July 9, 1969.

M. S. "Angela Davis: Esta mujer, alegre y profunda." *Romances*, September 1972, 14–15.

Mujeres. "Declaración del Comite por la Libertad de Angela Davis," July 1971, 12.

Nadelson, Regina. *Who Is Angela Davis? The Biography of a Revolutionary*. New York: Peter H. Wyden, 1972.

Newton, Huey P. "Cultura y Liberación." *Tricontinental*, no. 11 (1969): 100–104.

Petersen, Maurice. "Movies: Angela Davis." *Essence*, June 1972, 22.

Ramanathan, Lavanya. "Angela Davis Is Beloved, Detested, Misunderstood. What Can a Lifelong Radical Teach the Resistance Generation?" *Washington Post*, February 26, 2019.

Randall, Margaret. *To Change the World: My Years in Cuba*. New Brunswick, NJ: Rutgers University Press, 2009.

Reitan, Ruth. *The Rise and Decline of an Alliance: Cuba and African American Leaders in the 1960s*. East Lansing: Michigan State University Press, 1999.

Rivero, Raúl. "La otra Norteamerica." *Cuba*, November 1972, 10–13.

Rojas, Marta. "Intervienen delegaciones de otros países; jefes de organizaciones políticas y ministros del Gobierno Revolucionario en el II Congreso de la Federación de Mujeres Cubanas." *Granma*, November 27, 1974.

Rojas, Rafael. *Fighting over Fidel: The New York Intellectuals and the Cuban Revolution*. Princeton, NJ: Princeton University Press, 2016.

Salem, Sara. "On Transnational Feminist Solidarity: Angela Davis in Egypt." *Signs* 43, no. 2 (2018): 245–67.

Sawyer, Mark. *Racial Politics in Post-Revolutionary Cuba*. New York: Cambridge University Press, 2006.

Seidman, Sarah J. "Tricontinental Routes of Solidarity: Stokely Carmichael in Cuba." *Journal of Transnational American Studies* 4, no. 2 (2012): 1–25.

Seidman, Sarah J. "Venceremos Means We Shall Overcome: The African American Freedom Struggle and the Cuban Revolution, 1959–1979." PhD diss., Brown University, 2013.

Slutsky, Beth. *Gendering Radicalism: Women and Communism in Twentieth-Century California*. Lincoln: University of Nebraska Press, 2015.

Smith, Lois M., and Alfred Padula. *Sex and Revolution: Women in Socialist Cuba*. New York: Oxford University Press, 1996.

Springer, Kimberly. *Living for the Revolution: Black Feminist Organizations, 1969–1980*. Durham, NC: Duke University Press, 2005.

Stoner, K. Lynn. "Militant Heroines and the Consecration of the Patriarchal State: The Glorification of Loyalty, Combat, and National Suicide in the Making of Cuban National Identity." *Cuban Studies*, no. 34 (2003): 71–96.

Tice, Karen W. "The Politics of US Feminist Internationalism and Cuba: Solidarities and Fractures on the Venceremos Brigades, 1969–1989." *Feminist Encounters: A Journal of Critical Studies in Culture and Politics* 2, no. 1 (2018): 1–15.

Tietchen, Todd. *The Cubalogues: Beat Writers in Revolutionary Havana*. Gainesville: University Press of Florida, 2010.

Van Gelder, Sarah. "The Radical Work of Healing: Fania and Angela Davis on a New Kind of Civil Rights Activism." *YES!*, February 18, 2016.

Yara. "Imagen y colorido de Mayda." *Romances*, March 1971, 24–25.

Young, Cynthia. *Soul Power: Culture, Radicalism, and the Making of a U.S. Third World Left*. Durham, NC: Duke University Press, 2006.

Tactical *Negrificación* and White Femininity

Race, Gender, and Internationalism in Cuba's Angolan Mission

Lorraine Bayard de Volo

At the ideological heart of the Cuban Revolution is the commitment to liberation from oppressive systems at home and abroad. From early on, as it supported anti-imperialist struggles, revolutionary Cuba also officially condemned racism and sexism. However, the state's attention to racism and sexism has fluctuated—it has been full-throated at times, silent at others. In considering Cuba's legacy, this essay examines gender and race in its international liberatory efforts while also considering the human costs of armed internationalism. Why did women feature prominently in some instances and not others? As a "post-racial" society where "race doesn't matter," how are we to understand those occasions in which race officially *did* matter?

I focus on Cuba's Angola mission (1975–91) to explore the revolution's uneven attention to gender and race.[1] Rather than consistently battling inequities, the state approached gender and racial liberation separately and tactically, as means to military, political, and diplomatic ends. Through *negrificación* (blackening) of national identity, Cuba highlighted race to internationally legitimize and domestically mobilize support for its Angola mission.[2] In contrast, despite their high profile in the Cuban insurrection of the 1950s and 1980s defense, women were a relatively minor theme in the Angolan mission.

Several prominent studies note the international factors behind Cuba's racial politics, but they have a domestic focus, leaving international dynamics relatively

Radical History Review
Issue 136 (January 2020) DOI 10.1215/01636545-7857243

unexplored.[3] Here, I examine the international dynamics of race and gender in the Angola mission. While the state highlighted African ancestry internationally, women were a minor and primarily domestic theme. Few military women served in Angola, though many went as civilian internationalists. I suggest that military women's femininity was furthermore racialized, as idealized feminine combatants were typically represented as white and light-skinned women despite a diverse racial composition. Finally, regarding (in)visibility and Cuba's internationalism, I explore evidence of ambivalence and trauma among veterans that conflicts with the glowing testimonials of state media. Though these are predictable outcomes of armed conflict, military and civilian *internacionalistas* have no state-sanctioned public channel for critically assessing the mission in Angola or acknowledging psychological distress.

Racial and Gender Equality as Goals and Tools

Revolutionary Cuba adopted a single-issue framework, focusing on either race or gender, rather than an intersectional framework attending to the multiply oppressed. It outlawed discrimination, channeled Afro-Cubans and women into the public sphere of work, education, the military, and the Communist Party, and trusted economic redistribution to solve inequalities.[4] Problematically, Cuba "sought to use advances in the areas of race and gender to legitimize its activities and consolidate state power."[5] In doing so, it defaulted to representing Black soldiers as men and women soldiers as white. In sum, gender and racial equality, official revolutionary goals, were also tools to advance the state, yet Afro-Cuban women at the intersection of racial and gender oppression were largely absent from representations of internationalist New Men and Women.

From early on, Cuba represented its revolutionary promise and accomplishments to a global audience by embracing internationalism as well as racial and gender liberation. Addressing Latin American leaders in 1961, Che Guevara declared Cuba's solidarity with the world's oppressed peoples while also confirming Cuba's commitment to liberation from racial and gender discrimination. Cuba, he explained, "took many steps to affirm human dignity, one of the first having been the abolition of racial discrimination."[6] Che also remarked on advances in women's liberation, yet as scholars note, gender equality was relegated to a secondary status.[7] Fidel Castro declared, "The liberation of women is dependent upon the Revolution's success in attaining its primary objectives: to establish a wholly socialist economy and society."[8] Nonetheless, the state often touted women's advances as evidence of the revolution's success, and women's military participation was an early measure.[9] In celebrating the rebel triumph in 1959, Castro characterized women's participation as a rebel accomplishment: "We have proven that in Cuba it is not only men who fight. Women also fight."[10]

While women's equality was a secondary if unfinished goal, Cuba declared the race problem solved while shutting down independent Black organizing, which it viewed as divisive.[11] Despite claims of a raceless society, racism remains and racial politics follow "patterns of opening and retrenchment" according to state needs.[12] The literature indicates that in Cuba, international factors are key drivers of racial politics.[13] Cuba emphasized race to embarrass the United States for its lack of progress on racial equality and to promote socialism in the Global South.[14] With its Angola mission, Cuba departed from its previous claims of being a raceless society to selectively claim a Latin African identity.[15] In what follows, I explore how and why Cuba raised the issues of race and gender separately and tactically, depending upon the degree to which those issues supported its Angolan mission.

Tactical Negrificación: *Internacionalismo* and the Mission in Angola

In the name of *internacionalismo* (international solidarity), Cuba initiated Operation Carlota, entering the Angolan conflict in late 1975 as three Angolan rebel armies clashed when the Portuguese colonial power departed. It secretly sent 1,100 troops to support the leftist People's Movement for the Liberation of Angola (MPLA) and thwart South African military incursions.[16] Cuba ultimately sent tens of thousands of additional soldiers and support personnel. Over the course of sixteen years (1975–90), 377,033 Cuban combatants and over 50,000 Cuban civilian workers served in Angola, with 2,077 deaths.[17]

Operation Carlota significantly shaped African politics. It was pivotal in establishing MPLA control in Angola, ending South Africa's grip on neighboring Namibia, and toppling Apartheid itself.[18] Nelson Mandela thanked Cuba in 1991: "In Africa we are used to being victims of countries that want to take from us our territory or overthrow our sovereignty. In African history there is not another instance where another people has stood up for one of ours."[19] According to Piero Gleijeses, "Victory in Angola boosted Cuba's prestige in the Third World," with Cubans now "regarded as heroes in the Black world."[20]

Soon after the mission began, Castro proclaimed Cubans to be a "Latin-African people," an unprecedented acknowledgment of racial identity that linked it to solidarity with African peoples.[21] He explained, "Many are the things that unite us to Angola: our cause, our common interests, politics, ideology. But we are also united by blood . . . in the two senses of the word, blood of our ancestors and blood we shed together on the battlefields."[22] Jorge Risquet, the highest-ranking Cuban official in Angola, had declared in 1959 that the "revolution does not have a color, except the olive green color of the revolutionary army."[23] Yet in 1985, addressing the MPLA Congress, he too embraced the racial shared-origin story: "The Cuban and Angolan peoples have been together for a long time [and] African slaves, many of them from the territory that is now Angola, were part of the Cuban liberation army in the wars against Spanish colonialism."[24] Similarly, Cubans were said to be "returning" to Africa to aid Angola's independence and repel the mercenary and racist armies of the United States and Apartheid South Africa.

This was an instance of tactical negrificación, by which the state positioned Cuba as Black relative to other white-dominated nations, especially the United States and South Africa.[25] In contemporary Cuba, Kaifa Roland finds that the post-Soviet rise of tourism has racialized Cubans and Cuba itself as Black, in contrast to the racialized white Europe and North America. However, unlike this contemporary negrificación, in which Cubans experience themselves as "onerously black," the tactical negrificación of Cuba in its Angola mission aimed at racial pride.[26]

In part, tactical negrificación responded to symbolic dimensions of global Cold War politics. Cuba's Angolan mission came as the United States was reeling from defeat in Vietnam and the Watergate scandal. Leading into the 1976 elections, the Ford administration faced conservative criticism of US-Soviet détente plus fears that the United States was perceived as weak, as the early "victory of Soviet-backed forces in Angola [became] a symbol of United States helplessness."[27] The US press and policymakers obsessed about the USSR's role in Angola, with Cuba only occasionally and obliquely mentioned as a Soviet-backed force.

But Cuba did not escape blame, and President Gerald Ford vilified Castro as an "international outlaw" for sending troops to Angola.[28] Aiming at the heart of Cuban internacionalismo, the United States condemned Cuba for perpetuating the wrongs the revolution claimed to fight against, labeling Cuba and its Soviet allies as racist, imperialist aggressors. US Secretary of State Henry Kissinger accused Cuba of having "never had any historic interests" in Angola.[29] Taking up the attack, the *New York Times* called Cuba's Angola mission "a blatant military intervention by white powers from distant continents in the internal affairs of a black African country."[30] Similarly, an opinion editorial framed Cuban troops as "mercenaries" doing the bidding of their Soviet "paymaster."[31] Angolan rebels fighting against the MPLA denounced Cuban troops as a foreign army of occupation.[32]

In response, Cuba insisted it acted out of solidarity, with no desire to control Angola or exploit its resources, and that it had made its decision autonomously, without Soviet direction. In a 1976 article in *Verde Olivo*, the Cuban military magazine, an officer argued that unlike the United States, Cuba would never invade a country to subjugate it, as doing so is "antithetical to revolutionary principles."[33] Fifteen years later, Raúl Castro claimed: "All [internacionalistas who served in Angola] were moved by a single interest: to save and consolidate the fraternal Republic of Angola. . . . We have brought nothing back but the satisfaction of having done our duty and the remains of our comrades who fell."[34]

As reassurance particularly to African nations that its Angola mission was not an occupation, Cuba claimed to answer the call of its African "brothers"— brothers in the familial sense of shared blood, in the ideological sense of shared ideals, and as "brothers in arms."[35] As Fidel Castro put it in 1975, "We do not fold our arms when we see an African people, our brother that the imperialists want devoured, suddenly and brutally attacked by South Africa."[36] This was a fraternal, bilateral relationship, then, and not a Cuban occupation.[37] The image of Cuban Latin-Africans fighting alongside Black African brothers against imperialism and Apartheid combined internacionalismo with race-based liberation to produce a radical inversion of global racial power relations. In addition to bolstering criticism of the US government, it also helped Cuba frame the predominately white and vehemently anti-Castro Cuban exile community as "passionately racist."[38] Notably, this image of racial brotherhood was gendered masculine, thus challenging racial but not gender hierarchies.[39]

Domestic Legacies of Racial Politics and Internationalism

The Angolan mission's domestic legacy on race relations is less clear. Initially, Cuba selectively deployed dark-skinned Afro-Cuban soldiers, with the idea that they could blend in with local allies.[40] While this tactic was meant to evade the CIA, it also had the domestic effect of highlighting the courage and internationalist spirit of Afro-Cuban soldiers. In addition, Cuba named the mission Operation Carlota after an Afro-Cuban woman who died leading a 1844 slave uprising.[41] Aisha Finch finds that Carlota's actions and identity as a Black woman became "an intriguing metonym through which to read individual eruptions of black rage and the collective desires of black militancy."[42] Indeed, over 130 years later, on the anniversary of Carlota's slave uprising, the revolutionary state took up her memory, hailing Black identity while also tapping into the revolution's faith in women's abilities. Internationalists "returned" to Africa "to extend the legend of Carlota, the Cuban-African heroine," a framing emblematic of Cuba's tactical negrificación in which Cuban-ness evoked African ancestry.[43] Named after a woman rebel slave, Cuba's mission began with a recognition of the revolutionary potential of Afro-Cuban women; however, during the course of the mission, the gendered aspect of the reference receded.

Roughly half the Cuban population has African ancestry, and Afro-Cuban men were overrepresented in the rank-and-file of the military.[44] Furthermore, the Angolan struggle began as one against the white Portuguese colonial power followed by the intervention of Apartheid South Africa. The literature suggests, accordingly, that Cuba's aid to the independence struggles of Black Africans played well to the global subaltern. As Frank Taylor asserts, "Operation Carlota established beyond the shadow of doubt Fidel's credentials as 'one of the blackest men in the Americas.'"[45]

There is evidence that it encouraged Afro-Cuban support for the Angola mission.[46] For example, Reverend Abbuno González of the Cuban Pentecostal Church stated, "My grandfather came from Angola. So it's my duty to go and help Angola. I owe it to my ancestors."[47] Merida Rodrigues, a Black woman who had served as a civilian internacionalista in Angola, mentioned the "African heritage of slavery" in explaining her sense of obligation to help Angola. She was further motivated because "[Angola] had so many needs," which reminded her of her own poor and predominately Black community before the revolution.[48] However, as I discuss below, internationalists interviewed over a decade later did not highlight race as a motivator.

(In)Visible Gender

Normatively and numerically, Cuban soldiers were overwhelmingly men, but the form of masculinity adopted by the Cuban state was remarkably low-key. Fidel Castro's comments at the burial of internacionalistas illustrate the state's position throughout the mission: "It is not our intention at this solemn time to boast of our successes or to humiliate anyone, not even those who were our adversaries. Our country was not looking for military glory or prestige. . . . Even though we always acted with all the necessary firmness, at no time during the negotiating process did we utter an arrogant, dominating, or boastful word."[49] Indeed, only rarely were

Figure 1. *Verde Olivo* cartoon (March 21, 1976, by René de la Nuez), featuring Angola as a Black combatant and Cuba unnamed but represented as the inanimate globe "Solidarity." The two confront their Angolan enemies, the racially indistinct rats, as well as white imperialists: the United States (as Uncle Sam) and South Africa.

victories announced, and those were often described in terms of tactics more than heroics. Consistently, the state portrayed the military as disciplined soldiers doing their duty, motivated exclusively by solidarity, in marked contrast to greedy, racist, neoimperialist adversaries. Both sides performed a version of masculine strength that rendered them formidable adversaries, but in this rendering, Cuba claimed an honorable masculinity that it contrasted to its corrupt and dishonorable masculine adversary.

As the cartoon by René de la Nuez illustrates (fig. 1), Cuba also took pains not to outshine its Angolan ally and consistently portrayed its soldiers as playing in a supporting role alongside Black Angolans rather than leading in battle.[50] One Cuban leader explained, "We thought it would be much more dignified if the people we had helped talked about [our aid]."[51] This sensitivity arose in part because some African states viewed Cuba as an occupier on the continent.[52] Accordingly, this position of Cuban humility avoided offending African governments.

Given Cuba's 1960s baby boom and male draft, the Angolan mission did not need new sources of recruits, namely women, unlike in the 1980s War of All the People, in which women were the central focus and hundreds of thousands were mobilized into militias. Though a small number of Cuban military women served in Angola, gender was not central to the state propaganda, which focused instead on Afro-Cuban identity and *internacionalismo*.[53] The exceptions tended to involve Angolan women, mothers of male combatants or, after 1984, women of the anti–aircraft artillery units.

Early Cuban media references to women and Angola often focused on Angolan women, celebrating combatant motherhood in particular. A 1976 *Verde Olivo* article praised Angolan women in combat: "She wants to . . . demonstrate once again that she is capable of being just like you . . . to defeat the enemy of humanity. . . . She is going to defend the child of her womb. And take the rifle and shoot, just like you, for the child to live. So that all the children live."[54] Mariana Grajales, Cuba's mixed-race mother figure of the wars of independence, was also a common reference. In 1978, *Verde Olivo* celebrated International Women's Day by honoring mothers of military sons and daughters: "Dignified inheritors of Mariana Grajales' example, [who have] given to the country their precious children who made today's freedom possible . . . [and] who endure the absence of loved ones with legitimate revolutionary pride."[55] With such stirring references to maternal strength and suffering, Cuba adhered to traditional gendered divisions of war.

The Cuban media also hailed women in ways that more directly challenged gender norms, though these depictions were inevitably accompanied by references that confirmed military women's femininity was intact. Women were regularly described as "also there," offering unique feminine contributions: "The Cuban woman was also there [in Angola], an example of heroism, dedication, and bravery. In Angola, . . . women were the vital and decisive companions to men, contributing to the resurgence of peace and love."[56] The Women's Anti-Aircraft Artillery Regiment in Angola, established on International Women's Day in 1984, received Cuban media attention far out of proportion to its size. *Verde Olivo* featured artillery women stationed at the border of the US base in Guantanamo. These "brave and enthusiastic girls [*muchachas*]" hope to serve in Angola: "It still is not known who will [go to Angola], but there were tears of protest among those who feared they would not be selected."[57] As these examples illustrate, references to women's courage and revolutionary commitment were habitually balanced with feminine attributes—peace, love, and "tears of protest."

Articles covering internacionalistas such as the artillery women, especially articles oriented more toward mobilizing support than conveying news, were typically accompanied by photos of a few white and lighter-skinned women. This racialized representation was so common that I was surprised, upon seeing a group photo of the entire women's artillery regiment stationed in Angola, to find that its members were predominately mixed-race or darker-skinned Afro-Cuban women. The link between idealized femininity and whiteness most likely was not state policy so much as a manifestation of subconscious bias. Regardless, it demonstrates Afro-Cuban women's invisibility even as the state represented internationalism as a means of women's liberation.

Some articles indirectly addressed the question of women's virtue among so many men. Milagros Karina Soto, a political officer attached to a tank brigade, maintained that as the only woman in her unit, she has "received some of the most interesting and agreeable compliments" of her life: "I have never felt better about being a woman, because I sense, from the soldier to the highest officer, their respect and admiration for the *compañeras*. At times they care for us too much; they are afraid that we may be risking too much. . . . But we want to be with them anywhere they need us."[58]

Military women were unfailingly framed as eager, having earned their right to fight. Discussing artillery women, Fidel Castro rhetorically asked, "Could we deny women the opportunity of also participating?"[59] Their participation confirmed the revolution's support for women's equality. As Vilma Espín, head of the Federation of Cuban Women, explained, "women went to fight in Angola, fulfilling an internationalist duty. And they did not do it because there were not enough men to send there, but because our party believes that is also the right of women."[60]

Most Cuban women in Angola were civilian internacionalistas: medical personnel, teachers, journalists, entertainers, and construction workers. Victoria Brittain described "young women with pink earrings and ponytails," many of whom "had left a child at home with a grandmother for their two years in Angola."[61] However, each completed basic military training, and some were attacked and returned fire.[62] This militarized aspect of civilian work in Angola, which entailed stress and trauma as well as physical danger, was not part of official Cuban discourse.

In sum, Cuban coverage of women's participation in the Angola mission was a consistent but not prominent theme. While negrificación was primarily oriented to an international audience, representations of women addressed a domestic one, sometimes hewing to traditional gender relations, sometimes challenging them, but often tapping into a femininity racialized as white or lighter-skinned.

Internacionalista Ambivalence and Trauma

When it comes to memory, Angola now evokes ambivalence or even trauma for many Cubans. In her research with predominately civilian internacionalistas, Christine Hatzky found that most "were fundamentally persuaded not only of the success of the internationalist concept, but also that what they themselves were doing was right"; nonetheless, "In the memories of many Cubans . . . Angola remains a difficult phase in their history."[63] Most critically, among interviewees she found trauma, anxiety, stress, and despair to be common experiences.[64] Although the state legitimized the Angolan mission through claims to an African ancestry and the "return" to Africa to fight alongside their "brothers," Hatzky found little evidence of a special affinity for Africa in general or Angola in particular, and only a few of those interviewed mentioned searching for their African roots as a reason for volunteering.[65] It is not clear whether the importance of the Cuban connection to Africa had become diluted over time or if state sources during the mission did not accurately reflect public sentiment.

During my fieldwork, Cubans who readily spoke on a range of other topics were typically reluctant to speak about Angola in a formal interview setting. This hesitancy was likely influenced by the state secrecy that had surrounded the mission—a hesitancy compounded by my identity as a US citizen. But in more spontaneous moments, many Cubans raised Angola on their own, asserting that it was a mistake and waste of resources, a view often influenced by a perception of abandonment by their Angolan ally once the conflict was over.

Critical perspectives are also evident in artistic expressions.[66] For example, several Cubans who were reluctant to detail their own Angolan experience instead referred me to Frank Delgado's 1995 song "Veterano," which Robert Nasatir describes as "a bitter evocation of the personal cost of the Angolan conflict."[67] Delgado sings of having been ignorant of Angola until his unit was loaded onto a plane "without many explanations" and, "confused and with camouflage clothing . . . , we landed in a city called Luanda." He describes his mother as "truly alone, looking for me on a map written in Portuguese." He also recalls Angolans' fickle reception:

One day we were received with joy
another day that we expected the same
They insulted us and cursed us.

His lyrics also touch on the intentions of Cuban troops, which ranged from admirable to questionable. In acknowledging concerns for his abandoned mother, the dubious honor of some of his "brothers-in-arms," and even his own confusion over the mission, this song challenges the often-gendered tropes that bolstered Cuba's mission in Angola. The ambivalent and even bitter reflection resonates with Hatzky's findings but contrasts sharply with the official framing of the mission. Though the revolution's limited and selective representation of the individual internacionalista experience does not prepare us for evidence of ambivalence and trauma, such emotional and psychological costs are consistent with the literature on war. These sobering findings shine new light on Cuba's internationalism, underscoring its human costs.

Conclusion

In its mission in Angola, Cuba's overwhelmingly male military had sufficient numbers such that the state was not pressured to recruit women or otherwise challenge the gendered division of war. Yet race was a prominent theme, and through negrificación, Cuba legitimized its Angolan mission to a global audience. Though a racially mixed group of military women served, they were small in number, and the public face of the internacionalista woman was white or light-skinned. The Cuban military in Angola remained normatively and numerically masculine, and the racial pride generated from the negrificación of its international mission was predominately gendered masculine. Cuba's 1980s War of All the People defense mobilization helps contextualize these findings. In that case, men alone could not meet its recruitment goals, so the state actively courted women, often linking participation to women's liberation. In sum, Afro-Cuban men gained some recognition and status and white women were the feminine face of the Cuban internacionalistas. But Afro-Cuban women, doubly disadvantaged, remained largely invisible despite their representation in Cuba's female artillery units.

This research supports the argument that revolutionary Cuba's gender- and race-based liberatory efforts were secondary goals that ebbed and flowed according to their utility for realizing international and domestic military campaigns. It also sheds light on Black and mixed-race women's double disadvantage and invisibility in the internationalist project. Finally, it underscores the lingering damage of armed conflict and calls for an expanded understanding of the costs of armed internationalism.

Lorraine Bayard de Volo is a political scientist in the Department of Women and Gender Studies at the University of Colorado Boulder. Her areas of interest include gender, sexuality, and race as they relate to war and revolution in Latin America. She recently published *Women and the Cuban Insurrection: How Gender Shaped Castro's Victory* (2018). She is currently working on a book that takes a postcolonial, feminist approach to Cold War Cuba.

Notes

This work was supported by National Science Foundation Grant SES-0242269 and by a United States Institute of Peace grant.

1. Primary sources for this article include Cuban and US state reports, speeches, videos, archived interviews, and print media 1975–1991: *Verde Olivo* (the weekly military magazine), *Mujeres* (the monthly women's magazine), and *Granma* (the national daily newspaper). Seventeen years of print media was searched for gender or race references, yielding over 2,600 entries, which were then coded. This study also draws from fieldwork interviews and observations and from documents collected from several Cuban archives, including those of the Cuban Women's Federation.
2. Roland, "Tourism and the *Negrificación*."
3. Sawyer, "Unlocking the Official Story"; de la Fuente, *A Nation for All*.
4. Sawyer, *Racial Politics*, xviii; Smith and Padula, *Sex and Revolution*, 4.
5. Sawyer, "Unlocking the Official Story," 407.
6. Guevara, "Economics Cannot Be Separated."
7. Smith and Padula, *Sex and Revolution*; Chase, *Revolution within the Revolution*.
8. Lewis, Lewis, and Rigdon, *Four Women Living the Revolution*, xvii.
9. Bayard de Volo, *Women and the Cuban Insurrection*.
10. Smith and Padula, *Sex and Revolution*, 22.
11. Sawyer, "Unlocking the Official Story," 406–7; de la Fuente, *A Nation for All*.
12. Sawyer, *Racial Politics*, xix.
13. Sawyer, *Racial Politics*, xix; "Unlocking the Official Story," 408; de la Fuente, *A Nation for All*.
14. Sawyer, "Unlocking the Official Story," 405.
15. Roland, "Tourism and the Negrificación"; Sawyer, *Racial Politics*; Moore, *Castro, the Blacks, and Africa*.
16. Domínguez, *To Make a World Safe for Revolution*, 131; Gleijeses, *Conflicting Missions*.
17. R. Castro, "Raul Castro Welcomes Internationalists." See also Domínguez, *To Make a World Safe for Revolution*, 152.
18. Saney, "African Stalingrad," 82.
19. Mandela, "Castro Opens National Moncada Barracks Ceremony."
20. Gleijeses, *Conflicting Missions*, 380.
21. Moore, *Castro, the Blacks, and Africa*, 3.
22. F. Castro, "16th Anniversary of the Committees for the Defense."
23. Benson, *Antiracism in Cuba*, 132.
24. Risquet Valdes, "Seguiremos cumpliendo en Angola."
25. Roland, "Tourism and the *Negrificación*."
26. Roland, "Tourism and the *Negrificación*," 152.
27. Gelb, "U.S., Stung in Angola."
28. *New York Times*, "Castro Resumes."
29. Marcum, "Lessons of Angola," 407.
30. *New York Times*, "'Big Lie'; Gleijeses, *Conflicting Missions*, 321.
31. Safire, "Who Lost Africa?"
32. Hatzky, "'Latin-African' Solidarity," 162.
33. Ramírez Castillo, "Apoyo resuelto."
34. R. Castro, "Raul Castro Welcomes Internationalists."
35. Gleijeses, *Conflicting Missions*; Bayard de Volo, "Revolution in the Binary?"
36. F. Castro, quoted in Saney, "African Stalingrad," 91.

37. See Gleijeses, *Conflicting Missions*, 199.
38. de la Fuente, *A Nation for All*, 306.
39. Bayard de Volo, "Revolution in the Binary?"
40. This practice began in the 1960s at the request of leaders in Zaire and Guinea-Bissau (Gleijeses, *Conflicting Missions*, 88–89, 188). The State Department reported that 480 Black Cuban soldiers landed in Congo for transfer to Angola (Kissinger, "Cuban Clandestine Military Support").
41. Saney, "African Stalingrad," 95.
42. Finch, *Rethinking Slave Rebellion in Cuba*, 148.
43. R. Castro, "Raul Castro Welcomes Internationalists."
44. Moore, *Castro, the Blacks, and Africa*; Domínguez, "Racial and Ethnic Relations," 284.
45. Taylor, "Revolution, Race," 36.
46. Moore, *Castro, the Blacks, and Africa*, 331–32; Gleijeses, *Conflicting Missions*.
47. Saney, "African Stalingrad," 95.
48. Rodrígues, "Interview by Lyn Smith."
49. F. Castro, "Castro Honors Internationalists."
50. See Gleijeses, *Conflicting Missions*, 392.
51. Gleijeses, *Conflicting Missions*, 393.
52. Alao, *Brothers at War*.
53. Domínguez, *To Make a World Safe for Revolution*; Moore, *Castro, the Blacks, and Africa*.
54. de Arturo, "En este Día Internacional de la Mujer,"
55. Milián Castro, "La revolución ha dado posibilidades," 61.
56. *Mujeres*, "Entrevista con Rosario Fernández Pereda," 11.
57. Blaquier, "Días de sol radiante," 55.
58. *Juventud Rebelde*, 231.
59. Martín, *Respuesta a la escalada Sudafricana*.
60. Espín, "Vilma Espín Responds," 52.
61. Brittain, *Death of Dignity*, 7–8.
62. Hatzky, "'Latin-African' Solidarity," 162.
63. Hatzky, "'Latin-African' Solidarity,'" 163–64.
64. Hatzky, *Cubans in Angola*, 261.
65. Hatzky, *Cubans in Angola*; "'Latin-African' Solidarity," 163.
66. See also Alberto, *Caracol Beach*.
67. Nasatir, "El Hijo de Guillermo Tell," 58n5. Hatzky also mentions Delgado's *Veterano* as a key example of "the neglect and silence that accompanies the official success story of engagement in Angola" and the "(subversive) discursive strategies [that] have developed in the communicative memory of the Cuban population" that "call the official version of events [in Angola] into question." Hatzky, *Cubans in Angola*, 267.

References

Alao, Abiodun. *Brothers at War: Dissidence and Rebellion in Southern Africa*. London: British Academic Press, 1994.

Alberto, Eliseo. *Caracol Beach*. New York: Vintage, 2001.

Bayard de Volo, Lorraine. "Revolution in the Binary? Gender and the Oxymoron of Revolutionary War in Nicaragua and Cuba." *Signs* 37, no. 2 (2012): 413–39.

Bayard de Volo, Lorraine. *Women and the Cuban Insurrection: How Gender Shaped Castro's Victory*. Cambridge: Cambridge University Press, 2018.

Benson, Devyn Spence. *Antiracism in Cuba: The Unfinished Revolution*. Chapel Hill: University of North Carolina Press, 2016.

Blaquier, Elsa. "Días de sol radiante." *Verde Olivo*, June 1989, 54-8.

Brittain, Victoria. *Death of Dignity: Angola's Civil War*. Trenton, NJ: Africa World Press, 1998.

Castro, Fidel. "Castro Honors Internationalists, Views Socialism," December 7, 1989, Havana, Cuba, Latin American Network Information Center (LANIC), University of Texas at Austin. lanic.utexas.edu/project/castro/db/1989/19891207.html.

Castro, Fidel. "16th Anniversary of the Committees for the Defense," Speech, July 26, 1976, Havana, Cuba, Latin American Network Information Center (LANIC), University of Texas at Austin. lanic.utexas.edu/project/castro/db/1976/19760926.html.

Castro, Raúl. "Raul Castro Welcomes Internationalists." Speech, May 27, 1991, Havana Radio and Television Networks, LANIC, University of Texas at Austin. lanic.utexas.edu/project/castro/db/1991/19910527.html.

Chase, Michelle. *Revolution within the Revolution: Women and Gender Politics in Cuba, 1952–1962*. Chapel Hill: University of North Carolina Press, 2015.

de Arturo, Héctor. "En este Día Internacional de la Mujer, desde la heroica Angola." *Verde Olivo*, March 7, 1976, 8.

de la Fuente, Alejandro. *A Nation for All: Race, Inequality, and Politics in Twentieth-Century Cuba*. Chapel Hill: University of North Carolina Press, 2001.

Domínguez, Jorge I. "Racial and Ethnic Relations in the Cuban Armed Forces: A Non-Topic." *Armed Forces and Society* 2, no. 2 (1976): 273–90.

Domínguez, Jorge I. *To Make a World Safe for Revolution: Cuba's Foreign Policy*. Cambridge, MA: Harvard University Press, 1989.

Espín, Vilma. "Vilma Espín Responds to Written and Oral Questions about Women, the Family, Youth, and Life in Cuban Society." In *Three Decades after the Revolution: Cuban Women Confront the Future*, edited by Deborah Shnookal, 52. Melbourne, AU: Ocean Press, 1990.

Finch, Aisha. *Rethinking Slave Rebellion in Cuba: La Escalera and the Insurgencies of 1841–1844*. Chapel Hill: University of North Carolina Press, 2015.

Gelb, Leslie. "U.S., Stung in Angola, Forges Africa Policy." *New York Times*, April 16, 1976.

Gleijeses, Piero. *Conflicting Missions: Havana, Washington, and Africa, 1959–1976*. Chapel Hill: University of North Carolina Press, 2002.

Guevara, Ernesto "Che," "Economics Cannot Be Separated from Politics," Speech to Inter-American Economic and Social Council (CIES), sponsored by the Organization of American States (OAS) at Punta del Este, Uruguay, on August 8, 1961.

Hatzky, Christine. *Cubans in Angola: South-South Cooperation and Transfer of Knowledge, 1976–1991*. Madison: University of Wisconsin Press, 2015.

Hatzky, Christine. "'Latin-African' Solidarity: The Cuban Civilian Mission in Angola, 1975–1991." *Iberoamericana* 5, no. 20 (2005): 159–64.

Juventud Rebelde, October 1, 1988, 8–9, in *Cuba Annual Report, 1988*, Office of Research and Policy, Radio Marti Program, Voice of America, U.S. Information Agency (USIA), 230–31.

Kissinger, Henry. "Cuban Clandestine Military Support for MPLA in Angola," U.S. Department of State, 1975STATE266239_b3. November 20, 1975 (declassified 2006). wikileaks.org/plusd/cables/1975STATE266239_b3.html.

Lewis, Oscar, Ruth M. Lewis, and Susan M. Rigdon, *Four Women Living the Revolution: An Oral History of Contemporary Cuba*. Urbana: University of Illinois Press, 1977.

Mandela, Nelson. "Castro Opens National Moncada Barracks Ceremony: Mandela Addresses Event." Speech, Santiago de Cuba, Cuba, July 26, 1991. LANIC, University of Texas at Austin, lanic.utexas.edu/project/castro/db/1991/19910726-1.html.

Marcum, John A. "Lessons of Angola." *Foreign Affairs* 54, no. 3 (1976): 407–25.

Martín, Victor, dir. *Respuesta a la escalada Sudafricana* (video), La Habana, Cuba, Estudios de Cine y Televisión de las Fuerzas Armadas Revolucionarias (ECITVFAR), 1988.

Milián Castro, Arnaldo. "La revolución ha dado posibilidades reales a todas las mujeres para que desarrollen sus capacidades y aptitudes." *Verde Olivo*, March 19, 1978, 61.

Moore, Carlos. *Castro, the Blacks, and Africa*. Los Angeles: University of California Los Angeles, Center for African American Studies, 1988.

Mujeres, "Entrevista con Rosario Fernández Pereda." November, 1977, 11.

Nasatir, Robert. "El Hijo de Guillermo Tell: Carlos Varela Confronts the Special Period." *Cuban Studies* 39, no. 1: 44–59.

New York Times, "'Big Lie' in Angola." December 9, 1975.

New York Times, "Castro Resumes Attacks on U.S." May 11, 1976.

Ramírez Castillo, Adolfo. "Apoyo resuelto, decided, é irrestricto." *Verde Olivo*, May 2, 1976, 10.

Risquet Valdes, Jorge. "Seguiremos cumpliendo en Angola nuestro deber internacionalista: Declaró Risquet en el Congreso del MPLA." *Granma*, December 4, 1985.

Rodrígues, Merida. Interview by Lyn Smith. Lyn Smith Cuba Collection: Oral Histories of Women. U.S. Library of Congress (audio transcribed by author). English and Spanish Sound Recording. 1988.

Roland, L. Kaifa. "Tourism and the *Negrificación* of Cuban Identity." *Transforming Anthropology* 14, no. 2 (2006): 151–62.

Safire, William. "Who Lost Africa?" *New York Times*, April 14, 1977.

Saney, Isaac. "African Stalingrad: The Cuban Revolution, Internationalism, and the End of Apartheid." *Latin American Perspectives* 33, no. 5 (2006): 81–117.

Sawyer, Mark. *Racial Politics in Post-Revolutionary Cuba*. Cambridge: Cambridge University Press, 2006.

Sawyer, Mark. "Unlocking the Official Story: Comparing the Cuban Revolution's Approach to Race and Gender." *UCLA Journal of International Law and Foreign Affairs*, no. 5 (2000): 403–17.

Smith, Lois M., and Alfred Padula. *Sex and Revolution: Women in Socialist Cuba*. Oxford: Oxford University Press, 1996.

Taylor, Frank F. "Revolution, Race, and Some Aspects of Foreign Relations in Cuba since 1959." *Cuban Studies*, no. 18 (1988): 19–41.

Internationalizing the Revolutionary Family

Love and Politics in Cuba and Nicaragua, 1979–1990

Emily Snyder

On July 26, 1979, just one week after the Frente Sandinista de Liberación Nacional (FSLN, or Sandinistas) overthrew the US-backed Anastasio Somoza dictatorship in Nicaragua, its leaders reestablished diplomatic relations with Cuba. That same day, during a speech commemorating the twenty-sixth anniversary of the July 26, 1953, Moncada Barracks attack, Fidel Castro promised to the new Sandinista government an internationalist brotherhood. Even as he acknowledged the island's financial and material constraints, Castro offered Cuba's wealth of human resources—all the medics, teachers, and advisors Nicaragua needed to carry out its revolution.[1] More than twenty-nine thousand Cubans responded to Castro's call.[2] Over the span of the next decade, Cubans traveled to Nicaragua as *internacionalistas*—civilians who volunteered, usually for two years, to work on behalf of the revolution in health, education, construction, and the military—in addition to Cubans who went as experts, artists, and members of various solidarity brigades.[3]

Internationalism, always part of the revolutionary project, became personal for Cuban citizens in the late 1970s and 1980s as thousands of them participated in efforts abroad. If diplomacy is a "set of assumptions, institutions, and processes—a practice—for handling certain kinds of relations between human beings," internationalism was also one of Cuba's diplomatic strategies.[4] In the mid-1970s through the 1980s, this meant supporting countries in the midst of their anti-imperialist fights for socialism and national liberation. Part of Cuba's support involved sending

Radical History Review

Issue 136 (January 2020)   DOI 10.1215/01636545-7857259

© 2020 by MARHO: The Radical Historians' Organization, Inc.

civilian brigades overseas. Internationalist projects therefore fell between nonstate solidarity efforts and formal diplomacy. Volunteering on behalf of the state, Cuban citizens engaged in informal diplomacy.

Conversing with literature on gender and the Cuban Revolution, gender and foreign policy, and Cuban revolutionary diplomacy, this essay argues that Cuban ideas about gender, sexuality, and the family shaped internationalism to Nicaragua and within Cuba. It examines the relationship between internationalism and the New Man, revolutionary love and family, marriages Cuban internationalists solicited, and Nicaraguan students' experiences on the Isla de la Juventud (Isle of Youth), a small island off Cuba's southern coast.[5] Cuban collaboration with Nicaragua sprang from a gendered political discourse, and in turn the dynamics of gendered relationships between Cubans and Nicaraguans affected the internationalist campaigns. The Cuban state prophesied that the revolutionary New Man could be made anew in these efforts; duty and self-abnegation were paramount. Cuba's strategy to construct a "revolutionary family" through internationalist missions conscripted women as participants as well, even as leaders simultaneously designed policies that emphasized women's domestic responsibilities. This essay illuminates how Cubans and Nicaraguans navigated love and revolution as they actually unfolded in these campaigns, contributing to studies of social history on militancy and the family, as well as to emerging studies on the Cuban Revolution's 1980s and trans/international histories of the Sandinista Revolution.[6]

Family intersects with internationalism through three overlapping layers: state-state relations, state policy, and citizens' own construction of affinitive ties. That is, "family" operates as ideology, and as both a natural and a social formation.[7] Official discourse surrounding Cuban-Nicaraguan collaboration positioned the revolutions as members of the same family. Born from similar nineteenth-century independence wars against foreign intervention, shared pasts produced "sibling revolutions" that created a "fraternal and traditional brotherhood."[8] Yet Cuba, also partially responsible for the Sandinistas' victory, led the relationship; twenty years of revolutionary experience allowed Cuba to pass expertise down to Nicaragua, especially in education, healthcare, and the military.[9]

"Internationalism" projected commitment beyond the nation, but twentieth-century Cuban and Sandinista revolutions still understood the nation as the vehicle for revolutionary liberation. Cuban leaders sought to create the broader revolutionary family through love and the nation-state, which found ideological precedent in the nineteenth century. In the nineteenth century, strategic, legitimate, and consensual heterosexual love and then marriage would solidify the nation, binding together disparate interest groups, regions, and races.[10] In the twentieth century, defending the national revolution—and helping to foment revolution elsewhere—also required love, but it developed in partnership with the state, rather than with a lover.

Nation- and revolution-building was also racial. In Cuba, elite narrators of the nineteenth-century independence wars vaunted myths of a "raceless" nation, whereby citizens were "not white, not black, only Cuban."[11] In Nicaragua, nineteenth-century elites consolidated the nation's racial differences through *mestizaje* and in opposition to black and indigenous populations on the Atlantic Coast.[12] Sandinismo (the FSLN's revolutionary ideology) also reiterated nineteenth-century narratives of mestizaje as a solution to revolutionary consolidation, which continued to exclude black and Afro-descendant indigenous people through its emphasis that *mestizo* peasants, descended from indigenous populations that resisted Spanish colonialism, were the foundational twentieth-century revolutionaries.[13] In Cuba, revolutionary leaders led a campaign to eliminate racism and proclaimed its end in 1961.[14] Both discourses frustrated the ability to make racial claims within the revolution, and in the broader revolutionary family, there was little space for explicit blackness.

Within Cuba, the family operated as a site of state formation, contestation, and ideological battleground. In the messy years of revolutionary consolidation between 1959 and 1962, marriage, the politicization of youth, and new roles for women outside of the home produced anxiety about the destruction of the family.[15] Revolutionary leaders employed morality as a political mobilizer to counter such charges. Creating fitter, nuclear, socialist families would guard against capitalist imperialism.[16]

As the Cuban state moved to control health, education, and labor over the course of the 1960s, it became an intimate part of the family system.[17] The state sought to regulate sexuality through policies that included persecuting homosexuals, regulating abortion, and reeducating prostitutes.[18] Policing gender and sexuality also helped leaders reform the economy around volunteer labor and define the parameters of revolutionary youth identity.[19] The Family Code passed in 1975 was an attempt to legislate gender equality and alleviate women's "triple burden" of productive labor, reproductive labor, and political labor. It officially reinscribed the family as a partner in children's political and social development and called for men to share in work at home.[20] The Code also reinforced patriarchal norms by signaling the nuclear family as the preferred family structure. Legislating its way into the home, the state sought new ways to ways to harness familial power and labor and define acceptable roles for revolutionary women.[21]

Thus, the fact that Cuban leaders sought to construct the revolutionary family through internationalist missions demands attention to how the state's heteronormative attitudes toward marriage, child care, and gender informed internationalism. But considering the family as an ever-changing space where social affinities and gender relations are formulated also demonstrates how internationalism gave rise to new relationships that challenged both the state's view of internationalism and that of the women and men involved. Ultimately, mobility generated space for convulsive personal experiences, love within revolution, and new family dynamics.

Cuban Internationalism

In the 1960s, Cuban internationalism primarily took the form of aid to guerrilla movements in Latin America and Africa.[22] The 1966 Tricontinental Conference institutionalized Cuba as a revolutionary leader with the creation of the Organización de Solidaridad con los Pueblos de Asia, África, y América Latina (OSPAAAL, Organization of Solidarity with the Peoples of Asia, Africa, and Latin America). This watershed meeting called for greater internationalist solidarity in the "struggle against imperialism, colonialism, and neocolonialism in Africa, Asia, and Latin America."[23] Born from the Argentinian guerrilla leader Ernesto "Che" Guevara's convictions, Cuba felt compelled to support and lead other "Third World" and exploited countries to nationalist liberation through armed confrontation. Following Che's death in 1967 and Salvador Allende's 1970 election in Chile, Cuba adapted its foreign policy strategy to a shifting geopolitical landscape. In the 1960s, Latin American countries disengaged with Cuba under US pressure and the threat of Organization of American States (OAS) sanctions (apart from Mexico, which never severed relations), leaving the island diplomatically isolated. The Chilean Revolution provided Cuba its first diplomatic opening, and Peru followed by reestablishing diplomatic relations in 1972. By the middle of that year, Cuba's Ministerio de Relaciones Exteriores (MINREX, Ministry of Foreign Relations) reopened its Latin America Department, signaling the end of Cuba's hemispheric isolation.[24]

As part of this diplomatic shift, internationalism expanded from arming Marxist guerrilla movements to forging solidarity with a broader range of revolutionary governments. Counterrevolutionary resurgence and coups d'état in Uruguay, Chile, and Argentina in the 1970s required Cuban leaders to adjust their regional and global strategies to support revolutionary initiatives. Cuba's involvement in Angola heralded this new phase of internationalism. It institutionalized processes that would be applied to Nicaragua, assigning responsibility for managing cooperation agreements to the Comité Estatal de Colaboración Económica (CECE, State Committee for Economic Collaboration).[25] After intervening militarily in 1975 to push invading South African troops out of Angola, Cuba began sending brigades of civil volunteers to aid the Movimento Popular de Libertação de Angola (MPLA, Popular Movement for the Liberation of Angola).[26] Internationalist missions revived the excitement of the early years of the Cuban Revolution, at a time when the institutionalization of the 1970s shifted away from idealism and experimentation.[27] Voluntary labor abroad recapitulated, in work and in discourse, previous mobilizations; these new "brigades" and "armies" the government sent abroad to teach literacy, construct roads, or work in agriculture suggested that internationalists were part of a revolutionary tradition, and their work helped defend the ongoing revolution at home.[28]

Collaboration with Nicaragua differed from Cuban efforts in Angola, however. The Angolan government paid for Cuban support and crafted trade agreements that benefited the Cuban economy.[29] In contrast, Cuba supplied its human resources to Nicaragua without compensation, signaling that Cuban leaders saw nonmaterial benefits of collaboration.[30] Beyond the fact that Nicaragua had far less to give materially, Cuba operated according to a hemispheric priority. The success of another leftist revolution achieved through armed violence in Latin America meant that Cuba finally had an ally and a base to continue agitating for revolution across Central America.[31] Nicaragua also offered Cuba a nascent revolution through which it could radicalize its own young generation and revitalize its ossifying revolution.

Nicaragua received the second-highest number of Cuban internationalists after Angola. Official government figures report that approximately fifty thousand civilians went to Angola between 1975 and 1991.[32] In Nicaragua, the numbers were substantially lower: according to one study, Cuba sent 16,787 civilians between 1979 and 1990.[33] The majority were teachers; about two thousand worked in Nicaragua annually between 1980 and 1984.[34] Officials selected volunteers who possessed teacher certification, at least three years of teaching experience, and "appropriate" moral and political consciousness.[35] This meant membership in the Communist Party or in the Unión de Jóvenes Comunistas (UJC, Communist Youth), as well as in less selective mass organizations. Internationalists to both Cuba and Angola were supposed to be loyal revolutionaries with a proven record of model work and behavior, which included fitting into heterosexual gender molds.

The first teachers' brigade, Contingent Augusto César Sandino, assembled in October 1979, composed of 559 women (46.3 percent) and 641 men (53.7 percent).[36] On the surface, the roughly 50/50 gender split suggested that revolutionary leaders held men's and women's participation as internationalists to be equal. However, in October 1983, when the United States invaded Grenada, Cuban leaders changed their policy and sent female internationalists with children home, revealing that they continued to view women's roles as different from men's. Yet thousands of women went to Nicaragua before then, and their participation informed constructions of sacrifice, care work, and family.

Making the New Man in Nicaragua

Internationalist mobilizations shaped the Cuban Revolution's shifting definition of the New Man and his formation. In the 1960s, Cuba's New Man was defined by participating in mass organizations, volunteering to cut sugarcane, and putting the needs of the revolution before his own. Leaders argued that through proper education, Cuban citizens would develop a new consciousness, one motivated by moral incentives rather than material ones, that would eventually lead to the "abolition of the individual for the sake of the state."[37] In the 1970s, the new revolutionary generation came of age. Che Guevara had theorized that these youth would become "authentic revolutionaries," free from "original sin" because they were born and educated under the revolution.[38] Yet Cuban leaders edited the New Man archetype to include participation in a revolution's early phases. Paradoxically, Cubans who participated in the revolution and its early years could not truly be New Men, but the new generation also could not perfect itself without revolutionary experience. Through internationalist missions, youth would participate in processes similar to those of the early Cuban Revolution.

Fidel made the relationship between internationalism and the New Cuban Man explicit in a 1980 interview with the Sandinista newspaper *Barricada* upon his return from visiting Nicaragua. When *Barricada* asked Fidel to describe the main characteristics of the New Cuban Man, he answered,

> When we asked for teachers to teach in Nicaragua, in the most distant corners
> of Nicaragua, under very harsh conditions, 29,500 teachers with several years
> of experience offered to come. . . . That is the new man. . . . A man who can
> feel internationalism, that is, solidarity toward other peoples. A man who can
> feel solidarity toward his own brothers. A generous man, capable of sacrificing
> for others. . . . That is the new man.[39]

The meaning of New Man solidarity thus expanded from sacrificing alongside a fellow Cuban to leaving Cuba to sacrifice on behalf of another revolution. By bringing revolution or helping to solidify fledging governments in other recently liberated countries, Cubans performed their own transformation.

The New Man was predicated on rebel hegemonic masculinity, rooted in strength, courage, virility, and defined in opposition to femininity and homosexuality.[40] But if the gay man was antithetical to the New Man, women played a key role in New Man ideology.[41] As New Women, they created New Men as mothers, served as examples in laboring for and sacrificing their bodies to the state, took care of the home, and maintained traditional feminine beauty.[42] They were also internationalists, and their participation played an important role in the Cuban state's construction of guerrilla masculinity. The opposition between revolutionary masculinity and a feminized counterrevolution became a recurring theme in the revolution's early years, and appeared again in state discourse surrounding internationalism and Cuban teachers' missions to Nicaragua.[43] In 1980, Cuban media also cast the internationalist teachers sent to participate in the Sandinista's Literacy Crusade as brave, masculine revolutionaries, in contrast to the cowardly, feminine, US-backed Contras.[44]

The figure of the female *internacionalista* established revolutionary/counterrevolutionary opposition by emasculating Contra men. For example, one magazine article told the story of a female teacher's success in inverting a Contra's plan to humiliate her. The Contra soldier, frustrated that she would not leave her students despite repeated physical threats, put a snake in the drawer of her desk in order to "make her look ridiculous" in front of her students.[45] However, a student tipped the teacher off. The teacher asked for a machete and, in front of the class, killed the snake "to the admiration of all the students, and later, of the pueblo." She displayed masculine bravery by confronting the snake in public, turning the Contra's plan to feminize her (and by extension the Cuban missions) through humiliation on its head. Snakes in the Nicaraguan countryside were common, but Freudian notions of the snake as a phallic symbol underlaid the story and highlighted Contra emasculation. And using a female figure to represent a "battlefield triumph" followed the gendered logic that losses were psychologically greater when they came at the hands of women, thereby questioning the losers' masculinity.[46]

Other media also employed gender as a strategy to legitimate internationalists' moral and revolutionary cause while discrediting the counterrevolution. The Cuban television series *Por el mismo camino*, which aired in 1982, romanticized the manly sacrifice of the internacionalistas and wove the teachers' experience in Nicaragua into a readable narrative for the broader Cuban public. The accompanying graphic novel featured still shots from the show and dramatized the experiences of one group of teachers in Nicaragua. In the middle of the story, the teachers heard that the Contras had killed two Cuban teachers and four Nicaraguan students in Siuna. Tomás Borge, the Sandinista Minister of the Interior, delivered a condolence speech. He reported that the Cuban teachers had "died bravely, their clothes illuminated with sweat and mud from the road." In contrast, their attackers were "cowardly" and effeminate, wearing Christian Dior shirts and maintaining the "feminine smoothness of their lazy hands."[47] In this portrayal, sweat, grime, and bravery evidenced the Cubans' masculinity, while clean, designer clothes and soft hands feminized the imperialist enemy.

The story ends with the main teacher, Águedo Morales Reyna, assassinated by the counterrevolution.[48] Before knowing whether the assassinated teacher was Cuban or Nicaraguan, the Sandinista Minister of Agriculture, Jaime Wheelock, wrote a letter to Fidel Castro, which is reproduced as the final element in the book. He had just visited the site where Cuba was funding and building a new sugar mill—another token of internationalism—and upon leaving, passed a lone Cuban woman walking along the road. He writes, "That one Cuban teacher simply carrying out her beautiful internationalist mission taught me that maybe more than others, Cuba and Nicaragua are called upon to hold onto life, hope, and the right to redemption for our people." But the citizens of Cuba and Nicaragua must pay for this "destiny" through the "high cost of sacrifice."[49]

These accounts portrayed Cuban teachers fulfilling gendered visions of the New Man in Nicaragua. State political discourse feminized the enemy, and final victory rested with the stronger, more masculine, and ultimately moral revolution. Revolutionary nationalism turned on the ideology that heteronormative masculinity would assure the revolution's endurance in the face of North American imperialist aggression.[50] The New Man was the standard of revolutionary masculinity, and in the 1980s, he was an internationalist.

Revolutionary Love and the Family

As masculine subjects, internationalists theoretically sacrificed personal needs, family, and love for the revolution and Nicaragua.[51] Death surely constituted the most dramatic (and final) menace with which Cuban volunteers contended, but sacrifice came in many forms. Internationalists faced physical, external discomfort: teachers traversed inhospitable terrain, forged through rain, climbed mountains, walked long distances, endured mosquitos, and survived with limited provisions.[52] In addition to physical discomfort, they made sexual sacrifices. In the 1980s, the revolution required surrendering up the body, and its sexual impulses, abroad.

Somos Jóvenes, a new Cuban magazine that the government began publishing in 1977 to appeal to young people, discussed sexual sacrifice and what one should do about sex when away on an internationalist mission. One article responded to an anonymous letter from a male *internacionalista* who was concerned about the potentially negative health effects of masturbation. The editorial response posited that because it was void of love and meaning, masturbation should only be an antidote to sexual emergency. The article left the dimensions of "emergency" unaddressed—and bypassed the possibility of forming relationships with locals altogether. Instead, the writer assured the young, sexually frustrated *internacionalista* that he could "be sure that each person has the capacity to be able to temporarily control their sexual tensions."[53] In order to do this, he should focus on things that must be accomplished and direct his energy into chosen distractions, such as reading, writing, or a sport.[54] In other words, the state used the same argument it deployed to repress homosexuality: masturbation was unproductive for personal development, and by extension, for the revolutionary project.[55]

Furthermore, according to government policy and media, an *internacionalista* should be willing to sacrifice human love and relationships for the revolution. Love cannot be divorced from history, politics, or power relations.[56] Love within the Cuban Revolution was no exception, and revolutionary love revolved around the public good and the nation rather than a bourgeois desire for private love and family.[57] Accordingly, internationalists' desire to volunteer their labor abroad superseded their desire to stay in Cuba with a partner; love for serving the revolution transcended all other feelings.

A short story in *Somos Jóvenes* featured a young internationalist facing conflict and instructed readers about the relationship between amorous love and revolutionary love.[58] Isis, the heroine, is a young teacher preparing to leave for Nicaragua. She has to bid farewell to her boyfriend, Iván, for two years. Iván initially wants to break up with Isis for leaving him and for putting herself in a position where she might be killed. She refuses to cry when Iván threatens to leave her, but instead imagines her work instructing Iván in lessons of morality and consciousness, sure that in the end he will come around, because he too is a revolutionary. And he does, albeit reluctantly. Meanwhile, Isis forges ahead, bolstered by her father's communist sentiments and the memory of her mother, who died as a literacy worker in the Escambray Mountains during Cuba's Literacy Campaign in 1960. Significantly, Isis performs her socially expected labor of love as a woman through her relationship with Nicaragua as a member of a literacy brigade, rather than through a romantic partnership with a heterosexual man.

Cuba's revolutionary leaders promoted a particular version of love, and by extension, family. In the 1980s, *Mujeres*, the magazine mouthpiece of the Federación de Mujeres Cubanas (FMC, Federation of Cuban Women), profiled men and women who put their work for the revolution above intimacy with their spouse. For example, Asela and her husband Orlando met while studying in Poland and spent the subsequent decade moving between jobs and places, taking turns caring for their two children or leaving them with grandparents.[59] Asela gave birth to their second daughter in Poland while Orlando was in Havana; once she finished studying and returned to Cuba, Orlando left for Canada. When he returned, Asela got a job in Cárdenas, and Orlando continued to work in Havana. Then he went to Vietnam, and Asela considered going to East Germany. She says, "In the future, it might not be a training course in Germany, but an internationalist mission, who knows? Wherever they need our work, there we will be!"

Mujeres then highlighted Cecilia and Antonio, who also traded off time in Cuba with their children (and each other) and time abroad in the USSR, Poland, and Canada. Like Asela and Orlando, they relied on their parents for housing and childcare and always managed to time their travels so that one of them stayed with the children.[60] Reflecting ideals of the "New Couple," the husband performed childcare responsibilities alongside his equally revolutionary wife.[61] These families suggest that markers of the revolutionary family included long spans of separation from one's partner, prioritizing education and labor for the revolution over family life.

Internationalism also separated participants from their children. The press lauded leaving behind young children as one of the greatest "sacrifices" a woman could make. It represented both her revolutionary commitment and the importance of work to be done in Nicaragua. For instance, a *noticiero* (weekly newsreel) featured teachers convening and preparing to go to Nicaragua. The two internationalists who spoke first in the clip were women. One declared that upon arriving to Nicaragua, she was "prepared to do what is necessary." She explained, "In my case, I left my one-year-old boy with my mother, an elderly woman, and my husband . . . . If we are there for two years, my son will be 3-plus years [when I return], and he won't know me." Another woman in the circle of teachers spoke up next, saying that she also left a daughter, and that it had been very painful to leave her.[62]

Internationalist missions separated families, but extended familial labor, rather than governmental institutions, made such arrangements possible. One study of female internationalists confirmed that more than half of the five hundred women interviewed were mothers, with 73.7 percent leaving their children in the care of their parents or grandparents.[63] Going to Nicaragua, Cubans left their family behind, but were promised that they would find a new revolutionary family.[64] Yet internationalist labor depended on care work that the Cuban government obscured, leaving women to either arrange childcare with extended family members or, in the case of an absent partner, shoulder the entire burden themselves.

Family complicated the state's neat portrayals of revolutionary love. According to the state's narrative, love for the revolution and belief in solidarity propelled Cubans to volunteer for missions, despite relationships at home. In reality, a variety of reasons motivated civilian internationalists. In the case of Angola, these included the younger generation's desire to participate in heroic campaigns, and the opportunity to leave the parental home, improve their social and professional standing, travel, and attain material benefits.[65] The internationalists who went to Nicaragua volunteered for similar reasons. And, for some women, the ability to join husbands motivated some to volunteer themselves.[66] Being selected as an internationalist was a competitive process. As discussed above, candidates not only had to have demonstrated practical experience, but also vetted revolutionary militancy, evidenced through loyal service to the state and membership in mass organizations. These women were therefore model citizens. At the same time, some leveraged their political cachet for personal reasons, strategically placing themselves with their male partners.

Working in Nicaragua as a couple led to strengthened marriages for some, and dissolution for others. Gladys Chántez Oliva went to Nicaragua as a teacher alongside her husband, a military advisor. She remembered sharing worries with him about their children and parents they left back in Cuba, and her satisfaction at being able to take care of him. Gladys affirmed that their time in Nicaragua working toward the same goal strengthened their marriage.[67] However, Cuban officials' decision to evacuate women from Nicaragua after the Unites States invaded Grenada in 1983 negatively impacted other marriages. At the time, Guadalupe Espiñeira González, a doctor, was on mission along with her husband. They had a young daughter back in Cuba, and Guadalupe was sent home, but her husband was not. The husband remained in Nicaragua and met a Nicaraguan woman, and Guadalupe ended their marriage.[68] Gendered revolutionary logic thus influenced the ability of partners to be together and foreclosed even that slim possibility after 1983, as Cuba sent only men to Nicaragua after Grenada. The decision to pull women from Nicaragua, especially those with children, also reinforced traditional gender norms that held childcare as a maternal responsibility.

State discourse and policies surrounding internationalist missions reveal connections between care work and ideas of the revolutionary family, as well as contradictions in gendered revolutionary logic. While revolutionary culture celebrated the labor of internationalists, it simultaneously obscured the labor required to make the missions function. Officials expected extended family members to take on the work of raising children while their parents volunteered for missions. Then, according to official discourse, women selected as internationalists performed New Womanhood by subsuming family responsibility to the revolution. Constructing the "revolutionary family" came first, as women left the labor of caring for children and husbands to [female] relatives in Cuba. But Cuban leaders' decision to bar women internationalists after 1983 revealed the "revolutionary family's" primacy only superseded the nuclear family's to a certain point. Women could be loaned to construct the "revolutionary family," but only insofar as it was not dangerous, because their real responsibility was to raise children in Cuba.

Falling in Love on Mission: Marriage and Transnational Families

Internationalism relied on the labor of Cuban families, solidified or challenged marriages, and created *new* transnational families. Documents from the Cuban Ministry of Foreign Relations show internationalists demanding that the state recognize and facilitate marriages while they were on mission and facilitate family reunification after their departure. These *internacionalistas* and their Nicaraguan counterparts forged their own meanings of international solidarity, often challenging prescribed notions of "revolutionary love." They subverted the state's sexless and loveless narratives about internationalist missions. Internationalists across Nicaragua carved out spaces for affection and sex within revolutionary projects as they fell in love, had children, created new families, and in some cases, got married and emigrated.

The internationalists formed relationships despite the Cuban government's efforts to organize missions in a way that limited contact with locals outside of work. In order to cultivate a "together but separate ethos," Cuban doctors and health workers lived in spaces separate from Nicaraguans and were often prohibited from going anywhere alone.[69] The Cuban government feared defection and sought to keep its workers as isolated as possible. Emigration became even more politically charged after 125,000 citizens left Cuba for the United States in the Mariel Boatlift of 1980, which signaled widespread loss of faith in revolutionary leadership.[70] Internationalist defections of avowedly vetted revolutionaries clearly challenged the Cuban Revolution's legitimacy. Emigration through marriage, however, occupied murkier territory: going through legal channels, internationalists retained their revolutionary credentials although they no longer resided in Cuba. But, as discussed above, politics infused marriage, as Cuban leaders knew well.[71] Transnational love and marriage amended the Cuban Revolution's ideologies of revolutionary love. By falling in love, internationalists inserted eroticism back into the equation, and perhaps they saw themselves as shaping a new love, one that bound two revolutions together beyond solidarity and sacrifice.

Internationalist collaboration in Nicaragua created conditions and relationships that often facilitated marriage as a migration tactic. Although scholars have studied love and migration in relation to female sex workers during the Special

Period, internationalist emigration was primarily male.[72] By late 1982, a growing group of Cubans and Nicaraguans seeking to formalize their relationships compelled Cuban authorities to clarify the state's policies and processes governing marriage and migration. A "numerous group" of teachers had already married, and thirty more had plans to do so.[73] A 1976 law outlined procedures for Cubans wishing to contract marriages abroad.[74] But the legal, technical, and ideological discussions around Cuban-Nicaraguan marriage in 1980s reflect confusion over what the laws stipulated and which departments transacted marriages. At this same moment, the Cuban government discouraged Cubans in East Germany from returning to Cuba with East German spouses, citing fears of maladjustment.[75] Both cases suggest Cuban leaders saw transnational marriage (and family) as problematic; perhaps different places produced different challenges to official visions of collaboration and love.

In October 1982, the Cuban ambassador to Nicaragua convened a meeting in Managua with representatives from each Cuban ministry that worked with or sent people to Nicaragua. The meeting clarified the government's rules and regulations for marriages and migrations. For Cubans to marry Nicaraguans, they needed to obtain an *hago constar* (affidavit) from the Minister or the highest Cuban government official they reported to. The Ministry of Foreign Relations then authenticated this document, which needed to expressly state that the proposed marriage would not affect the mission that the person was carrying out. In other words, the signatories had to swear that they did not go abroad for the purposes of contracting a marriage.[76]

According to one official, the most challenging aspect of allowing marriage was ensuring "militancy," and finding "definitive solutions" to ensure the marriages would "not affect the feelings and the will of the internationalist, of the revolutionary, of the communist."[77] Here, romance potentially threatened the internationalists' inner will and militancy, as if personal relationships and the sexuality they implied were direct threats to revolutionary sentiment. This requirement reinforced official Cuban views on revolutionary commitment and love: that is, that marriages could only proceed if they did not detract from the revolutionary mission—otherwise affective ties required sacrificing.

Cubans also had to present the desire to marry before the last six months of their time in Nicaragua, as well as a birth certificate and a sworn declaration of relationship status, providing a divorce certificate if applicable.[78] Fear of insincere marriage reigned. One Cuban official characterized transnational marriage as "very complicated," because in Cuba the "migratory procedures are *just like those of any other citizen who wants to abandon the country*" (emphasis added).[79] In the aftermath of the Mariel Boatlift, when Cuban leadership feared desertion of the revolutionary project, the official's complaint insinuated that Cubans married Nicaraguans as a strategy to leave the country. This was not the desired outcome of internationalist missions, but rather a subversive cooptation of Cuban informal diplomacy.

Migration to another revolutionary Caribbean country also placed in question Cuba's revolutionary "expertise" and its ability to capture the loyalty of the younger generation.

Furthermore, marriage represented the only avenue a Cuban could use to bring a Nicaraguan partner to Cuba, or return to Nicaragua.[80] Any other relationship arrangement, even one that involved children, afforded no travel rights to the couple. For an unmarried Cuban father to bring children back to Cuba, he had to recognize them through the Consular Office and obtain the mother's permission for the children to leave. This patriarchal policy likely deterred fathers from returning to Cuba with children born to them in Nicaragua, defaulting responsibility for offspring to the Nicaraguan mother unless the Cuban man chose otherwise. The Cuban state held fatherhood to be optional; motherhood, unavoidable.

The 1982 meeting outlining marriage and migration procedures concluded with resolutions to print the regulations for distribution to Internationalist Brigade Chiefs and hire an assistant to help the Chief of the Consular Office in Managua deal with the likely increase of marriage petitions.[81] However, bureaucratic inefficiency compounded Cuba's reluctance to sanction the emigration of those who were supposed to embody the archetype of the New Man. Cubans' relationships with Nicaraguans challenged the Cuban government's prohibitions on traveling to and from the island apart from in an official capacity. Traveling to Nicaragua to further a relationship during the 1980s was not itself outright illegal. Instead, the Cuban government produced "legal uncertainty" through the law—or enforced norms—in order to impede movement and maintain social control.[82] A marriage requirement, approval through Immigration Office to leave the country, and flight ticket purchases in US dollars combined to complicate or make it nearly impossible for Cubans to travel to Nicaragua. Yet legal uncertainty also created space for Cubans to contest the law—which they did in numbers.

In the fall of 1986, the Nicaraguan embassy in Cuba complained to Manuel Piñeiro, head of the America Department (the institution within the Communist Party of Cuba responsible for secret foreign relations and maintaining connections with Latin American revolutionary movements) about the problems continuously arising from Nicaraguan-Cuban marriages and the difficulties Cubans faced in moving to Nicaragua. From Nicaragua's perspective, Cuba had no official avenue to authorize its citizens' exits, which resulted in a "long and tedious" process, especially for doctors.[83] Then, once Cubans completed the immigration requirements to leave, they had to buy their plane ticket to Nicaragua in US dollars—not only making the trip financially prohibitive, but also, technically illegal because the dollar was criminalized.[84] The Cuban government allowed Nicaraguans to travel to Cuba by taking collaboration flights run by CECE for free.[85] But the rules differed for Cubans. Cubana de Aviación charged Cubans USD $228 from Managua to Havana, and USD $223 for the return—an exorbitant amount.[86]

Cubans and Nicaraguans did not accept this requirement without protest. The Cuban embassy in Nicaragua wrote to MINREX in Havana to figure out a solution to complaints about ticket pricing.[87] Cuban citizens also wrote to the Ministry of Foreign Relations, motivated by love, family, and possibly the desire to leave Cuba. Unable to afford the price in dollars, Cubans argued to pay it in pesos. By 1987, Cubans seeking to travel to Nicaragua inundated the America Department with requests. Fed up, the head of the Nicaraguan Section called a meeting with the Immigration Office and the National Bank of Cuba to sort out the inconsistency. The National Bank of Cuba reported that it had "clear instructions" not to sell Cubans flights in Cuban pesos, so Immigration agreed that it would not approve Cubans to leave the country if the bank did not approve the ticket sale in Cuban pesos.[88] Officials hoped this would prevent people from petitioning the America Department to allow the sale of tickets in pesos. They also floated the desire to end the policy allowing Nicaraguans to take CECE's flights for free, which would further restrict unofficial movement between Cuba and Nicaragua.

The letters Cubans wrote to Isidoro Malmierca, the Minister of Foreign Relations, provide glimpses into the dynamics of transnational relationships, the marriage process, and citizens protesting policy. For example, Manuel Durán Legón, a teacher, had a baby with his Nicaraguan girlfriend during his time on mission. He was not able to marry her due to an incomplete divorce and lack of documentation, but after returning to Cuba and finalizing the divorce, he wanted to return to Nicaragua at the end of 1981. Durán asked Malmierca for the opportunity to join a mission again in order to marry his girlfriend and formalize his family before returning to Cuba. Apparently, he had been told after returning to Cuba the first time that he would be able to return on a flight to Nicaragua without extending his mission. Failing that, the only way Durán could get back to Nicaragua and carry out the immigration process was to volunteer to go back on mission.[89] It is unclear if Durán returned to Nicaragua in 1982, but he reappears in the archive, writing to Malmierca again in 1989 to seek permission to travel to Nicaragua. Durán went through the process of obtaining permission to be able to visit his son back in 1982, securing approval to travel through the Immigration Office, his passport bought and authorized. But when he attempted to purchase the flight, he was asked to pay in US dollars, and this presumably impeded his visit. Frustrated, he asked Malmierca, "How is it possible to require payment in dollars, if I am a Cuban worker who receives my salary in Cuban pesos? Is there a legal way by which a Cuban citizen can acquire the dollar?"[90] Durán exposed the paradox of traveling to Nicaragua: the act itself was not illegal, but the only way to complete it was by breaking the law.

Another internationalist, Juan Miguel Vésente, asked Malmierca if he could pay the passage to Nicaragua in Cuban pesos to visit his wife. He had met and married his Nicaraguan wife while on a mission. After earning her degree in medicine, she solicited a residential visa for Cuba, but it was denied because she owed two years of social service to Nicaragua. She then asked for a visitation visa, but could not afford the airfare. Once again, Vésente appealed to Malmierca to help him reunite with the wife he had not seen for eighteen months and would not see for two more years should he not be able to pay for the ticket in Cuban pesos.[91] Malmierca's response is absent from the archive, but it seems unlikely that he approved Vésente's petition.

Marriages and relationships were a byproduct of internationalist missions in Nicaragua, and also very human responses to an otherwise abstract political project. While the Cuban revolutionary government did not explicitly outlaw these relationships, it discouraged them through bureaucratic inconsistences and by impeding Cubans' ability to leave Cuba. Romantic relationships challenged revolutionary rhetoric about internationalist missions, which revolved around themes of self-sacrifice and the priority of the collective over the individual. The government was loath to lose some of its most necessary citizens to individualistic love. But love and sex existed alongside internationalism, and internationalists' desire to maintain emotional and physical connections with their partners and children endured well after the end of their mission.

Internationalism on the Isla de la Juventud

As Cuban internationalists went to Nicaragua, Nicaraguans came to Cuba to study. The Cuban Revolution's largest internationalist project unfolded in the form of boarding schools on the Isla de Pinos, renamed the Isla de la Juventud in 1978. In the 1970s, the *escuelas en el campo* concept defined the island and saw widespread installation. Escuelas Secundarias Básicas en el Campo (ESBEC, Secondary Schools in the Countryside), boarding schools spanning the seventh to ninth grade, operated on the premise that manual labor, usually agricultural, constituted an essential element of revolutionary education. Students studied for half of the school day and worked in the fields for the other half. Five to six hundred students lived in each school, placed throughout the countryside, for weeks or months at a time. In the early 1970s, the government stocked the schools with children from mainland Cuba. Beginning in 1977, however, Cuba "offered" schools on the Isla de Pinos to foreign governments Cuba had relations with and that were in the midst of their own revolutionary struggle, such as Angola and Mozambique.

Nicaraguans arrived on the Isla just three months after the triumph of the Sandinista Revolution in 1979 and populated ESBEC #53, Carlos Fonseca Amador, named for the founder of the FSLN. A second school, Amistad Cuba-Nicaragua, opened in March 1980. Many students in the early classes had participated in the revolution: 40 percent of the 515 students that came in the spring of 1980 fought with the FSLN to overthrow Somoza's dictatorship.[92] Cuban news outlets featured these children, highlighting both their revolutionary credentials and Cuba's role in training them for the next phase of Nicaragua's revolutionary consolidation.[93] Cuba would provide Nicaraguans with a different kind of revolutionary education, one earned not in battle but in the classroom and fields.

For all the triumphant press, many Nicaraguan students had trouble adapting to life in Cuba. Out of the first group of 603 students, 545 completed three years.[94] The Sandinista government gave students little preparation about what to expect and enforced minimal screening.[95] It only required parent permission and the ability to travel alone—which likely excluded women with children. One student remembered her physical education teacher inviting whoever wanted to study in Cuba to sign up.[96] Therefore, for many the transition from Nicaragua to the escuelas en el campo was radical.[97] In Cuba, students found themselves without their families and with different soap, different food, different schools, and different rules that monitored their whereabouts. As a result of the labor and conditions in the schools, many students sought to leave the Isla and return to Nicaragua.[98]

Nicaraguans' maladjustment to Cuba's escuelas en el campo was widespread. In order to help his students, the director of Carlos Fonseca petitioned the FMC in the fall of 1979 to select local families to "adopt" a Nicaraguan student. The FMC called the program "Madres Combatientes Internacionalistas" (Combatant Internationalist Mothers), modeled off the preexisting Movimiento de Madres Combatientes por la Educación (Movement of Combatant Mothers for Education), which organized women to volunteer in local schools.[99] However, the labor required of FMC women on the Isla to help the schools function differed. Instead of working inside the schools or alongside teachers, the revolution's internationalism solicited their skills as mothers and caretakers. Nicaraguan students visited their Cuban families' houses on the weekends to be taken care of by a Cuban mom. She did laundry, cooked, and cared for the Nicaraguan student, providing them with a family and love.[100] The program was a resounding success; though it began with Nicaraguans, it spread to other schools and nationalities once students and administrators saw the benefits of connecting with local women and families.[101] Relationships forged between the Cuban families and Nicaraguan students were tight, as some families brought their Nicaraguan student back to the mainland with them for vacations and kept in touch once their student returned to Nicaragua. Nicaraguan students who return to the Isla still seek out their Cuban families to visit and reconnect, attesting to how important local Cuban women were to their lives on the Isla.

Paralleling Cuban internationalism in Nicaragua, internationalist collaboration on the Isla de la Juventud also forged new families. Sex ratios within the schools likely informed sexual practices: males significantly outnumbered females in secondary and preuniversity schools, and the Carlos Fonseca Military Academy was exclusively male. Only 29 percent of the Escuela Amistad Cuba-Nicaragua's incoming 1980 class was female; by 1989, the gender disparity continued, with a 25 percent female enrollment at Amistad Cuba-Nicaragua and 30 percent at Carlos

Fonseca.[102] Though students formed relationships within the schools, the uneven sex ratios ostensibly drove males to find partners outside of the schools. They dated women they met during their free time on weekends and through their sponsorship by families. Unsurprisingly, some of these relationships resulted in children.[103]

Nicaraguan students also got pregnant. In the early 1980s, protocol for pregnancy within secondary and preuniversity schools called for both the woman and the baby's father to be sent back to Nicaragua.[104] Abortion was not an option, and both parties lost their scholarships. As a result, some young women carried out their own abortions to avoid penalty.[105] After a few years, the Cuban state permitted students to obtain legal abortions, and likely encouraged this option over either returning to Nicaragua or having the baby.[106] In at least two cases, Nicaraguan women neither returned to Nicaragua nor had abortions, instead carrying their pregnancies to term and giving birth on the Isla.[107] Officials had established a daycare (*círculo infantil*) in La Fe, a suburb of Nueva Gerona, to accommodate other foreign students studying on the Isla who arrived to the Isla already pregnant. The Nicaraguan mothers were able to drop their babies off for daycare while they went to school. In another case, Illeana D'Carmen Espinoza got pregnant her last year of preuniversity, at age nineteen.[108] She was given the choice of abortion—after seeking "permission"—or having the baby. She chose to have the baby, graduated eight months pregnant, and returned to Nicaragua to give birth.

The Cuban state intervened when Nicaraguan female students became pregnant, but not when Nicaraguan men impregnated Cuban women. The state was responsible for the Nicaraguan students within the school, and it extended its patriarchal reach into the family and Cuban women's sexuality to include Nicaraguan women. For female Nicaraguan students, then, attending school on the Isla meant relinquishing some degree of control over sexuality to the Cuban state. However, though state policy suggested that being a young, unmarried mother was incompatible with being a revolutionary student, some Nicaraguan women held otherwise.

Conclusion

Internationalism informed the core of Cuba's foreign policy strategy in the 1980s. As Cubans left the island for years to complete missions, internationalist projects affected broad swaths of the population. This essay has examined the gendered logics of Cuban internationalism in the 1980s and demonstrated how mobility gave rise to new relationship dynamics. In Cuba, revolutionary sacrifice and the constructions of the New Man evolved to emphasize an internationalist volunteerism, albeit an internationalism predicated on guerrilla masculinity. Yet, Cuban women also participated as internationalists, despite—and sometimes because of—family. Once in Nicaragua, many Cubans fell in love, inherently challenging the revolutionary government's definition of love as self-sacrifice for collective, rather than personal, goals. By soliciting marriages, Cuban internationalists compelled leaders to clarify emigration policy and confront their revolutionaries' desires. And, as Cuba sent internationalists to Nicaragua, Nicaraguan students came to study on the Isla. They navigated everyday difficulties in boarding schools with the help of Cuban women. In both Cuba and Nicaragua, internationalist collaboration created new, transnational relationships and families.

Cuban policies surrounding internationalism both in Nicaragua and Cuba illuminate state attitudes toward gender, sexuality, love, and care work. The Cuban state had always expected women to subsume love and family responsibilities to the revolution, while still raising children and caring for the home. The onset of internationalist missions continued in this vein: leaving children evidenced women's revolutionary sacrifice. At the same time, Cuban leaders held care work to be women's responsibility, sending home internationalists with young children, recruiting women on the Isla de la Juventud to adopt foreign students, and leaving the offspring of unmarried Cuban fathers in the care of their Nicaraguan mothers. Ultimately, women's labor constructed the revolutionary family with little governmental support.

Assessing internationalist collaboration between Cuba and Nicaragua also reveals the Cuban leaders' continued emphasis on heteronormative and legally "legitimate" nuclear families. They envisioned a de-eroticized revolutionary family bound by ideology, work, education, and neat national boundaries, rather than romantic love, sex, offspring, and transnational families. But internationalism created space for new relationships and individuals to shape their own experiences abroad, challenging both the state's lingering emphasis on familial legitimacy, as well as individual views of revolutionary love. Considering Cuba's internationalism with the Sandinista Revolution through the lenses of gender and sexuality exposes the internal logic of the Cuban Revolution, its transnational dimensions, and the intimate consequences of foreign policy in the private lives of citizens. This approach wrestles with what it meant to Cubans and Nicaraguans to leave, be left, and navigate inter/transnational cooperation.

Emily Snyder is a history PhD candidate at Yale University. Her dissertation, "Untangling Revolutions: Cuban and Nicaraguan Collaboration in the Cold War Caribbean, 1979–1990," takes connections between the Cuban and Sandinista Revolutions as points of departure to examine how collaboration shaped each revolution's process, the shifting meanings of revolution/counterrevolution, and individual experiences of exchange. She graduated from the University of Florida in 2013, and her work can also be found in *Cuban Studies*.

Notes

I would like to thank the two anonymous reviewers and the issue editors, Michelle Chase and Isabella Cosse, for their thoughtful reading and suggestions, which greatly improved the article. I also thank Anne Eller, Carlos Hernández, Sarah Sklaw, and Naomi Sussman for their reading and comments during the piece's development and revision.

1.   Castro, "Discurso del XXVI aniversario," 3.

2. Rojas, "El aula verde," 13.

3. *Internacionalista* was a professional term referring to a category of Cuban collaborators who completed years of service.

4. Sharp, *Diplomatic Theory*, 13.

5. Ernesto "Che" Guevara theorized that the New Man would be a new kind of individual, born of revolutionary struggle, who was willing to sacrifice himself for liberation projects, putting the needs of the collective above his own. He was anti-imperialist, (inter) nationalist, straight, heroic, and the model to which every socialist subject should aspire. Guevara, "Socialism and Man."

6. Cosse, "Infidelities"; Tinsman, *Partners in Conflict*. On the state of Cuban Revolution historiography, see Lambe and Bustamante, "Cuba's Revolution from Within."

7. Rapp, Ross, and Bridenthal, "Examining Family History," 175.

8. Hernández Pardo, "Entrevista con Daniel Ortega y Sergio Ramírez."

9. Camacho Albert, "Partió hacia Nicaragua brigada médica"; García, "Nacionalidad: Cubano-Nicaragüense."

10. Sommer, *Foundational Fictions*, 24.

11. Ferrer, *Insurgent Cuba*; Guerra, *The Myth of José Martí*. On putatively raceless republicanism elsewhere in the Americas, see for example Lasso, *Myths of Harmony*.

12. Hooker, "Race and the Space of Citizenship."

13. Hooker, "'Beloved Enemies.'"

14. Benson, *Antiracism in Cuba*; de la Fuente, *A Nation for All*.

15. Chase, *Revolution within the Revolution*, 170–208.

16. Hynson, "Sex and State Making," 2.

17. Padula and Smith, *Sex and Revolution*, 147.

18. Hynson, "Sex and State Making," 19–62; Hynson, "Count, Capture, and Reeducate"; Sierra Maduro, "El trabajo os hará hombres."

19. Guerra, "Gender Policing," 269.

20. Baldacci, "Consumer Culture," 23.

21. Baldacci, "Consumer Culture," 123–58.

22. Chile is a notable exception.

23. Barcia, "Locking Horns," 212.

24. Harmer, *Allende's Chile*, 170–71.

25. Hatzky, *Cubans in Angola*, 194.

26. Gleijeses, *Visions of Freedom*.

27. Institutionalization included joining the Soviet trade bloc, which meant turning away from moral incentives towards material ones and relying on subsidies to fuel the economy. Leaders overhauled legal, judicial, and party structures over the course of the 1970s and passed a new constitution. See Mesa-Lago, *Cuba in the 1970s*; Pérez-Stable, *The Cuban Revolution*, 121–52.

28. Kapcia, *Cuba in Revolution*, 102.

29. Hatzky, *Cubans in Angola*, 152.

30. Internationalists who went to Angola were not aware that the MPLA was paying the Cuban government for their labor. It is possible that the Sandinistas paid for some of the services and personnel supplied by Cuba, but evidence suggests that cooperation with Nicaragua was not economically beneficial to Cuba. For example, commercial agreements reflect a two-to-one exchange, by which Nicaragua received twice as many imports from Cuba as it exported. Ricardo Cabrisas to Luis Carrión, "Protocolo sobre el intercambio

comercial," May 12, 1988 (personal archive of Michel Vazquez de Oca); Michel Vazquez de Oca, interview by author, Havana, Cuba, December 16, 2017.

31. Oñate, "The Red Affair."

32. The actual number probably falls between 44,000 and 49,000. Hatzky, *Cubans in Angola*, 153–55.

33. Angel García Pérez-Castañeda, "El internacionalismo de Cuba en la colaboración económica y científico-técnica: Esbozo histórico de un cuarto de siglo de la Revolución Socialista Cubana 1963–1988," cited in Hatzky, *Cubans in Angola*. I suspect both Angola and Nicaragua's statistics are inflated due to the reports' summation methods: the Ministry of Education lists the number of collaborators per year and then totals them, not accounting for people who spent more than one year abroad. See Batista Girbau, "La colaboración educacional," 13; and Jiménez Rodríguez, *Mujeres sin fronteras*, 97.

34. Jiménez Rodríguez, *Mujeres sin fronteras*, 97.

35. Jiménez Rodríguez, *Mujeres sin fronteras*, 97.

36. Batista Girbau, "La colaboración educacional," 13. Another article reported 550 women and 650 men. See Escobar Casas, "Una hermosa tarea."

37. Guevara, "Socialism and Man," 212.

38. Guevara, "Socialism and Man," 212; Guerra, *Visions of Power*, 230–35.

39. *Barricada*, "Fidel entrevistado por *Barricada*," 3.

40. Bayard de Volo, *Women and the Cuban Insurrection*, 90.

41. Bejel, *Gay Cuban Nation*; Sierra Maduro, "El trabajo os hará hombres."

42. Guerra, "Gender Policing," 275–79; Baldacci, "Consumer Culture," 21.

43. Bayard de Volo, *Women and the Cuban Insurrection*.

44. The Literacy Crusade lasted from March to August 1980. Sandinista leaders modeled the campaign after the Cuban Literacy Campaign of 1960 and sought to increase literacy as well as political support for the revolution. Miller, *Between Struggle and Hope*.

45. Bravo, "Una bella misión," 41–43.

46. Bayard de Volo, *Women and the Cuban Insurrection*, 212.

47. Rodríguez Torres, *Por el mismo camino*, 47.

48. On the assassination of the real Áquedo Morales, see *Cuba Internacional*, "Dispuestos miles de cubanos," 3.

49. Rodríguez Torres, *Por el mismo camino*, 94–95.

50. Sierra Madero, "El trabajo os hará hombres," 315–16.

51. Castro, *Fidel Castro y la religión*, 261–63.

52. Rodríguez Torres, *Por el mismo camino*, 46–47; *Cuba Internacional*, "Cuba y Nicaragua marchan"; Benitez, "El maestro cubano," 11.

53. Carrobello, "Por favor no publicar mi nombre."

54. Carrobello, "Por favor no publicar mi nombre," 43.

55. Sierra Maduro, "El trabajo os hará hombres."

56. Hamilton, *Sexual Revolutions in Cuba*, 74.

57. Butler, "Deconstructing an Icon," 62–65.

58. Santos, "Floreciéndole a la vida."

59. González Cabrera, "Esa muchacha aparentemente frágil."

60. González Cabrera, "Juntos, todo resulta fácil."

61. Baldacci, "Consumer Culture," 98.

62. Noticiero No. 945, November 22, 1979, Archivo Fílmico de Arte e Industria Cinematográficos, Havana, Cuba (ICAIC).

63. Jiménez Rodríguez, *Mujeres sin fronteras*, 14.

64. *Cuba Internacional*, "Maestros cubanos."

65. Hatzky, *Cubans in Angola*, 93.

66. Niurka Pérez Rojas, interview by author, Havana, Cuba, February 24, 2018.

67. Jiménez Rodríguez, *De las mujeres*, 214–15.

68. Jiménez Rodríguez, *De las mujeres*, 215.

69. Anderson, "Health Care Reform," 205.

70. García, *Havana USA*, 59; de los Angeles Torres, *In the Land of Mirrors*, 113.

71. Hynson, "Sex and State Making," 63–90.

72. Babb, "Sex and Sentiment"; Cabezas, *Economies of Desire*; Fusco, "Hustling for Dollars"; Stout, "Feminists, Queers and Critics." The Special Period refers to the years following 1989 when the Cuban economy collapsed after the dissolution of the Soviet Union, resulting in severe material shortages.

73. Dirección Jurídica, Reunión en la Embajada de Cuba en Nicaragua, October 29, 1982, 3, Nicaragua, box 2, folder 1982, Archivo Central del Ministerio de Relaciones Exteriores de Cuba, Havana, Cuba (hereafter ACMINREX).

74. Dirección Jurídica, Circular No. 27/76, December 10, 1976, Nicaragua, box 2, folder 1976, ACMINREX.

75. Domínguez, *To Make a World Safe for Revolution*, 98. Thanks to Michelle Chase for suggesting this comparison and line of analysis.

76. José Viera Linares to Héctor Rodriguez Llompart, 1, Nicaragua, box 2, folder 1982, ACMINREX.

77. Julián López Díaz to José Machado Ventura, August 20, 1982, Nicaragua, box 2, folder 1982, ACMINREX.

78. Dirección Jurídica, Reunión en la Embajada de Cuba en Nicaragua, 3–4. An earlier memo put the number at three months. Authorities enforced (or theoretically enforced) the *hago contestar* requirement after October 1982.

79. Dirección Jurídica, Reunión en la Embajada de Cuba en Nicaragua, 3–4.

80. Dirección Jurídica, Reunión en la Embajada de Cuba en Nicaragua, 4–5.

81. Dirección Jurídica, Reunión en la Embajada de Cuba en Nicaragua, 5–6.

82. Pérez Martín, "Entre la redención y la resistencia."

83. José Raúl Vira Linares to Roberto González Caro, September 24, 1986, Nicaragua, box 4, folder 1986, ACMINREX.

84. Dirección Jurídica to Giraldo Mazola, June 23, 1987, Nicaragua, box 4, folder 1987, ACMINREX; Manuel Munsulí Gómez to Manuel Piñeiro Losada, February 27, 1986, Nicaragua, box 4, folder 1986, ACMINREX; Manuel Piñeiro to Isodoro Malmierca, September 9, 1986, Nicaragua, box 4, folder 1986, ACMINREX.

85. Dirección Jurídica to Giraldo Mazola, 1. CECE managed internationalist operations.

86. Manuel Munsulí Gómez to Manuel Piñeiro Losada.

87. Manuel Munsulí Gómez to Manuel Piñeiro Losada.

88. Dirección Jurídica to Giraldo Mazola.

89. Manuel Durán Legrá to Malmierca, November 20, 1981, Nicaragua, box 2, folder 1982, ACMINREX.

90. Manuel Durán Legrá to Malmierca, April 15, 1989, Nicaragua, box 5, folder 1989, ACMINREX.

91. Juan Miguel Vésente to Malmierca, December 30, 1987, Nicaragua, box 4, folder 1987, ACMINREX.

92. Colina, "Otra ESBEC."
93. Escobar Casas, "Nicaragua"; González, "Recuerdos de la batalla."
94. "Trabajo investigativo: Sobre las escuelas internacionales en la Isla de la Juventud," 1986, box 11, folder 225, Archivo Histórico Municipal de la Isla de la Juventud, Nueva Gerona, Isla de la Juventud, Cuba (hereafter AHM).
95. Omar Morales to Malmierca, April 30, 1988, 3–4, Nicaragua, box 4, folder 1988, ACMINREX.
96. Johanna Malespin García, interview with author, Darío, Nicaragua, January 23, 2019.
97. Marlen Villavicencio Batista, interview with author, Nueva Gerona, Isla de la Juventud, Cuba, January 30, 2018.
98. Omar Morales to Malmierca, 3; Garrido Pérez, *Memorias*, 17, 21–24.
99. Garrido Pérez, *Memorias*, 44–45; *Mujeres*, "Las Madres Combatientes."
100. Cascaret, "Un nuevo combate"; Villavicencio Batista, interview.
101. Villavicencio Batista, interview.
102. Colina, "Otra ESBEC"; Luis Sires Pérez, Proyección del curso escolar 89/90, p. 7, box 16, folder 388, AHM.
103. Alejandro Hernández Solis, interview with the author, Managua, Nicaragua, February 5, 2019.
104. Garrido Pérez, *Memorias*, 54; Villavicencio Batista, interview.
105. Illeana D'Carmen Espinoza, interview with the author, Rivas, Nicaragua, January 25, 2019.
106. Abortion policy changed over the years; deregulation by 1979 made it accessible and contributed to the [re]creation of an "abortion culture." Bélanger and Flynn, "The Persistence of Induced Abortion in Cuba," 13.
107. Villavicencio Batista, interview.
108. D'Carmen Espinoza, interview.

References

Anderson, Kristin. "Health Care Reform in Sandinista Nicaragua, 1979–1990." PhD diss., University of Texas at Austin, 2014.
Babb, Florence. "Sex and Sentiment in Cuban Tourism." *Caribbean Studies* 38, no. 2 (2010): 93–115.
Baldacci, Alexis. "Consumer Culture and Everyday Life in Revolutionary Cuba, 1971–1986." PhD diss., University of Florida, 2018.
Barcia, Manuel. "'Locking Horns with the Northern Empire': Anti-American Imperialism at the Tricontinental Conference of 1966 in Havana." *Journal of Transatlantic Studies* 7, no. 3 (2009): 208–17.
Barricada. "Fidel entrevistado por *Barricada*: Nadie puede discutir papel de vanguardia a sandinistas." July 29, 1980, 3.
Batista Girbau, Jorge. "La colaboración educacional cubana en Nicaragua." Unpublished report, Biblioteca del Ministerio de Educación, La Habana, Cuba, n.d.
Bayard de Volo, Lorraine. *Women and the Cuban Insurrection: How Gender Shaped Castro's Victory.* Cambridge, UK: Cambridge University Press, 2018.
Bejel, Emilio. *Gay Cuban Nation.* Chicago: University of Chicago Press, 2001.
Bélanger, Danièle, and Andrea Flynn. "The Persistence of Induced Abortion in Cuba: Exploring the Notion of an 'Abortion Culture.'" *Studies in Family Planning* 40, no. 1 (2009): 13–26.

Benitez, José. "El maestro cubano de Waspado Central." *Cuba Internacional*, no. 12 (1981): 10–11.

Benson, Devyn Spence. *Antiracism in Cuba: The Unfinished Revolution*. Chapel Hill: University of North Carolina Press, 2016.

Bravo, Ernesto. "Una bella misión." *Cuba Internacional*, no. 9 (1983): 41–43.

Butler, Krissie. "Deconstructing an Icon: Fidel Castro and Revolutionary Masculinity." PhD diss., University of Kentucky, 2012.

Cabezas, Amalia. *Economies of Desire: Sex and Tourism in Cuban and the Dominican Republic*. Philadelphia: Temple University Press, 2009.

Camacho Albert, René. "Partió hacia Nicaragua brigada médica de Santiago de Cuba." *Granma*, August 6, 1979, 1.

Carrobello, Caridad. "Por favor no publicar mi nombre." *Somos Jóvenes*, no. 90–91 (1987): 42–43.

Cascaret, Alicia. "Un nuevo combate: El estudio." *Mujeres* 20, no. 5 (1980): 21.

Castro, Fidel. "Discurso del XXVI aniversario del asalto al Cuartel Moncada." *Granma*, July 26, 1979: 3–4.

Castro, Fidel. *Fidel Castro y la religión: Conversaciones con Frei Betto*. México, D.F.: Siglo Veintiuno Editores, 1988.

Chase, Michelle. *Revolution within the Revolution: Women and Gender Politics in Cuba, 1952–1962*. Chapel Hill: University of North Carolina Press, 2015.

Colina, Sergio. "Otra ESBEC para estudiantes nicaragüenses abre sus puertas en la Isla de la Juventud." *Victoria*, April 10, 1980.

Cosse, Isabella. "Infidelities: Morality, Revolution, and Sexuality in Left-Wing Guerrilla Organizations in 1960s and 1970s Argentina." *Journal of the History of Sexuality* 23, no. 3 (2014): 415–50.

Cuba Internacional. "Cuba y Nicaragua marchan juntas hacia el futuro," no. 12 (1981): 3.

Cuba Internacional. "Dispuestos miles de cubanos a sustituir a maestro asesinado," no. 2 (1982): 3.

Cuba Internacional. "Maestros cubanos en Nicaragua," no. 1 (1980): 5.

de la Fuente, Alejandro. *A Nation for All: Race, Inequality, and Politics in Twentieth-Century Cuba*. Chapel Hill: University of North Carolina Press, 2001.

de los Angeles Torres, Maria. *In the Land of Mirrors: Cuban Exile Politics in the United States*. Ann Arbor: University of Michigan Press, 1999.

Domínguez, Jorge. *To Make a World Safe for Revolution: Cuba's Foreign Policy*. Cambridge, MA: Harvard University Press, 1989.

Escobar Casas, Reynaldo. "Una hermosa tarea." *Cuba Internacional*, no. 2 (1980): 11–12.

Escobar Casas, Reynaldo. "Nicaragua: Generación de la victoria." *Cuba Internacional*, no. 3 (1980): 38–40.

Ferrer, Ada. *Insurgent Cuba: Race, Nation, and Revolution, 1868–1898*. Chapel Hill: University of North Carolina Press, 1999.

Fusco, Coco. "Hustling for Dollars: *Jineterismo* in Cuba." In *Global Sex Workers: Rights Resistance, and Redefinition*, edited by Kamala Kempadoo and Jo Doezema, 151–66. New York: Oxford University Press, 1998.

García, Julio. "Nacionalidad: Cubano-Nicaragüense, Ocupación: Revolucionario." *Granma*, July 23, 1980, 1.

García, Maria Cristina. *Havana USA: Cuban Exiles and Cuban Americans in South Florida, 1959–1994*. Berkley: University of California Press, 1997.

Garrido Pérez, Waldo. *Memorias y Reencuentros*. Managua: Bitecsa, 2011.

Gleijeses, Piero. *Visions of Freedom: Havana, Washington, Pretoria, and the Struggle for Southern Africa*. Chapel Hill: University of North Carolina Press, 2013.

González Cabrera, Heidy. "Esa muchacha aparentemente frágil." *Mujeres* 19, no. 12 (1979): 8–10.

González Cabrera, Heidy. "Juntos, todo resulta fácil." *Mujeres* 22, no. 4 (1982): 62–63.

González, Cristina. "Recuerdos de la batalla." *Somos Jóvenes*, no. 20 (1980): 12–14.

Guerra, Lillian. *The Myth of José Martí: Conflicting Nationalisms in Early Twentieth-Century Cuba*. Chapel Hill: University of North Carolina Press, 2005.

Guerra, Lillian. "Gender Policing, Homosexuality, and the New Patriarchy of the Cuban Revolution, 1965–1970." *Social History* 35, no. 3 (2010): 268–89.

Guerra, Lillian. *Visions of Power in Cuba: Revolution, Redemption, and Resistance, 1959–1971*. Chapel Hill: University of North Carolina Press, 2012.

Guevara, Ernesto "Che." "Socialism and Man in Cuba." In *Che Guevara Reader: Writings on Politics and Revolution*, edited by David Deutschmann, 212–28. North Melbourne, AU: Ocean Press, 2001.

Hamilton, Carrie. *Sexual Revolutions in Cuba: Passion, Politics, and Memory*. Chapel Hill: University of North Carolina Press, 2012.

Harmer, Tanya. *Allende's Chile and the Inter-American Cold War*. Chapel Hill: University of North Carolina Press, 2011.

Hatzky, Christine. *Cubans in Angola: South-South Cooperation and Transfer of Knowledge, 1976–1991*. Madison: University of Wisconsin Press, 2015.

Hernández Pardo, Héctor. "Entrevista con Daniel Ortega y Sergio Ramírez: Con el fortalecimiento de la Revolución en Nicaragua se fortalece también el Movimiento de los No Alineados." *Granma*, September 4, 1979, 4.

Hooker, Juliet. "'Beloved Enemies': Race and Official Mestizo Nationalism in Nicaragua." *Latin American Research Review* 40, no. 3 (2005): 14–39.

Hooker, Juliet. "Race and the Space of Citizenship: The Mosquito Coast and the Place of Blackness and Indigeneity in Nicaragua." In *Blacks and Blackness in Central America: Between Race and Place*, edited by Lowell Gudmundson and Justin Wolfe, 246–78. Durham, NC: Duke University Press, 2010.

Hynson, Rachel. "'Count, Capture, and Reeducate': The Campaign to Rehabilitate Cuba's Female Sex Workers, 1959–1966." *Journal of the History of Sexuality* 24, no. 1 (2015): 125–53.

Hynson, Rachel. "Sex and State Making in Revolutionary Cuba, 1959–1968." PhD diss., University of North Carolina at Chapel Hill, 2014.

Jiménez Rodríguez, Nancy. *De las mujeres y sus memorias*. La Habana: Casa Editorial Verde Olivo, 2011.

Jiménez Rodríguez, Nancy. *Mujeres sin fronteras*. La Habana: Editoria Política, 2008.

Kapcia, Antoni. *Cuba in Revolution: A History since the Fifties*. London: Reaktion Books, 2008.

Lambe, Jennifer, and Michael Bustamante. "Cuba's Revolution from Within: The Politics of Historical Paradigms." In *The Revolution from Within: Cuba, 1959–1980*, edited by Michael Bustamante and Jennifer Lambe, 3–32. Durham, NC: Duke University Press, 2019.

Lasso, Marixa. *Myths of Harmony: Race and Republicanism during the Age of Revolution, Columbia 1975–1831*. Pittsburgh, PA: University of Pittsburgh Press, 2007.

Mesa-Lago, Carmelo. *Cuba in the 1970s: Pragmatism and Institutionalization*. Albuquerque: University of New Mexico Press, 1978.

Miller, Valerie. *Between Struggle and Hope: The Nicaraguan Literacy Crusade.* Boulder, CO: Westview Press, 1985.

Mujeres. "Las Madres Combatientes." 21, no. 8 (1981): 53.

Oñate, Andrea. "The Red Affair: FMLN-Cuban Relations during the Salvadoran Civil War, 1981–92." *Cold War History* 11, no. 2 (2011): 133–54.

Padula, Alfred, and Lois Smith. *Sex and Revolution: Women in Socialist Cuba.* New York: Oxford University Press, 1996.

Pérez Martín, Amalia. "Entre la redención y la resistencia: El rol político y sociohistórico del derecho en Cuba posrevolucionaria." Paper presented at "New Voices in Cuba Studies: Graduate Student Symposium," Harvard University, Boston, MA, November 30, 2018.

Pérez-Stable, Marifeli. *The Cuban Revolution: Origins, Course, and Legacy.* New York: Oxford University Press, 1999.

Rapp, Rayna, Ellen Ross, and Renate Bridenthal, "Examining Family History." *Feminist Studies* 5, no. 1 (1979): 174–200.

Rodríguez Torres, Nilda. *Por el mismo camino.* La Habana: Editorial Gente Nueva, 1982.

Rojas, Marta. "El aula verde." *Cuba Internacional,* no. 10 (1981): 12–13.

Santos, Mercedes. "Floreciéndole a la vida." *Somos Jóvenes,* no. 42 (1983): 32–33.

Sharp, Paul. *Diplomatic Theory of International Relations.* New York: Cambridge University Press, 2009.

Sierra Maduro, Abel. "El trabajo os hará hombres: Masculinización nacional, trabajo forzado y control social en Cuba durante los años 60." *Cuban Studies,* no. 44 (2016): 309–49.

Sommer, Doris. *Foundational Fictions: The National Romances of Latin America.* Berkeley: University of California Press, 1991.

Stout, Noelle. "Feminists, Queers and Critics: Debating the Cuban Sex Trade." *Journal of Latin American Studies* 40, no. 4 (2008): 721–42.

Tinsman, Heidi. *Partners in Conflict: The Politics of Gender, Sexuality, and Labor in the Chilean Agrarian Reform, 1950–1973.* Durham, NC: Duke University Press, 2002.

Transgressing Che

Irina Layevska Echeverría Gaitán, Disability Politics,
and Transgendering the New Man in Mexico,
1964–2001

Robert Franco

Clutching a cigarette in her hand, the disability rights and transgender activist Irina Layevska Echeverría Gaitán stares off screen at the interviewer as the smoke collects around her. The camera is rolling, but the shot remains frozen on her face, framed by a mop of black hair and a shelf full of books behind her. Even in the grainy footage, her thick eyebrows are clearly furrowed as she collects her thoughts. "Che spoke of the creation of the New Man," she utters, "and the New Man does not yet exist. There are men who are new, but there is no New Man."[1]

Born in 1964 to Communist parents who were later arrested during the 1968 student protests, Echeverría Gaitán was a child of the Mexican student and leftist movements that emerged in the wake of the Cuban Revolution. In her infancy, she began showing signs of muscle and nerve degeneration in her arms and legs, which would eventually be diagnosed as Charcot-Marie-Tooth disease and would worsen as she aged. Her disability, however, did not stop her from participating in various leftist parties and organizations in Mexico and abroad. Bearing a striking resemblance to Ernesto "Che" Guevara, Echeverría Gaitán modeled herself after Che's "New Man" in her youth. At age thirty-six she began transitioning to a woman, adding a new layer of radicalism to her militancy.

Radical History Review
Issue 136 (January 2020)   DOI 10.1215/01636545-7857271
© 2020 by MARHO: The Radical Historians' Organization, Inc.

In this article, I use the life of Echeverría Gaitán, pieced together from interviews, her 2008 *testimonio* (testimonial text) titled *Carta a mi padre* (*Letter to My Father*), and a 2011 documentary about her life, *Morir de pie* (*Die Standing*), as a lens to examine the circulation and appropriation of the discursive New Man and the figure of Che Guevara by a broad set of actors from leftist revolutionaries to sexual rights activists in Mexico. While for many, these models of revolutionary masculinity did not align with individuals like Echeverría Gaitán due to her medical struggles and gender identity, I argue that those excluded from the heteronormative able-bodied ideal of militancy—gay men, women, trans folk, and those with disabilities—used the futurist, universal, and self-developmental aspects of the New Man to reject exclusionary leftist politics. I contend that the New Man as an aspirational yet abstract goal enabled the formulation of radically transgressive subject positions and provided a discourse with which to construct a militant identity that was inclusive and oppositional to the masculinist and ableist revolution.

In his 1965 essay "El socialismo y el hombre en Cuba" ("Socialism and Man in Cuba"), Che Guevara outlined the utopian citizens known as the New Man and Woman. "To build communism it is necessary," he writes, "simultaneous with the new material foundations, to build the new man and woman."[2] Highlighting the ways capitalism constructed a consciousness of individualism and the myth of the self-made man, Guevara argued that these new men and women needed to have values such as moral perfection, community centeredness, and a willingness to sacrifice private interests for collective transformation. In the initial phases of revolution, these characteristics of selflessness and moral strength were embodied in the vanguard—soldiers like Fidel Castro who set aside commitments to family for their comrades and country. Guevara, however, envisioned that self-development and education through physical work and integration into cadres would enable the birth of an entire society of New Men and Women, making these subjects always both aspirational and in the process of becoming.[3]

As it spread across Latin America, the New Man became a figure of contestation, particularly in the generational divides of the Left over armed struggle, sexual liberation, and feminism.[4] Popular and literary iterations of the New Man made him a patriarchal and masculinist figure, rejecting "sexual deviants" such as homosexuals and sex workers as counterrevolutionary.[5] Women, while less clearly incorporated into the revolution's construction of the utopian citizen, were able to use the figure of the New Woman to vocalize their revolutionary valor, echoing similar ableist discourses of physical capability as those of the New Man.[6] Echeverría Gaitán's disability and gender affirmation, on the other hand, put into question prevailing ideas of who could embody the New Man and New Woman.

Despite the normative connotations of physical perfection and gendered order applied to the New Man and New Woman, marginalized subjects could still draw upon these figures to create meaning in their own lives. Designated male at birth, Echeverría Gaitán fashioned herself using the rubric of the New Man early in her life, even modeling her appearance after Che Guevara. While this gender performance had as much to do with concerns for safety as admiration for Che, her appropriation of the New Man allowed her to lay claim to a revolutionary identity while distancing herself from the disablism and sexism of her contemporaries. Later, Echeverría Gaitán drew on the New Man's ideals of self-construction to embrace her feminine identity as a New Woman.

Echeverría Gaitán's transformation from New Man to New Woman invites us to consider a number of epistemological tensions. As scholars of testimonio literature have discussed, writing a "life story" involves the selective use of memory in the construction of historical narratives about the self and subaltern truth. Similarly, Echeverría Gaitán's testimony is an act of retroactive reconstruction that interprets past experiences and events as a journey of recognizing how she has always understood herself.[7] And given that I draw from materials recorded from before and after the date she indicates she began changing her gender expression, her narrative elucidates how testimonies are shaped by the particular historical moments during which they are recounted. Whether it is her proclaiming her desire to inhabit the New Man amid the crises on the Left during the 1990s, or her framing of herself as a New Woman after the politicization of Mexico's transgender movement two decades later, her testimony is a striking example of how the subjective act of reconstructing a life story changes over time.

Despite its remarkability, Echeverría Gaitán's life has been overlooked in the history of leftist struggle. A new wave of biographical work and studies of leftist private life, however, urges us to more seriously consider stories like hers, for they reveal how the creation of new subjectivities often entails challenging, usually for the better, the dominant moral paradigms of revolutionary movements.[8]

Transgressing Temporality

Echeverría Gaitán's life story gives us an exceptional account of revolutionary action in the years after the Cuban Revolution. But it is not without its limits. She cannot always disclose full names of individuals or exact dates of events, either due to the shortcomings of memory, the need to protect fellow militants, deteriorated relationships, or a combination of all three. Furthermore, since narrating her life is a political act, it is under the constant process of revision.[9] Interviews from the 1990s, for instance, show Echeverría Gaitán confessing her desire to be a New Man while expressing hope for a socialist futurity upon the dissolution of the Soviet Union. In contrast, narrating her testimonio in 2008 served as an outlet for her frustrations with the disablism and transphobia she was encountering in Mexico City. Updated interviews with me in 2018, meanwhile, occurred after significant legal gains in her gender affirmation, which were crucial to her understanding of self. With the opportunity to reassess her life trajectory, she now asserts that she has, in fact, always been striving to be a New Woman.

Scholars have theorized how the bodily alienation and forced gender assignments that often mark the adolescence of sexual and gender minorities generate such heterogeneous experiences of time and identity.[10] In the case of Echeverría Gaitán, although she was read and treated as a disabled man for many years, she narrates her experiences entirely in the feminine. She is and always has been Irina, an experience of trans temporality that insists on the continuity of self between her early childhood and the moment she met her namesake (the nurse who cared for her in Moscow).[11] Never shifting gender pronouns, mentioning a dead name from childhood, or even providing a birth date in her testimonio, she in many ways occupies a queer sense of time that Jack Halberstam defines as "the perverse turn away from the narrative coherence of adolescence."[12]

Echeverría Gaitán's experiences are also intersectional. Littered throughout her writings and interviews are multidimensional experiences of disablism coupled with violent rejections of her displays of femininity, informing and constituting one another.[13] Her testimonio, in fact, opens with her earliest and most tangible memory—the stinging sensation of an operation—highlighting how the corporeal alienation wrought by disability can precede the bodily difference of being transgender.[14] Ableist barriers further structured her experiences of time around the fear and expectation of delay—a reorientation of temporality that Alison Kafer and others characterize as "crip time."[15] She was, for example, enrolled in classes designed for learning disabilities despite the fact that hers was a physical one, and her father beat her for the protracted manner in which she ate.[16]

Despite the heterogeneous temporalities and intersectional experiences that punctuate her life story, one is nevertheless struck by the way Echeverría Gaitán gives it order. In her testimonio, she indicates the linear passage of time with the various stages of her muscle and nerve degeneration. And although she is resistant to embrace a temporal shift in pronouns that would give her narrative a male past and female present, she does recognize her process of affirmation in terms of a fixed beginning and end. To that effect, she does not identify as a trans woman (*transexual* or *trans*), arguing that *trans* is not a permanent designation of a person but rather a temporary term that describes the process of gender affirmation.[17]

The understanding of trans time as transitional is indicative of what Alba Pons Rabasa has shown to be a result of the adoption of the medical model of transgender in Mexico during the late 1990s and early 2000s. In this model "the discursive shift from transgender as a political identification and political strategy to the medical categorization . . . has converted transgender into a phase through which the subject passes in his or her 'process of transition.'"[18] Echeverría Gaitán's comments in *Carta a mi padre* reveal her engagement with these discursive shifts in order to give her life a sequential order: "Transexuality was only a process. What am I? A woman. Who am I? Irina. Who was I? Irina. I was hidden, repressed, scared, but I was there. All I needed was a process to be born, and here I am."[19] Using a language of birth, she situates her eventual arrival as the culmination of a process of gaining the language and knowledge necessary to articulate her identity. But slip-pages in this chronological timeline remain as she also expresses herself as always having existed.

Thus, although the chronic nature of Charcot-Marie-Tooth disease and the asynchronism of her gender identity—that is, her identification as Irina even as she was inscribed in the historical record and the memories of her contemporaries as a different gender—resist a division of before and after, Echeverría Gaitán organizes her life around a temporal regime of transition and futurity. Rather than character-ize this as a case of transnormative narration in which trans histories conform to the linear conventions of a transition story, scholars must take into account the political ideologies that also govern temporalities.[20] I maintain that Echeverría Gaitán's pre-sentation of a narrative of transition is due to her commitments to the futurist pro-ject of socialism and the revolutionary subjectivity espoused in Che Guevara's uto-pian citizen. Based on developmental discourses, this subjectivity can be achieved by developing one's militancy, which leads to a transcendental moment of rebirth into revolutionary consciousness that frees one from a painful personal history.[21] The logic of a future-oriented self-construction and erasure of past trauma figures heavily in the testimony of Echeverría Gaitán who, in addition to her own dead name, never mentions her parents' names, likely due to her strained relationship with them.[22]

Overall, in ways similar to how trans histories have been coded to fit an ideo-logical project of distinguishing a chaotic past from a stable future, the New Man and New Woman give coherence to Echeverría Gaitán's life.[23] This emphasis on the potentiality of futurity pushes us to further question curative imaginaries of dis-ability that uphold compulsory able-bodiedness and to expand the trans historicist imperative to search for accounts of gender variability in the past ("trans before trans") by also asking who is "trans after trans"—a project especially crucial in a region such as Latin America that is consistently presented as existing in a time "before" or outside of sexual modernity.[24]

Admiring the New Man

Irina Layevska Echeverría Gaitán was born on October 12, 1964, between two of the most profound events to mark the late twentieth century: the Cuban Revolution of 1959 and the 1968 Tlatelolco Massacre. The former made Cuba a major exporter of revolutionary ideas and culture to the Global South, particularly after the publica-tion of Che Guevara's "Socialism and Man in Cuba."[25] For a younger generation of activists and leftists in Mexico disillusioned by the USSR, Cuba provided a new way of envisioning social change at a time when the promises of redistribution from the Mexican Revolution (1910–1920) were coming to a halt. The latter, meanwhile, was a generational clash of political discontent regarding the democratic legacy of the

Mexican Revolution and the government's failure to fulfill its promises to reduce widespread inequality. Tlatelolco left an indelible mark on Mexican society, shattering the tenuous façade of political stability under the Institutional Revolutionary Party (PRI).[26]

Echeverría Gaitán's birth, as fate would have it, was also a product of the Cuban Revolution—her parents met while at a march in support of the revolution in July of 1963. Her mother, Yolanda Gaitán, was a militant of the Mexican Communist Party (PCM) and worked for the party from 1962 to 1968, while her father, Rodolfo Echeverría, rose through the party's ranks. In October of 1968, when Echeverría Gaitán was about to celebrate her fourth birthday, her father returned from a trip to Moscow and was arrested in the crackdown following the student massacre. While he had managed to escape the bloodshed at Tlatelolco, he was rounded up with other student activists and sent to the dreaded Lecumberri prison where he would spend the next three years incarcerated.[27] With the arrest of her father, Echeverría Gaitán's mother took over the household while also serving as head of the Comité de Familiares de Presos Políticos (Committee of the Relatives of Political Prisoners).[28]

As the child of Communist militants, Echeverría Gaitán's upbringing was further influenced by the gender, sexual, and family politics of the PCM. In the years after its founding in 1919, the PCM positioned itself as the moral alternative to the Mexican government and Catholic Church. It did so by emphasizing militant decency in its publications and making labor and policy demands based on the nuclear family such as restrictive protections for women's work and a male-centered family wage.[29] Propaganda in the newspaper *El Machete* (1924–38) also mocked homosexuals and sex workers, with some of the most virulent homophobia and heterosexism coming from prominent members such as Diego Rivera.[30] The PCM's approach to women's issues was no more progressive, as strict gender divides and *machista* (sexist) attitudes were rampant despite the indispensable work of women within the party.[31] Overall, the PCM in these early decades reflected the homophobic and sexist attitudes that were widespread in Mexican society before the Cuban Revolution.

Growing up in a communist family during the Cold War was a formative experience for Echeverría Gaitán and her two sisters. Despite stigmatization from neighbors, her parents remained fiercely loyal to communist ideals, which they imparted to their children. "I was educated," explains Echeverría Gaitán, "with a morality that we in those days called revolutionary morality."[32] Her mother also championed revolutionary ideas in the home, teaching her children about contraception and sexually transmitted diseases. However, Echeverría Gaitán discloses, "homosexuality was very badly viewed. My mother had friends who were gay and lesbian, but she could not stand the possibility of her children being that way."[33]

Although Mexico's 1968 generation challenged sexual taboos and incorporated some levels of tolerance into their friendships, the PCM remained hostile to many of these new trends.[34]

Upon the arrest of her father in 1968, Echeverría Gaitán's weekends were spent visiting the infamous Lecumberri prison. By then she was around four years old and had begun showing signs of her illness. She needed to walk with orthopedic shoes, which caused onlookers to stare and guards to mock her during visits. As her muscle issues progressed, her family turned a blind eye and refused to discuss the matter. Echeverría Gaitán recalls that her mother would say things like, "Nothing is wrong, everything is normal, we are a normal family." In her testimonio, Echeverría Gaitán dismisses this emphasis of normalcy, a disablist discourse constructed to erase difference in favor of a universal ideal, by characterizing it as her mother's "fantasy."[35]

Despite her mother's disablism, Echeverría Gaitán remained fairly close with her, whereas her relationship with her father was characterized by conflict. Though she initially admired him for his arrest as a revolutionary, their relationship deteriorated upon his release in 1972. Echeverría Gaitán claims that her father was abusive, humiliating her and attacking her physically. He demanded she act as an *hombrecito* (tough man), perhaps reflecting the anxieties around the emasculation of disabled youth who are urged to "fight it like a man."[36] Echeverría Gaitán states that while she was aware of her desire to be a woman throughout her life, it was these early clashes with her father that stirred her desire to explore her femininity in order to express her emotions.[37]

In July 1972, Echeverría Gaitán's father took her to Romania for a leg operation after her family had petitioned the USSR for medical support. Soon after their arrival, she remembers him abandoning her at the hospital to travel around Europe to conduct party affairs. For Echeverría Gaitán, this was yet another example of her father's abuse and absence. However, as she slowly pushed him away, she found solace in the figure of Che Guevara, whose condition of asthma gave Echeverría Gaitán a sense of kinship with the revolutionary.[38]

Che for me was more than an emblematic person. Che became my image of an ideal father. My biological father, we had a very conflictive relationship. . . . My mother, in her bedroom, had a very large portrait of Che. It was not the typical image. He did not have a beret and had short hair, with a trimmed beard. I dreamed that he was my dad and I talked to him. I always said "Papa" to him. But it was not only the image. Che was a man who had a very strong physical disability. He had an asthma that prevented him from doing many things. In the most agitated or most complicated moments of the armed struggle in which he participated, asthma beat him, but it never defeated him. He never complained. And so I wanted to be like him.[39]

Che Guevara served as substitute father figure for Echeverría Gaitán—one who did not abuse her and shared her physical difficulties. By keeping a portrait of Che in their home, her mother initiated the process of her daughter's self-construction in his image.

Aiming for Che

In 1979, Echeverría Gaitán was sent to Moscow's Central Clinical Hospital. Known as the "Kremlin Hospital," it offered the highest quality medical care in the Soviet Union and catered to highly ranked party officials and esteemed "foreign comrades" such as Diego Rivera.[40] Since the right to free health care was extended to foreigners, Echeverría Gaitán was able to stay for over a year and was joined by other foreign guests getting medical attention.[41] Manuel Marulanda Vélez, cofounder of the Revolutionary Armed Forces of Colombia—People's Army (FARC), tutored her in leftist theory; Daniel Ortega, one of the leaders of the Sandinista National Liberation Front in Nicaragua (FSLN), shared her medical wing; and Palestine Liberation Organization (PLO) chairman, Yasser Arafat, allegedly attempted to marry her mother. In Moscow she would also meet Irina, a nurse whose attentive care impacted Echeverría Gaitán so much that she adopted her name.[42]

Away from most of her family and more mature than during her time in Romania, Echeverría Gaitán felt a sense of freedom to begin exploring her gender and sexuality in Moscow. About a year into her stay, she began dating a boy from Iraq. When he would refer to her as his boyfriend, she remembers that she would correct him and demand to be called his girlfriend. After their first sexual encounter, she notes that he finally began believing that she was a woman, stating it was because she made love like one. She writes, "I felt so realized and complete. . . . He was the first to accept me as a woman." The time and space away from her family, while freeing, was also temporary. Returning to Mexico in 1981 "forced me to hide all emotion."[43]

In 1981, Echeverría Gaitán also began using a wheelchair, a shift in mobility that further conflated her body with her disability (fig. 1).[44] As a result, she began radicalizing her militancy. Around 1984, frustrated with the messages of caution imposed on her, she went to Nicaragua to aid in a literacy campaign. While there, however, she claims that she took up arms and other duties such as training injured and disabled guerillas to use weaponry. She also asserts that the Contras overran her rural camp and almost killed her. She managed to escape, however, by flinging herself off her wheelchair and crawling away: "Without realizing it, I crossed the border with Costa Rica and came upon their encampment. I fired my gun and hit a few. The Sandinista National Liberation Front decorated me."[45] Whether or not Echeverría Gaitán truly did accomplish this extraordinary feat matters less than her narration of the event, which articulates her desire to occupy the role of the sacrificial New Man.

Figure 1. Echeverría Gaitán in Moscow, wearing a beret and beginning to use a wheelchair. Photo courtesy of Irina Layevska Echeverría Gaitán.

In fact, when asked why she went to Nicaragua, she stated she felt like if she was going to die, she wanted a romantic death like Che Guevara.[46]

While Echeverría Gaitán was recovering in Moscow and fighting in Nicaragua, the terrain of sexual politics was rapidly changing as a visible and vocal gay and lesbian movement emerged in Mexico by the end of the 1970s.[47] The demands for greater rights and respect from gay men and lesbians were initially met with visceral homophobia from militants of the PCM, even as the movement endorsed a socialist agenda. During a solidarity march for the Cuban Revolution held on July 26, 1978, gay men and lesbians connected their liberation to the goals of the revolution by chanting "Socialism without Sexism" and "Revolution in the Factory and the Sheets." They were met with jeers from members of the Communist Party, who refused to march alongside them and called them "faggots."[48] By 1980, however, the conversation around sexual politics began to shift as the sexual rights movement's leaders made contact with PCM officials. As a result, during its XIX Congress in 1981, the party officially endorsed feminism and freedom of sexual orientation as part of its defense of individual privacy, although this moderate tolerance would wax and wane over time.[49]

The Communist Party's long-standing opposition to sexual liberation stands in stark contrast to the policies of the Workers' Revolutionary Party (PRT), a Mexican Trotskyist opposition party that Echeverría Gaitán would join in the late 1980s, a little over a decade after its founding in 1976. Although it also supported the Cuban Revolution, the PRT did not follow the homophobic line of Castro. It even had an organized collective of lesbian and gay militants known as the Homosexual Work Commission. Following the example of the United Secretariat of the Fourth International, in 1979 the PRT adopted a resolution calling for the abolition of women's oppression and an end to the discrimination of sexual minorities.[50]

For many members of the sexual rights movement, the Cuban Revolution was initially prominent in their political imaginary during these years of activism. As Braulio Peralta, a militant of the Mexican gay and lesbian movement noted, "In '68 we all adored Fidel Castro, we did not criticize Stalin, we believed that the socialist bloc represented hope . . . with a future for everyone, including homosexuals. Now we know all too well that this was not true."[51] While Peralta constructs a memory of disappointment and failure after the Cuban Revolution, others like Arturo Vázquez Barrón reconcile the hopes of revolution with the homophobia that followed 1959. In his words, "Our fight was for what we called socialism without sexism . . . to purge socialism of the remnants of homophobia."[52]

The opposing attitudes of Peralta and Vázquez Barrón demonstrate Cuba's contested image and the divergent ways its revolutionary ideals of liberation and autonomy could be interpreted. For some, the homophobia of the Cuban experience after 1961 served as a cautionary tale regarding the continued repression of sexual minorities under socialism. For others, the liberatory promises of Cuba could be salvaged: they believed socialism without sexism could be achieved by defending the emancipatory aspects of the Cuban Revolution while reforming the homophobia of leftists. This plasticity of the image of Cuba and belief in its redemption would serve Echeverría Gaitán in the years to come.

Breaking with her communist upbringing, Echeverría Gaitán joined the PRT in 1988. She claims this was due to her disagreement with former PCM leaders to ally with moderate sectors of the PRI in the 1988 presidential elections, but it is also likely that the PRT's tolerance towards sexual minorities appealed to her. "In the PRT there was respect and comradery in regards to diverse gender and sexual minorities," she recalls, "which was not the case in the PCM."[53] By 1993, Echeverría Gaitán had risen through the ranks of the PRT to become part of its Central Committee. Although some of her fellow militants expressed disdain or pity toward her, most others recognized her tenacity and ability to organize.[54]

Throughout this period, Echeverría Gaitán remained a fierce advocate of the revolutionary promises of socialism and the Cuban Revolution. With the onset of the "Special Period" of economic crisis after the 1991 dissolution of the Soviet Union, Echeverría Gaitán spearheaded the PRT's Committee of Solidarity "¡Va por Cuba!," which brought crucial supplies to the island. Between 1991 and 1994, during some of the island's worst shortages, the group sent three boatloads of diesel oil to Cuba. During her third mission to the island in 1994, Echeverría Gaitán married Nélida Reyes Guzmán, another PRT militant and Cuba sympathizer. Their marriage was a socialist partnership, with equality between them and a mutual dedication to defending the revolution.

The Special Period in Cuba and the fall of the Berlin Wall in 1989 gave Echeverría Gaitán cause for reflection in the face of the downward trajectory of revolutionary movements that marked the decade. In an undated interview from the 1990s, Echeverría Gaitán expressed her disappointment in the collapse of the Socialist Bloc, but a continued hope in the futurist project of the New Man. Claiming that her entire life had been dedicated to the formation of herself into a New Man and recalling the speech by Castro on the need to educate future generations to be like Che, she stated,

"What do I hope for? Well I do not expect something utopian. I just hope the people wake up. . . . Che talked about the New Man, and the New Man does not yet exist. There are new men, but there is no New Man. There will be one, two, three."[55]

Echeverría Gaitán's meditations on the New Man speak to her desire for a plurality of possibilities for the future of revolutionary militancy. Noting the lack of a true utopian subject in her lifetime, Echeverría Gaitán emphasized the potential for diversity in the New Man to come—perhaps hinting at gender variability but certainly asserting her hopes for a revolutionary figure that did not carry the sexism and ableism of her contemporaries. Yet the realities of the late 1990s in the terrain of leftist politics, and in her personal life, also meant projecting these hopes into an indeterminate future.

During these years of armed struggle and leftist activity in Mexico and abroad, the aims of living up to the New Man, combined with her resemblance to Che, made Echeverría Gaitán's militancy distinct. She writes how the discovery of her appearance to him in the 1980s dramatically changed her understanding of self:

I needed an anchor to hold on to, and I found it when I was lent a beret at school and one of my friends commented: "Hey, you look a lot like Che Guevara." You cannot imagine what that was like for me; it was like a glass of cold water in the desert. I finally had an identity. I had never liked the one I had from childhood, but with this discovery I could have a personality to hold onto without being suffocated.[56]

With a beret and beard in the style of Che, Echeverría Gaitán constructed herself as a revolutionary in his image. In addition to imitating his appearance, she adopted her own interpretation of the moral and ethical code of the New Man. Her performance, however, clashed with the *machismo* (sexism) of her fellow militants, who were surprised to learn that she cooked and washed dishes. They would also become enraged when their girlfriends and wives would come to Echeverría Gaitán to vent their frustrations about their relationships.[57]

Echeverría Gaitán changed the appearance of the traditional revolutionary figure to include her disability. She also formed an alternative identity, one that cloaked her transgender subjectivity. This performance of Che and the New Man, however, was not the crystallization of masculinity or a "reidealization of hyperbolic heterosexual gender norms."[58] Rather, her version was a redefining of what the New Man could be, for it did not carry the machismo of previous iterations. In fact, she claims it enabled her to test the boundaries of her femininity and embody a revolutionary womanhood. She writes, for example, that she grew out her hair under the auspices of being a rebel. But in reality, it was one of the few opportunities she had to express her womanhood.[59] Echeverría Gaitán recalls attempting to promote her femininity while also embodying these iconic signs of rebellion and masculinity. By collapsing the gender binaries into one another in her memory of revolutionary activity, she is able to resolve the psychological conflict and temporal disjunction that she feels upon seeing past photos of herself ("I am seeing someone who I was but at the same time I did not want to be").[60]

Echeverría Gaitán's self-construction as Che, furthermore, lays bare the necessity that undergirds gender performances for survival. In her words, "What happens is that when you are living in a society where masculinity is so central and you have been taught that you have to be a man, well, I could not upset my family, much less my mother. And so it was better to appear as Che than as something else."[61] Intuiting the ways that her family's insistence on hypermasculinity coincided with the increasing demands of her disability as she shifted to a wheelchair, Echeverría Gaitán built a gender performance that appeased her social circle. Resembling Che, Echeverría Gaitán could stake a claim to the aspects of revolutionary masculinity that were open to her—such as clothing and facial hair—yet at the same time allow her to manage her gender identity without incurring punishment during a period when she was already being treated with great hostility.[62]

Becoming Irina

Starting in 2000, Echeverría Gaitán began to lose her eyesight as muscular dystrophy affected her optic nerves. For aid in confronting this new crisis, she appealed to Cuba. After a number of exams with Cuban physicians, she was told she would eventually lose her eyesight. Upon her return to Mexico, she contemplated committing suicide, but was stopped by her wife Nélida, who emphasized her need to mourn, give in to her emotions, and explore her femininity. It was then that Echeverría Gaitán began to seriously inquire what it meant for her to be a woman. Her first step was trying on a dress belonging to her wife, which she marks as the day she became the true Irina: August 24, 2001. She would begin hormone treatment and change her appearance soon after (fig. 2).

The years leading up to Echeverría Gaitán's gender affirmation witnessed the rapid expansion of the transgender movement in Mexico, with groups such as Eón Inteligencia Transgenérica (Aeon Transgender Alliance) emerging in Mexico City from the mid-1990s onward. The politicization of the transgender movement involved an alliance with sexologists and the deployment of medical discourses in

Figure 2. Irina in the late 2000s. Photo courtesy of Irina Layevska Echeverría Gaitán.

order to make rights-based claims. Such discourses included establishing *transgender* as a transitory clinical category with the end goal being a subject's sense of concordance between sex and gender.[63]

Echeverría Gaitán's narration of her affirmation, particularly the ways she frames it as a transition that ended upon seeing herself as a woman, demonstrates the acquisition of this knowledge. By framing her gender affirmation as a process, she is able to reconcile it with her political commitment to constant self-construction. The expansion of her political commitments also reflects the gradual radicalization of her consciousness. For this reason, she concludes her *testimonio* discussing both her continued battles to make Mexico City a more accessible space, and the legal struggle to have her gender affirmation recognized in the civil registry (a right that was won in Mexico City in 2008). Presenting her affirmation as complete also reasserts a vital sense of agency over her body. While Echeverría Gaitán attests to feelings of corporal failure due to her disability throughout her life, it was the chronological rubicon of puberty that presented a newer sensation of untimeliness and loss of her bodily autonomy.[64] As an adult, however, she was able to regain control over her gender expression, which represents a crucial turning point in her militancy. So while she was always Irina, she can also provide a date for when Irina appeared.

Echeverría Gaitán's changing relationship to her body and identity meant ending her resemblance to Che Guevara. As she recounts,

I went to Cuba and when I arrived at the hotel, I looked at myself in the mirror. I removed my beard and mustache and went to Loma El Taburete, Che's last campsite before going to Bolivia. I climbed the hill in my wheelchair, three kilometers on pure dirt, I fell several times but I kept getting up until I arrived. And at the foot of a tree that was at the edge of the cabin, among the stars. . . . I thanked him and said goodbye to that physical image.[65]

In *Exile and Pride*, Eli Clare explains that the daily struggle of disabled folk to navigate an inaccessible world is often framed as a metaphoric mountain.[66] For Echeverría Gaitán, this mountain was both symbolic and literal. During her journey to Loma El Taburete, Echeverría Gaitán resolved that her gender did not constitute a separate aspect of either her disability or her militancy. In fact, transitioning became the most radical expression of her revolutionary identity. Without the need for gender performance in the image of Che, Echeverría Gaitán contends she can focus more attention on playing her part in constructing a new world, even if "doing it as a woman is very complicated in a world dominated by a patriarchal culture where the left is also contaminated by macho concepts and methods."[67]

Echeverría Gaitán's changing appearance, however, did not mean a departure from Guevara's utopian citizen. Rather, in transitioning she further expanded the image of the revolutionary figure. When asked about who could occupy the role of the New Man, Echeverría Gaitán reinterpreted the words of Che, replying,

> Che referred to the New Man as a concept of humanity, not as a gender, just as we refer to *Man* as the human species. But that *New Human Being* will not come alone, it is a process of formation that will give rise to ideological self-formation from the breaking of vices and attitudes of selfishness, to build a community for the benefit of all. That being the case, the concept is inclusive for gays, lesbians, trans folk, and all expressions of gender dissidence, regardless of their disability status.[68]

In this reformulation, the New Man becomes a concept for all of humanity, including sexual minorities and those with disabilities. By reflecting on the New Man after assuming the gender expression she had always felt, Echeverría Gaitán was able to reinterpret the language of Guevara to make the New Man a universal figure of any gender who combines the futurist goals of socialism with a desire for broad inclusion. Using discourses of the Cuban Revolution, Echeverría Gaitán proposes a disabled and trans futurity that is invested in incorporating marginalized minorities who were excluded from the utopian visions of past generations and celebrates their differences as part of the liberatory and emancipatory revolution.

For an individual undergoing the process of gender affirmation, however, the gendering of this human being is crucial. Echeverría Gaitán does not identify as a gender neutral New Human Being, but rather as a New Woman. By interviewing her in 2018, I provided Echeverría Gaitán with the opportunity to rework her past as she had always experienced it. When asked, for instance, if she felt she was still part of the futurist and socialist vision of Che Guevara, she responded, "I have dedicated my entire life to my ideological self-transformation to become the New Woman, for the construction of socialism, not the one that they wanted to impose with Stalin, but a real one."[69] While in past interviews Echeverría Gaitán had emphasized her self-construction as the New Man—possibly indirectly hinting at its gender variance—in this instance she was able to explicitly express her true desire to make herself a New Woman.

Historically, the figure of the New Woman was "constantly present" in revolutionary images but "did not play a central role in official discourse."[70] Echeverría Gaitán's reinterpretation of the New Woman, on the other hand, makes her central to revolutionary discourse. She is, nevertheless, complementary to the New Man. Even while she elevates Che Guevara to a universal model, stating that he "remains a key piece of my existence to build myself as a New Woman," she retains the gender difference he delineated between New Man and Woman.[71] Echeverría Gaitán thus invites us to reconsider the contested desires for the mutability of gender in the process of transitioning, as her shift from one revolutionary model (the New Man) to another (the New Woman) is coded along a binary and given a conceptual framing as rebirth.

Affirming herself as a New Woman put Echeverría Gaitán in confrontation with her social circle. Most of her family disowned her upon hearing the news. Pondering the rejection from her family, specifically her father, she writes, "There's something I do not understand: you have gay friends, dad, and you do not treat them like you treat me."[72] Although she still affiliates with the PRT, she also notes that the party had mixed responses to her transition. "The reaction was diverse," she states. "There were those who supported me and were allies in my rebirth. There were also those who got angry and stopped talking to me, others got scared, and others, well, they left and promised to return and never did."[73] She also claims she was expelled from the Zapatista Army of National Liberation (EZLN) for "gender betrayal."[74]

Not everyone reacted to Echeverría Gaitán's transition with visceral rejection. Some reexamined their revolutionary principles to find acceptance. One friend, referred to only as "Luis" in her testimonio, stands out because of his acceptance of her gradual transformation.[75] Luis fulfilled Echeverría Gaitán's vision that the ideals of liberation and autonomy espoused in revolutionary discourse could be inclusive of transgender individuals. And despite some initial difficulties, her wife Nélida Reyes Guzmán also remained at her side. Reyes Guzmán states that she learned the importance of "problematizing your own prejudices and then working on them. . . . What I discovered in my process with Irina is that love has no gender."[76] Their marriage enabled Reyes Guzmán to reconfigure her partnership to make room for Echeverría Gaitán's self-construction.

In the end, Echeverría Gaitán's clashes with family and fellow militants expose some of the central contradictions regarding sexual politics. First is the known existence and even friendships with sexual minorities alongside the violent public rejection of their rights. Second is the differentiation of transgender rights from gay and lesbian rights, with the latter seemingly enjoying greater acceptance. Her parents' and comrades' relationships with gay men and women were not free of sexism, and their rejection of her gender affirmation highlights how misogyny extends into transmisogny.[77] Though her disability—likely read as outside of her control—did not preclude her from participating in revolutionary activities, entering womanhood was seen as a transgressive choice that did. Their negative reactions highlight a general anxiety around the role of the feminine body on the Left and foreshadowed the controversy that transgender inclusion continues to elicit among contemporary progressive movements.[78]

Conclusion

When he introduced the concept of the New Man and Woman in 1965, Che Guevara did not reckon with the masculinist and exclusionary politics of the period. He did, however, propose a futurist vision of development that required constant self-construction in order to achieve revolutionary consciousness. For a generation of feminists, sexual rights activists, and disabled revolutionaries born in the aftermath of the Cuban Revolution, these principles laid the foundation for expanding who could participate in building a new world.

Armed with a gun and a vision of Che, Irina Layevska Echeverría Gaitán was one of these revolutionaries. As a youth, Echeverría Gaitán was expected to occupy the role of the virile New Man envisioned by her parents. However, the social stigma and lack of accessible public spaces that constructed her disability, the cultural values that emasculated her body, and the conservative sexual politics that rejected her gender identity alienated her from the masculinist, able-bodied revolutionary subject embodied by men like her father.[79] She nevertheless drew on the models of Guevara, the New Man, and New Woman at different moments in her life to make meaning of her gender identity and disability, all the while amending them to her militancy and refuting their sexist, ableist, and transphobic iterations.

Echeverría Gaitán documented her engagement with these ideals by writing her own testimonio, published as the Left was resurging in Latin America during the region's "Pink Tide" and Mexico's transgender movement was making landmark legal gains. Imparting her memories gave Echeverria Gaitán the opportunity to dispute the restrictive gender ideals of her family and, above all, the Left. While her contemporaries rejected the identitarian politics she championed, Echeverría Gaitán demonstrated how revolutionary praxis could be reconciled with the cultural turns that would mark the last decades of the twentieth century and whose unresolved legacies continue to haunt political activism today.

Robert Franco is a doctoral candidate in the Department of History at Duke University. He is currently a 2019–2020 Predoctoral Fellow for Excellence through Diversity at the University of Pennsylvania. He is completing his dissertation, which examines the issues of homophobia, heterosexism, and antagonism toward sexual politics in the Mexican Left.

Notes

Thank you to Irina Layevska Echeverría Gaitán for sharing your story. Jocelyn Olcott, Pete Sigal, Kevan Antonio Aguilar, and Farren Yero, in addition to the two anonymous reviewers who generously provided me with thoughtful feedback. I would also like to extend my gratitude to the editors of this special issue, Michelle Chase, Isabella Cosse, Heidi Tinsman, and Melina Pappademos, for their patience and guidance.

1. *Morir de pie.*
2. Guevara, "Socialism and Man," 217.
3. Guevara, "Socialism and Man," 227.
4. Barr-Melej, *Psychedelic Chile*, 158–61, 234; Lancaster, *Life Is Hard*, 40, 175; with some differences of interpretation, Markarian, *Uruguay*, 126–32.
5. Lumsden, *Machos, Maricones, and Gays*, 58–61; Porbén, *La revolución deseada*, 25–26.
6. On these questions see Rodríguez, *Women, Guerrillas, and Love*, 46; 108–9; Montoya, *Gendered Scenarios*, 8; and Serra, *The "New Man,"* 109. For more on women's roles in revolutionary movements, see Chase, *Revolution within the Revolution*; Kampwirth, *Women and Guerrilla Movements*; and Oberti, *Las revolucionarias*.
7. James, *Doña María's Story*, 123; Arias, *The Rigoberta Menchú Controversy*; Olcott, "Cold War Conflicts."
8. See Cosse, "Infidelities"; Green, *Exile within Exiles*; Leibner, *Camaradas y compañeros*; Olcott, "'A Plague of Salaried Marxists'"; Salgado, "'A Small Revolution'"; Silva Schultze, *Aquellos comunistas*; and Vaughan, *Portrait of a Young Painter*.
9. Halberstam, *In a Queer Time and Place*, 77.
10. Dinshaw et al., "Theorizing Queer Temporalities"; See also Lau, "Between the Times"; and Snorton, *Black on Both Sides*.
11. Bychowski et al., "'Trans°historicities,'" 662–64.
12. Dinshaw et al., "Theorizing Queer Temporalities," 182.
13. Clare, "Body Shame, Body Pride," 261–62.
14. Crenshaw, "Demarginalizing," 139–40. For more on the construction of disability, see Davis, *Bending over Backwards*; and McRuer, "We Were Never Identified."
15. Kafer, *Feminist, Queer, Crip*, 26–27.
16. Echeverría Gaitán, *Carta a mi padre*, 21, 37.
17. While the use of transgender (*transgénero*) has been gaining ground in recent decades, breaking from the historic designation of *travesti*—subjects who adopt feminine expressions in dress and language but who are traditionally placed on the spectrum of homosexual desire—Echeverría Gaitán does not use this term. Lewis, *Crossing*, 6–7.
18. Pons Rabasa, "From Representation to Corposubjectivation," 395.
19. Echeverría Gaitán, *Carta a mi padre*, 81.
20. Bychowski et al., "'Trans°historicities,'" 664.
21. Saldaña-Portillo, *The Revolutionary Imagination*, 66.
22. In order to obtain this information, I had to ask her and other acquaintants directly.
23. Carvajal, "Image Politics and Disturbing Temporalities," 627–28.
24. Kafer, *Feminist, Queer, Crip*, 33–34; Devun and Tortorici, "Trans, Time, and History," 524; Muñoz, *Cruising Utopia*; Quiroga, *Tropics of Desire*, 16. For more on the curative model, see Kim, *Curative Violence*.
25. Cheng, *Creating the "New Man"*; Drinot, *Che's Travels*; and Brown, *Cuba's Revolutionary World*.

26. See Keller, *Mexico's Cold War*, 53–57; Walker, *Waking from the Dream*, 93; Rivas
     Ontiveros, *La izquierda estudiantil en la UNAM*, 176–77; Estrada, *1968, estado y
     universidad*, 128–29; Pensado, *Rebel Mexico*, 150–51; and Zolov, *Refried Elvis*, 107–15.
27. For more on the history of Lecumberri, see García Ramírez, *El final de Lecumberri*;
     Frazier and Cohen, "Defining the Space of Mexico '68"; and McCormick, "The Last
     Door."
28. Irina Layevska Echeverría Gaitán, email interview with the author, August 8–12, 2018.
29. Lear, *Picturing the Proletariat*, 87–91, 109–10.
30. Balderston, "Poetry, Revolution, Homophobia," 57.
31. Olcott, *Revolutionary Women*, 38.
32. *Morir de pie.*
33. Echeverría Gaitán interview.
34. Carr, *Marxism and Communism*, 240.
35. Echeverría Gaitán, *Carta a mi padre*, 19; 24; Lennard J. Davis, "Introduction," 4.
36. Wilson, "Fighting Polio Like a Man," 121.
37. Fernández, *10 ingobernables*, 32.
38. Echeverría Gaitán, *Carta a mi padre*, 38.
39. *Morir de pie.*
40. Richardson, "The Dilemmas of a Communist Artist," 62; Graham, *Moscow Stories*, 243;
     Voslensky, *Nomenklatura*, 216–17.
41. Hazanov, "Porous Empire," 248–49; Studer, *The Transnational World*, 71.
42. Fernández, *10 ingobernables*, 17.
43. Echeverría Gaitán, *Carta a mi padre*, 42.
44. Siebers, "Disability," 24.
45. Fernández, *10 ingobernables*, 13.
46. Fernández, *10 ingobernables*, 17–19.
47. Laguarda, *Ser gay en la ciudad de México*, 57.
48. Hernández, *Entrevistas*, March 20, 2000, 14.
49. Carr, *Marxism and Communism*, 288–89.
50. De la Dehesa, *Queering the Public Sphere*, 80–82; 89–90.
51. Peralta, *Entrevistas*, October 20–November 17, 2001, 23.
52. Vázquez Barrón, *Entrevistas*, July 25, 2000, 8.
53. Echeverría Gaitán interview.
54. *Morir de pie.*
55. *Morir de pie.*
56. Echeverría Gaitán, *Carta a mi padre*, 40.
57. Fernández, *10 ingobernables*, 24–25.
58. Butler, *Bodies That Matter*, 125.
589. Echeverría Gaitán, *Carta a mi padre*, 40.
60. *Morir de pie.*
61. *Morir de pie.*
62. Halberstam, *In a Queer Time and Place*, 77.
63. Pons Rabasa, "From Representation to Corposubjectivation."
64. Echeverría Gaitán, *Carta a mi padre,* 39; Freeman, "Introduction," 163.
65. *Morir de pie.*
66. Clare, *Exile and Pride*, 1–2.
67. Echeverría Gaitán interview.

68. Echeverría Gaitán interview.
69. Echeverría Gaitán interview.
70. Serra, *The "New Man,"* 109.
71. Echeverría Gaitán interview.
72. Echeverría Gaitán, *Carta a mi padre*, 63.
73. Echeverría Gaitán interview.
74. Fernández, *10 ingobernables*, 21; Fernández, "La revolucionaria que se travestía del Che."
75. Echeverría Gaitán, *Carta a mi padre*, 77.
76. *Morir de pie.*
77. Serano, "Skirt Chasers," 226–30.
78. Rodríguez, *Women, Guerrillas, and Love*, 32–35; Riddell, "Divided Sisterhood"; Whittle, "Where Did We Go Wrong?"
79. Wilson, "Fighting Polio Like a Man," 121; Barounis, "Cripping Heterosexuality," 381–88.

References

Arias, Arturo, ed. *The Rigoberta Menchú Controversy*. Minneapolis: University of Minnesota Press, 2001.

Balderston, Daniel. "Poetry, Revolution, Homophobia: Polemics from the Mexican Revolution." In *Hispanisms and Homosexualities*, edited by Sylvia Molloy and Robert McKee Irwin, 57–75. Durham, NC: Duke University Press, 1998.

Barounis, Cynthia. "Cripping Heterosexuality, Queering Able-Bodiedness: *Murderball, Brokeback Mountain*, and the Contested Masculine Body." In *The Disability Studies Reader*, edited by Lennard J. Davis, 381–97. New York: Routledge, 2013.

Barr-Melej, Patrick. *Psychedelic Chile: Youth, Counterculture, and Politics on the Road to Socialism and Dictatorship*. Chapel Hill: University of North Carolina Press, 2018.

Brown, Jonathan C. *Cuba's Revolutionary World*. Cambridge, MA: Harvard University Press, 2017.

Butler, Judith. *Bodies That Matter: On the Discursive Limits of "Sex."* New York: Routledge, 1993.

Bychowski, M. W., Howard Chiang, Jack Halberstam, Jacob Lau, Kathleen P. Long, Maria Ochoa, and C. Riley Snorton. "'Trans°historicities': A Roundtable Discussion." *TSQ: Transgender Studies Quarterly* 5, no. 4 (2018): 658–85.

Carr, Barry. *Marxism and Communism in Twentieth-Century Mexico*. Lincoln: University of Nebraska Press, 1992.

Carvajal, Fernanda. "Image Politics and Disturbing Temporalities: On 'Sex Change' Operations in the Early Chilean Dictatorship." *TSQ: Transgender Studies Quarterly* 5, no. 4 (2018): 621–37.

Chase, Michelle. *Revolution within the Revolution: Women and Gender Politics in Cuba, 1952–1962*. Chapel Hill: University of North Carolina Press, 2015.

Cheng, Yinghong. *Creating the "New Man": From Enlightenment Ideals to Socialist Realities*. Honolulu: University of Hawai'i Press, 2009.

Clare, Eli. "Body Shame, Body Pride: Lessons from the Disability Rights Movement." In *The Transgender Studies Reader 2*, edited by Susan Stryker and Aren Z. Aizura, 261–65. New York: Routledge, 2013.

Clare, Eli. *Exile and Pride: Disability, Queerness, and Liberation*. Durham, NC: Duke University Press, 2015.

Cosse, Isabella. "Infidelities: Morality, Revolution, and Sexuality in Left-Wing Guerrilla Organizations in 1960s and 1970s Argentina." *Journal of the History of Sexuality* 23, no. 3 (2014): 415–50.

Crenshaw, Kimberlé. "Demarginalizing the Intersection of Race and Sex: A Black Feminist Critique of Antidiscrimination Doctrine, Feminist Theory, and Antiracist Politics." *University of Chicago Legal Forum*, no. 140 (1989): 139–68.

Davis, Lennard J. *Bending Over Backwards: Disability, Dismodernism, and Other Difficult Positions*. New York: New York University Press, 2002.

Davis, Lennard J. "Introduction: Disability, Normality, and Power." In *The Disability Studies Reader*, edited by Lennard J. Davis, 1–14. New York: Routledge, 2013.

De la Dehesa, Rafael. *Queering the Public Sphere in Mexico and Brazil: Sexual Rights Movements in Emerging Democracies*. Durham, NC: Duke University Press, 2010.

Devun, Leah, and Zeb Tortorici. "Trans, Time, and History." *TSQ: Transgender Studies Quarterly* 5, no. 4 (2018): 518–39.

Dinshaw, Carolyn, Lee Edelman, Roderick A. Ferguson, Carla Freccero, Elizabeth Freeman, J. Halberstam, Annamarie Jagose, Christopher S. Nealon, and Tan Hoang Nguyen. "Theorizing Queer Temporalities: A Roundtable Discussion." *GLQ: A Journal of Lesbian and Gay Studies* 13, no. 2–3 (2007): 177–95.

Drinot, Paulo, ed. *Che's Travels: The Making of a Revolutionary in 1950s Latin America*. Durham, NC: Duke University Press, 2010.

Echeverría Gaitán, Irina Layevska. *Carta a mi padre: Testimonio de una persona transexual con discapacidad*. Mexico City: CONAPRED, 2008.

Estrada, Gerardo. *1968, estado y universidad: Orígenes de la transición política en México*. México, D.F.: Plaza Janés, 2004.

Fernández, June. *10 ingobernables: Historias de transgresión y rebeldía*. Madrid: Libros del K. O., 2016.

Fernández, June. "La revolucionaria que se travestía del Che." *Pikara Online Magazine*, February 23, 2015. www.pikaramagazine.com/2015/02/la-revolucionaria-que-se-travestia -del-che/.

Frazier, Lessie Jo, and Deborah Cohen. "Defining the Space of Mexico '68: Heroic Masculinity in the Prison and 'Women' in the Streets.'" *Hispanic American Historical Review* 83, no. 4 (2003): 617–60.

Freeman, Elizabeth. "Introduction." *GLQ: A Journal of Lesbian and Gay Studies* 13, no. 2–3 (2007): 159–76.

García Ramírez, Sergio. *El final de Lecumberri: Reflexiones sobre la prisión*. México: Porrúa, 1977.

Graham, Loren R. *Moscow Stories*. Bloomington: Indiana University Press, 2006.

Green, James N. *Exile within Exiles: Herbert Daniel, Gay Brazilian Revolutionary*. Durham, NC: Duke University Press, 2018.

Guevara, Ernesto Che. "Socialism and Man in Cuba." In *Che Guevara Reader: Writings on Politics and Revolution*, edited by David Deutschmann, 212–28. Melbourne, AU: Ocean Books, 2003.

Halberstam, J. *In a Queer Time and Place: Transgender Bodies, Subcultural Lives*. New York: New York University Press, 2005.

Hazanov, Alexander. "Porous Empire: Foreign Visitors and the Post-Stalin Soviet State." PhD diss., University of Pennsylvania, 2016.

Hernández, Juan Jacobo. *Entrevistas*. Archivo Histórico del Movimiento Homosexual en México, 1978–1982. México: ENAH-Colectivo Sol CONACYT, Publicaciones digitales UNAM, 2004.

James, Daniel. *Doña María's Story: Life History, Memory, and Political Identity*. Durham, NC: Duke University Press, 2000.

Kafer, Alison. *Feminist, Queer, Crip*. Bloomington: Indiana University Press, 2013.

Kampwirth, Karen. *Women and Guerrilla Movements: Nicaragua, El Salvador, Chiapas, Cuba*. University Park: Pennsylvania State University Press, 2002.

Keller, Renata. *Mexico's Cold War: Cuba, the United States, and the Legacy of the Mexican Revolution*. New York: Cambridge University Press, 2015.

Kim, Eunjung. *Curative Violence: Rehabilitating Disability, Gender, and Sexuality in Modern Korea*. Durham, NC: Duke University Press, 2017.

Laguarda, Rodrigo. *Ser gay en la ciudad de México: Lucha de representaciones y apropiación de una identidad, 1968–1982*. México: CIESAS, 2009.

Lancaster, Roger N. *Life is Hard: Machismo, Danger, and the Intimacy of Power in Nicaragua*. Berkeley: University of California Press, 1992.

Lau, Jacob R. "Between the Times: Trans-Temporality, and Historical Representation." PhD diss., University of California, Los Angeles, 2016.

Lear, John. *Picturing the Proletariat: Artists and Labor in Revolutionary Mexico, 1908–1940*. Austin: University of Texas Press, 2016.

Leibner, Gerardo. *Camaradas y compañeros: Una historia política y social de los comunistas del Uruguay*. Montevideo: Trilce, 2011.

Lewis, Vek. *Crossing Sex and Gender in Latin America*. New York: Palgrave Macmillan, 2010.

Lumsden, Ian. *Machos, Maricones, and Gays: Cuba and Homosexuality*. Philadelphia: Temple University Press, 1996.

Markarian, Vania. *Uruguay, 1968: Student Activism from Global Counterculture to Molotov Cocktails*, translated by Laura Pérez Carrara. Oakland: University of California Press, 2017.

McCormick, Gladys. "The Last Door: Political Prisoners and the Use of Torture in Mexico's Dirty War." *The Americas* 74, no. 1 (2017): 57–81.

McRuer, Robert. "We Were Never Identified: Feminism, Queer Theory, and a Disabled World." *Radical History Review*, no. 94 (2006): 148–54.

Montoya, Rosario. *Gendered Scenarios of Revolution: Making New Men and New Women in Nicaragua, 1975–2000*. Tucson: University of Arizona Press, 2012.

Morir de pie. Directed by Jacaranda Correa. México: Mediam9, Martfilms, FOPROCINE, Canal 22, 2011.

Muñoz, José Esteban. *Cruising Utopia: The Then and There of Queer Futurity*. New York: New York University Press, 2009.

Oberti, Alejandra. *Las revolucionarias: Militancia, vida cotidiana y afectividad en los setenta*. Buenos Aires: Edhasa, 2015.

Olcott, Jocelyn. "Cold War Conflicts and Cheap Cabaret: Sexual Politics at the 1975 International Women's Year Conference." *Gender and History* 22, no. 3 (2010): 733–54.

Olcott, Jocelyn. "'A Plague of Salaried Marxists': Sexuality and Subsistence in the Revolutionary Imaginary of Concha Michel." *Journal of Contemporary History* 52, no. 4 (2017): 980–98.

Olcott, Jocelyn. *Revolutionary Women in Postrevolutionary Mexico*. Durham, NC: Duke University Press, 2005.

Pensado, Jaime M. *Rebel Mexico: Student Unrest and Authoritarian Political Culture During the Long Sixties*. Stanford, CA: Stanford University Press, 2013.

Peralta, Braulio. *Entrevistas*. Archivo Histórico del Movimiento Homosexual, México, 1978–1982. México: ENAH-Colectivo Sol CONACYT, Publicaciones digitales UNAM, 2004.

Pons Rabasa, Alba. "From Representation to Corposubjectivation: The Configuration of Transgender in Mexico City." *TSQ: Transgender Studies Quarterly* 3, no. 3–4 (2016): 388–411.

Porbén, Pedro. *La revolución deseada: Prácticas culturales del hombre nuevo en Cuba*. Madrid: Editorial Verbum, 2014.

Quiroga, José. *Tropics of Desire: Interventions From Queer Latino America*. New York: New York University Press, 2000.

Richardson, William. "The Dilemmas of a Communist Artist: Diego Rivera in Moscow, 1927–1928." *Mexican Studies/Estudios Mexicanos* 3, no. 1 (1987): 49–69.

Riddell, Carol. "Divided Sisterhood: A Critical Review of Janice Raymond's The Transsexual Empire." In *The Transgender Studies Reader*, edited by Susan Stryker and Stephen Wittle, 144–58. New York: Routledge, 2006.

Rivas Ontiveros, José René. *La izquierda estudiantil en la UNAM: Organizaciones, movilizaciones y liderazgos (1958–1972)*. México: Universidad Nacional Autónoma de México, Facultad de Estudios Superiores Aragón, 2007.

Rodríguez, Ileana. *Women, Guerrillas, and Love: Understanding War in Central America*. Minneapolis: University of Minnesota Press, 1996.

Safa, Helen. "Hierarchies and Household Change in Postrevolutionary Cuba." *Latin American Perspectives* 36, no. 1 (2009): 42–52.

Saldaña-Portillo, María Josefina. *The Revolutionary Imaginary in the Americas and the Age of Development*. Durham, NC: Duke University Press, 2003.

Salgado, Alfonso. "'A Small Revolution': Family, Sex, and the Communist Youth of Chile during the Allende Years (1970–1973)." *Twentieth Century Communism* 8 (2015): 62–88.

Serano, Julia. "Skirt Chasers: Why the Media Depicts the Trans Revolution in Lipstick and Heels." In *The Transgender Studies Reader 2*, edited by Susan Stryker and Aren Z. Aizura, 226–33. New York: Routledge, 2013.

Serra, Ana. *The "New Man" in Cuba: Culture and Identity in the Revolution*. Gainesville: University Press of Florida, 2007.

Siebers, Tobin. "Disability, Pain, and the Politics of Minority Identity." In *Foundations of Disability Studies*, edited by Matthew Wappett and Katrina Arndt, 17–28. New York: Palgrave Macmillan, 2013.

Siebers, Tobin. *Disability Theory*. Ann Arbor: University of Michigan Press, 2008.

Silva Schultze, Marisa. *Aquellos comunistas: (1955–1973)*. Montevideo: Taurus, 2009.

Snorton, C. Riley. *Black on Both Sides: A Racial History of Trans Identity*. Minneapolis: University of Minnesota Press, 2017.

Studer, Brigitte. *The Transnational World of the Cominternians*, translated by Dafydd Rees Roberts. Houndmills, UK: Palgrave Macmillan, 2015.

Vaughan, Mary Kay. *Portrait of a Young Painter: Pepe Zúñiga and Mexico City's Rebel Generation*. Durham, NC: Duke University Press, 2015.

Vázquez Barrón, Arturo. *Entrevistas*. Archivo Histórico del Movimiento Homosexual en México, 1978–1982. México, ENAH-Colectivo Sol CONACYT, Publicaciones digitales UNAM, 2004.

Voslensky, Michael. *Nomenklatura: The Soviet Ruling Class*, translated by Eric Mosbacher. Garden City, NY: Doubleday, 1984.

Walker, Louise. *Waking from the Dream: Mexico's Middle Classes after 1968*. Stanford, CA: Stanford University Press, 2013.

Whittle, "Where Did We Go Wrong? Feminism and Trans Theory—Two Teams on the Same Side?" In *The Transgender Studies Reader*, edited by Susan Stryker and Stephen Wittle, 194–202. New York: Routledge, 2006.

Wilson, Daniel J. "Fighting Polio Like a Man: Intersections of Masculinity, Disability, and Aging." In *Gendering Disability*, edited by Bonnie G. Smith and Beth Hutchison, 73–104. New Brunswick, NJ: Rutgers University Press, 2004.

Zolov, Eric. *Refried Elvis: The Rise of Mexican Counterculture*. Berkeley: University of California Press, 1999.

Insurgent Intimacies

Sex, Socialism, and Black Power in the Dutch Atlantic

Chelsea Schields

In the days after May 30, 1969, on Curaçao, rumors circulated that Cuban operatives had quietly planted themselves on the small Caribbean island, radicalizing its populace and fomenting a dramatic uprising. That day, a strike begun among dockworkers in the capital city of Willemstad quickly assumed the dimensions of anticolonial revolt as thousands of the city's working class and urban poor joined in demonstration, eventually setting fire to large parts of the historic downtown. Cuban influence on these insurgent Antilleans would have been easy for witnesses to spot, as the leaders of the May 30 revolt donned army fatigues styled in the image of Fidel Castro. Auguring fear of a communist takeover on the island, conservative newspapers ran headlines quoting the island's radical youth: "'WE ARE BIG FANS OF FIDEL CASTRO.'"[1]

While historians have since debated the extent to which Cuba influenced the May 30 uprising, the most compelling and unique contributions of Antilleans to global radicalism remain unexplored.[2] For it was not the events of May 30 that marked the creative apotheosis of Antillean radicalism. As this article contends, it was their imaginative arguments for gender emancipation and sexual freedoms that set Antillean radicals apart from other New Left movements. In articulating demands for sexual rights, Antilleans drew lessons from the Cuban Revolution and the Black Power movement. Socialism's purported ability to eradicate prostitution—an accomplishment that Fidel Castro celebrated in 1966—inspired

Radical History Review

Issue 136 (January 2020)   DOI 10.1215/01636545-7857283

© 2020 by MARHO: The Radical Historians' Organization, Inc.

Antilleans to theorize sex and desire beyond the bounds of capitalism.[3] Radical activists likewise embraced Black Power's exaltation of blackness and its potential to revitalize romantic love among *and between* black men and women. Their articulations of a revolutionary masculinity premised not on a "vigorous revindication of black manhood"[4] but rather on emotional availability, respect, and mutuality—for straight and same-sex-desiring men alike—is perhaps one of the most remarkable features of the movement's gender and sexual politics, and a far cry from dominant articulations of Cuba's "New Man" or the Black Panthers' "brother on the block."[5]

Though sex emerged seemingly everywhere as a political issue in the 1960s, Antilleans put forward distinctive arguments for the political importance of intimacy. In frequent allusions to the sexual violence of slavery, leftists connected violence and desire, revealing the troubling imbrication of intimacy in the very foundations of inequality that leftists fought to dismantle. As residents of overseas territories of the Netherlands, Antilleans struggled against the effects of second-class citizenship and the abiding material and psychic trauma of colonial racism. Linking sex to past and present abuses, Antilleans claimed sexual self-determination and the right to pleasure as revolutionary acts. As one commentator in 1971 poignantly offered, "The great struggle for INDEPENDENCE, mental and sexual, will take place in large part in the bedroom."[6]

This article thus considers the centrality of sexual politics to the imaginaries of Antillean leftists and explores the Atlantic currents that informed debates on gender and sexuality. Drawing on over fifteen years of radical periodicals, I argue that leftists viewed sexual revolution not as discrete from class struggle and antiracist activism but indeed as its most foundational component. Illuminating the transmission of these ideas across the Atlantic world, this article reconceives both the substance and geography of the sexual revolution. Until now, this history has largely been told from the vantage of Europe and North America and featured an overwhelmingly white cast of characters.[7] Historian Todd Shepard has aptly termed the reproduction of these narratives "vanilla history," which serves to "erase the importance of people of color; vanilla histories of sex pretend that its multiple valences and diverse forms are best ignored."[8] Returning to the creative invocation of sexual liberation within decolonization struggles not only broadens the scholarly view of the many ways in which sex became politicized in the 1960s, but it also draws vital attention to the formation of what Christopher Lee has termed the *communitas* or imagined "community of feeling" that could bind nonstate actors across the Global South in their efforts to realize and anticipate new worlds.[9] It was the promise of liberated sexuality that inspired Antillean activists to combine and adapt revolutionary Atlantic movements as they fought stridently to build their own. Placing the Caribbean and its diaspora at the center of the sexual revolution thus offers us new ways to approach the history of sexuality and empire, viewing intimacy not only as a tool of colonial coercion but rather as the central terrain of transnational anticolonial insurgency.

Atlantic Circuits and Antillean Students

In 1970, a government-appointed commission published a report on the causes of the May 30 uprising. It impugned students returning from study in the Netherlands who brought with them "new ideas about social and sexual behavior" which they propagated "with the express purpose of persuasion."[10] Indeed, against the backdrop of economic decline and enduring racial discrimination in the Antilles, many Antillean youths in the 1960s made use of government-funded scholarships to pursue higher education in the Netherlands.[11] In Europe, Antillean students encountered peers from other parts of the colonial world following emergent liberation struggles in their home countries. What's more, spatial proximity among Antilleans in the Netherlands enabled Leeward Islanders and Curaçaoans, for example, to interact more frequently than they would have in the Antilles.[12] Their common status as "outsiders" in the Netherlands mobilized greater feelings of unity across racial, gender and cultural divides.[13]

These factors combined to radicalize Antillean students in the 1960s, sparking the creation of several leftist groups. Under the editorship of Antillean university students Harold Hollander, Harold Arends, and Marlene Eustatia, the first issue of *Kambio* appeared in the Netherlands in 1965.[14] In anonymously authored articles covering topics from anticolonial movements to Marxist ideology, *Kambio* criticized lingering colonial forces in the Antilles and debated the prospects of a working-class revolution. As other leftists entered the fray, *Kambio* became known as an excessively ideological paper. Its critics—many of whom were fellow leftists and former collaborators—dismissed as "romantic Marxism" the paper's academic treatment of leftist thought and its seeming estrangement from the revolutionary class of Antillean laborers.[15]

Hoping to address the situation on the ground, a group of recently returned graduates on Curaçao began publishing *Vitó* in 1966. In the run-up to the paper's appearance, a small group of young people orbiting around Stanley Brown, *Vitó's* eventual editor-in-chief, organized protests and demonstrations in Willemstad. Perhaps in part because of the group's visibility, *Vitó* enjoyed a wide distribution, circulating nearly fifteen thousand issues across the Dutch Antilles, the Netherlands, and Cuba.[16] The only independently owned paper on Curaçao, *Vitó* featured extensive coverage of local news, reader-submitted content, and anonymously authored columns including "Black Panther on Curaçao" and "Open Letter to Women." From 1968 until the paper's dissolution in 1971, contributors to *Vitó* published anonymously, making authorship difficult to identify. Yet by most accounts, *Vitó* and *Kambio's* core participants resembled each other: they drew from an emerging group of university-educated light-skinned and black individuals—most but not all of whom were men.[17] Their message also appealed to the Afro-Curaçaoan laborers with whom *Vitó* organized. As Brown recalled, laborers in the oil refining industry were "influenced as much as I was by Fidel Castro and Che Guevara, Black Power and Black Panther."[18]

Taking up the mantle of student radicalism in the Netherlands after the May revolt, a younger generation of students began publishing *Kontakto Antiano* in 1969. This bimonthly journal aimed to forge connections among an increasingly dispersed Antillean population in the Netherlands. In addition to describing academic and activist events organized or attended by Antillean students, *Kontakto Antiano* also featured reader-submitted pieces including poetry, practical tips for navigating Dutch social service bureaucracies, and meditations on metropolitan life. One distinguishing feature of *Kontako Antiano* was its robust group of Antillean women contributors. Yet all three leftist publications took up questions of sexual morality and gender discrimination—a fact that Antillean authorities attributed to the liberal climate of the 1960s Netherlands. But the idea that "the island stood defenseless against Dutch-imported moral decay"[19] minimizes the other radicalizing forces—both homegrown and transnational—that shaped Antillean imaginaries. As we will see, Antilleans looked beyond the continent for inspiration, tracking emerging ideas about sexuality, socialism, and antiracism from Cuba to the United States.

Prostitution and the Promise of Socialism

Like others throughout the colonial world, Antillean leftists longed for political independence and the social and economic modernization that would ensure its achievement. New standards of sexual practices and behaviors, some argued, would be crucial for producing radical change across the Antilles. Cuba's example became particularly appealing to leftists in the 1960s with the decline of once-powerful oil-refining industries on both Aruba and Curaçao. Antillean policy makers insisted that tourism would stymie shocks to insular economies—a move that leftists feared would invite new occupiers. They pointed to the transformation of Havana—once a hedonistic tourist destination, now a stronghold of socialism—as evidence of the promise of socialism to restore equality. The purported moral regeneration of the Cuban Revolution and its putative answer to prostitution offered Antilleans a socialist solution to their sexual woes.

Leftists were alarmed at the prospect of tourism and the potential increase in prostitution not least because of the historic precedent established during World War II, when thousands of US soldiers arrived to safeguard Aruba and Curaçao's oil refineries. Popular press sources at the time lamented the scandalous situation in the port environs, with youngsters routinely scandalized by the presence of copulating couples on beaches and in the back rooms of bars and cafes.[20] In an effort to address these conditions, a committee made up of colonial officials and representatives from the Catholic Church urged the construction on Curaçao of Campo Alegre, a government-sanctioned brothel that opened its doors in 1949. To cater to the assumed preferences of foreign clientele and to protect the chastity of local womanhood, only light-skinned foreign women were permitted to work in the brothel.[21]

In the 1960s, the specter of a renewed influx of "Yankee dollars" sent the Left searching for answers to this particular vestige of Dutch colonialism. After 1966, Antillean leftists seized on Cuban leader Fidel Castro's declaration that the Cuban Revolution had "nearly eliminated" prostitution. Castro's announcement came at the end of a six-year campaign to rehabilitate an estimated thirty- to forty-thousand sex workers. According to Rachel Hynson, the revolutionary regime initially treated sex workers as victims of capitalist exploitation. By 1962, however, Cuban authorities viewed the persistence of prostitution as an affront to the revolution's success and soon deployed sex workers to labor on collective farms. Although sex work persisted underground, Castro's 1966 statement "symbolized the supposed success and culmination of the campaign against sex work."[22]

Antillean leftists applauded this alleged triumph in Cuba. In 1967, an author in *Kambio* proclaimed, "Before Castro, Havana, the cheerful tourist city, counted hundreds of brothels for twelve- and fourteen-year-old daughters of the poor."[23] The article attributed the disappearance of prostitution to the revolution's victory over American imperialism. Without a similar revolution in the Antilles, however, there would be no defense against the corrupting influences of foreign capital. The article opined, "A government faced with serious economic downturn and that clings to tourism as a singular solution . . . must fully realize the consequences and develop guarantees to protect the community from the possible excesses inherent in flourishing tourism."[24] Several months later, another article in *Kambio* warned that the intrusion of American capital in prerevolutionary Cuba had led not only to an increase in prostitution, but also "sharpening discrimination" and "the loss of national identity."[25] Cuba's socialist experiment, it seemed, could help Antilleans to resolve precisely the same sexual, social, and political issues that rankled the Dutch islands.

Within the dual imperatives of socialist revolution and sexual liberation, however, leftists struggled with whether prostitution was the ultimate form of exploitation or a perfectly acceptable element of a sexually liberated society. Writing in 1971, an anonymously authored piece in *Vitó* exclaimed, "What Fidel Castro achieved, and what we also hope to achieve on Curaçao, is to be able to end the exploitation of people. . . . The system of prostitution here on Curaçao . . . is a form of exploitation that does not fit with our socialist system."[26] Elsewhere, however, *Vitó* offered a flexible appraisal of the problem, and one that differed markedly from Castro's own approach. A cover story on Campo Alegre contended, "*Vitó* is not against prostitution in general" because voluntary sexual relationships between adults, single or married, or "whether between people of the same sex," should be protected by the law.[27]

These conflicting statements reflected *Vitó*'s commitment to destabilize the prevailing order by all possible means. Incorporating those deemed marginal to society was one of the primary ways *Vitó* activists hoped to accomplish this.

Such an approach differed markedly from Cuba's in the 1960s, which increasingly viewed those who did not conform to revolutionary standards for appropriate masculinity and femininity as counterrevolutionaries, interning suspected sex workers and same-sex-desiring men in forced labor camps.[28] Though inspired by the egalitarianism of the Cuban Revolution, some Antillean leftists nevertheless saw socialism as a chance not to eradicate but rather to redeem multiple forms of intimacy.

Antilleans' selective celebration of the Cuban Revolution attests to the perceived urgency of the so-called "prostitution question" on Curaçao. The Campo Alegre brothel continued to be a controversial topic even after the brothel opened with full government approval in 1949. Despite *Vitó*'s plea for the acceptance of various forms of sexuality, the majority of leftists viewed Campo Alegre not only as an issue of women's equality, but perhaps most importantly as a particular manifestation of the corrosive effects of American imperialism. Perhaps because employees of Campo Alegre were not Antillean women but foreign nationals who stayed only temporarily on the island, leftist commentators said comparatively less about sex workers themselves and focused rather on the structural issues that gave rise to prostitution. Diagnosing the issue this way, Antillean radicals found in Cuba a model of a Caribbean nation that, through socialism, defeated neoimperialism and redressed its social consequences.

Black Power in the Bedroom

Curiously, while many US Black Power activists went to Cuba in search of socialist conceptions of racial solidarity, activists among the Antillean diaspora did not build similar bridges between socialism and antiracism.[29] For some Antillean leftists, it seemed that class revolution would not guarantee racial justice. The eradication of racism would first and foremost demand a deep and thoroughgoing examination of social attitudes and norms within the ranks of the leftist movement itself, a commitment that Antillean leftists found modeled in the US Black Power movement.[30] Here, too, activists insisted that the rewards of antiracist activism would be experienced in the bedroom. Binding activists' engagement with these radical Atlantic movements was thus a shared concern with the erotic promise of class and racial liberation.

The increased international influence of the US Black Power movement and, in particular, the Black Panther Party, after 1966 shaped the tenor of Antillean activism.[31] It was through the language of Black Power that Antillean women found ways to rebuke male comrades and to radicalize the leftist movement toward consensus on the topic of women's social and sexual equality. Several women commentators railed against the hypocrisy of Antillean men "whose mouths are full with BLACK POWER and who jump at the chance to sleep with a white woman."[32] Others criticized long-standing perceptions about white femininity and beauty. In a pamphlet distributed on Curaçao and reprinted in *Kontakto Antiano* in 1970, activists rallied black women to "think black, be black, feel proud." "Wear a shorter miniskirt," the article continued; "Show your liberated black thighs, let go of your shame. The Black Panthers can prove to you: THE BLACKER THE BERRY, THE SWEETER THE JUICE."[33] Black Power offered Antillean women a vocabulary for addressing not only antiblack racism prevalent in the Netherlands and the Antilles, but also the psychic effects of internalized racism.

Many male leftists were persuaded by these arguments, eventually taking up the charge to reeducate male readership on revolutionary gender roles. Encouraging women's social and sexual emancipation, some reasoned, would deepen intimate ties and romantic affection among couples. In a 1970 article titled "Attractive Masculinity" in *Kontakto Antiano*, the author outlined defining characteristics of attractive manhood, including patience, responsibility, and the free expression of emotions with one's intimate partner.[34] Still others longed for closer intimacy premised on equality. Guillermo Rosario dedicated his poem "Women's Emancipation" to "Antillean women in Holland." It read,

Never believe the one
Who wants to keep you in servitude
Whether as property inside the bedroom
Or in the kitchen as a queen

I want to love you without domination
On a foundation of greater tolerance
For you to be a friend, with an equal role
Contributing and sharing equally.[35]

Although it is difficult to discern whether these ideas touched the intimate corners of people's romantic lives, this vision of revolutionary gender roles is nevertheless remarkable in its departure from contemporary leftist movements. In 1950s–1960s Cuba, the image of the "brashly confident" hypermasculine guerilla warrior inspired not only loyalty to the revolution but also a whole generation of revolutionaries across the globe.[36] The Black Panthers, a group particularly influential to *Vitó*, initially linked "black liberation to the regaining of 'black manhood.'"[37] In the wider Caribbean, too, offshoots of the Black Power movement in Belize, Bermuda, and Trinidad "emphasiz[ed] the recuperation of black manhood and the assertion of black male power."[38] Though women were at every turn involved in these struggles, the dominant conception of revolutionary action remained masculine in orientation. In a striking reversal, in the pages of Antillean radical publications it was women who were enlisted to act with greater militancy and men who were called on to reflect and defer.

Power and Pleasure

It was in discussions about the sexual emancipation of women and same-sex-desiring men that the sexual revolution in the Dutch Atlantic reached perhaps its most creative form. For many commentators believed that until the most marginalized members of society enjoyed a right to sexual pleasure, Antillean society could not be free. Yet, in making the case for the revolutionary potential of pleasure, Antillean leftists did not promote a facile understanding of "free love." Instead, they saw in sex the potential for radical transformation precisely because sex had for so long served as a site of subjugation and cruelty.

Allusions to slavery permeated discussions on women's sexual emancipation. One editorial written by a twenty-six-year-old woman titled "Which one of us is the whore?" attacked male sexual privilege and called on women to reject "living like slaves."[39] One "open letter to women" appearing in *Vitó* offered similar advice: "REMEMBER NOT TO HAVE SEXUAL RELATIONS WITH A MAN WHO TREATS YOU LIKE A SLAVE."[40] An editorial running in *Kontakto Antiano* contended that men as well as women should be instructed on the importance of female pleasure. The author stated, "People must also tell [women] that they have just as much right to sexuality as Antillean men and that sexuality is one of the few pleasures in life, for both rich and poor." She closed her article with a plea for women to embrace sexual pleasure and reject oppression: "Sexuality, Yes! Slavery, No!"[41]

Others connected the legacy of sexual violence to contemporary manifestations of racism. Writing in 1968, one author in *Vitó* criticized the servile attitudes of the "Curaçao white," the light-skinned progeny of white men and women of African descent: "the result of a lot of free and forceful fucking by white men and their black slaves. My grandmother and her mother."[42] Far from being reductive or hyperbolic, statements such as these reflected the very real ways in which intimacy and power were profoundly interlinked during slavery and the colonial past. As many scholars maintain, Europeans constructed racial ideologies by attributing to blackness a host of deviances, with sexual profligacy foremost among them—an ascription that also served to condone the sexual violation of the enslaved.[43] If slavery was maintained at the site of the bedroom, then leftists suggested liberation would be achieved there, too. Women's sexual pleasure was thus endowed with revolutionary potential precisely because of the legacies of sexual subjugation that characterized slavery and its afterlife.

It was not only women, however, who were invited to share in the fruits of a new insurgent intimacy. In April 1969, *Vitó* featured an "Interview with a Homosexual" as its centerfold story. Rebuking the social isolation of men who sought the erotic company of other men, the author concluded, "There are roughly 1,500 people on Curaçao who are homosexuals. Who speaks about their problems, their struggles with integration, the emancipation of the homosexual within our community?

Their only recourse here on Curaçao is *Vitó*. This vanguard movement is for the groups who are abused, whether black people, the laborer, the homosexual, youth, or women."[44]

Leftist groups in the Netherlands also sought solidarity with Antillean men who identified and organized as homosexuals. In 1971, *Kontakto Antiano* covered the formation of an Antillean group formed to "bring emancipation to our people, using homosexuality as our point of action."[45] These activists asked how organizing around homosexuality could "change the antiquated structures, colonial and capitalist, that exist in the Antilles."[46] At least for this group, social acceptance of male same-sex eroticism would help to challenge the attitudes and institutions that collaborated in the oppression of same-sex-desiring individuals and Antillean society broadly.

The popular narrative of the global 1960s often touts the alliances among various New Left groups while assuming the discrete quality of each. The 1970 constitutional convention held by the Black Panther Party and attended by members of the Gay Liberation Front, among others, is one example of a successful effort to build a mass movement across particular interests.[47] But in the Dutch Atlantic, it was not merely that the sexual revolution, decolonization, and the rise of the Black Power movement overlapped and drew together diverse interlocutors; neither did Antilleans conceive of struggles for socialism, sexual emancipation, and antiracism as separate. For Antillean radicals of the Dutch Atlantic, the elimination of colonialism, capitalism, and racism each required coordinated transformations in the intimate lives of Antilleans.

Conclusion

In recovering Antillean arguments for the intertwined pursuit of sexual emancipation, socialist revolution, and antiracism, this article has sought to restore to knowledge one of the most imaginative aspects of Antillean leftist activism. Through developing their gender and sexual politics, Antillean leftists appropriated lessons from the Cuban Revolution and Black Power movement, in the process arriving at ideas about gender norms and sexual freedoms that were markedly different from those that shaped emancipatory struggles in Cuba and the United States. Yet, Antilleans embraced these liberatory movements for their promise to transform interpersonal interactions into revolutionary acts of intimacy. In seeking to create new norms suited for a revolutionary age, Antillean radicals powerfully laid claim to sexuality as a key element of self-determination.

These discussions emphasize that the sexual revolutionaries of the 1960s were not just white Euro-Americans who believed making love and waging war to be incompatible. Antillean views on the repressive and emancipatory potential of sex served to distinguish the sexual revolution in the Dutch Atlantic from contemporaneous debates on sex in continental Europe. Whereas the leftist movements of mainland Europe connected sexual repression, or the absence of sex and pleasure, to fascism and militarism,[48] in the Dutch Atlantic it was not the absence of sex but in fact its abusive prevalence that helped to explain numerous problems, whether regarding women's inequality, economic dependence, or the survival of colonial attitudes and institutions. It was precisely these uneven relations of power that would make sex a potent site for political transformation in the global age of decolonization.

Chelsea Schields is assistant professor of history at the University of California, Irvine. With Dagmar Herzog, she is coeditor of the forthcoming *Routledge Companion to Sexuality and Colonialism*. She is currently completing a book manuscript about the sexual politics of decolonization in the Dutch Antilles.

Notes

1. Aalders, "Kambio in Haagsche Post," *Amigoe*, August 19, 1967. Delpher.nl, resolver.kb.nl /resolve?urn=ddd:010463549:mpeg21:a0145 (accessed August 19, 2019).
2. Historian Gert Oostindie concluded that Cuba did not intervene in the May 30 uprising. Oostindie, "Woedend vuur," 19.
3. Hynson, "'Count, Capture and Reeducate,'" 151.
4. Macpherson, *From Colony to Nation*, 257.
5. On the gender politics of the Cuban Revolution, see Michelle Chase, *Revolution within the Revolution*; and Guerra, "Gender Policing." On gender dynamics in the US Black Panther Party, see Robyn Spencer, *The Revolution Has Come*; and Tracye Matthews, "'No One Ever Asks.'"
6. Amzand, "Muhé Antiyano: usa bo sintí!" *Kontakto Antiano*, December 1971. Internationaal Instituut voor Sociale Geschiedenis, Amsterdam, the Netherlands (hereafter IISG).
7. For notable exceptions, see Andrew Shield, *Immigrants in the Sexual Revolution*; and Shepard, *Sex, France, and Arab Men*.
8. Shepard, *Sex, France, and Arab Men*, 16.
9. Lee, "Between a Moment and an Era," 25–26.
10. "30 Mei 1969: Rapport van de Commissie tot onderzoek van de achtergronden en oorzaken van de onlusten welke of 30 mei 1969 op Curaçao hebben plaatsgehad," 201, KITLV Collection, Leiden University, Netherlands.
11. Oostindie, "Black Power, Popular Revolt," 247.
12. In the 1960s, the Netherlands Antilles consisted of six islands: Aruba, Curaçao, and Bonaire in the southern Caribbean; and the Leeward islands of St. Maarten, Saba, and St. Eustatius.
13. Koot and Ringeling, *De Antillianen*, 139.
14. "Kambio in druk op NA," *Amigoe*, September 30, 1966. Delpher.nl, resolver.kb.nl/resolve ?urn=ddd:010463029:mpeg21:a0088 (accessed August 19, 2019).
15. "'Wij kunnen het de Nederlanders,'" *Amigoe*, October 21, 1965. Delpher.nl, resolver.kb .nl/resolve?urn=ddd:010462448:mpeg21:a0106 (accessed August 19, 2019).
16. Circulation figure cited in Rutgers, "'Trinta di Mei a bini,'" 216. *Vitó* maintained a subscription swap with *Granma* in Cuba; see Brown, "Stanley Brown," 18.
17. I draw this information from several interviews with *Kambio* and *Vitó*-affiliated authors. See footnotes 14, 15, and 30. On Curaçao, light-skinned individuals of mixed European

and African descent might be racialized as white whereas in the Netherlands these individuals were often racialized as people of color. See footnote 30 on the evolving racial politics of the *Kambio* and *Vitó* movements.

18. Brown, "Stanley Brown," 16.
19. Brown, "Stanley Brown," 202.
20. Schields, "'This Is the Soul of Aruba Speaking,'" 201.
21. Sex workers at Campo Alegre hailed largely from the Dominican Republic and Colombia. Kempadoo, *Sexing the Caribbean*, 92.
22. Hynson, "'Count, Capture, and Reeducate,'" 151.
23. "Gangsters Go Home," *Kambio*, September 1967, 3, no. 5. IISG.
24. "Gangsters Go Home."
25. "Toerisme: Panacee of doos van Pandora?" *Kambio*, December 1967, 3, no. 7. IISG.
26. "Prostitutanan den Cayanan di Willemstad," *Vitó*, January 9, 1971. IISG.
27. "Muher di bida den kanyanan di Willemstad," *Vitó*, February 1, 1969. IISG.
28. Guerra, "Gender Policing," 268.
29. Reitan, *The Rise and Decline of an Alliance*.
30. Participants in both *Kambio* and *Vitó* claimed that the politicization of blackness after the May 30 uprising fissured the relationship between predominantly Afro-Curaçaoan laborers and light-skinned intellectuals. See Hollander, "Harold Hollander," 51–52; and Brown, "Stanley Brown," 18.
31. On the early history of the Black Power movement and Black Panther Party, see Bloom and Martin, *Black against Empire*, 36–44.
32. "Di kon homber pretu ta prefera di drumi ku un muhe blanku riba un muhe pretu," *Vitó*, November 23, 1968. IISG.
33. "Segun 'Black Panthers,'" *Kontakto Antiano*, February 1970. IISG.
34. "Homber atraktivo," *Kontakto Antiano*, April 1970. IISG.
35. Guillermo Rosario, "Muhé Emansipa," *Kontakto Antiano*, May 1973. IISG.
36. Chase, *Revolution within the Revolution*, 45–46.
37. Matthews, "No One Ever Asks," 242.
38. Quinn, "Introduction," 17.
39. "Karta abierta na hende muhe," *Vitó*, June 20, 1970. IISG.
40. "Karta abierta na hende muhe," *Vitó*, May 9, 1970. IISG.
41. Amzand, "Muhé Antiano: usa bo sintí!" *Kontakto Antiano*, December 1971. IISG.
42. "Curaçao's Black God," *Vitó*, December 25, 1968. IISG. This edition of *Vitó* appeared in English so that it could be distributed to tourists.
43. For this argument, see Hartman, *Scenes of Subjection*; Morgan, *Laboring Women*; and Garraway, *The Libertine Colony*.
44. "Entrevista ku un HOMO-SEKSUAL," *Vitó*, April 5, 1961. IISG.
45. "Homosekswalidat . . . punta di akshon!" *Kontakto Antiano*, March 1971. IISG.
46. "Homosekswalidat . . . punta di akshon!"
47. Katsiaficas, "Organization and Movement."
48. On this argument, see Herzog, *Sex after Fascism*, ch. 4.

References

Bloom, Joshua, and Waldo E. Martin Jr. *Black against Empire: The History and Politics of the Black Panther Party*. Oakland: University of California Press, 2013.

Brown, Stanley. "Stanley Brown." In *Curaçao, 30 Mei 1969: Verhalen over de revolte*, edited by Gert Oostindie, 12–23. Amsterdam: Amsterdam University Press, 1999.

Chase, Michelle. *Revolution within the Revolution: Women and Gender Politics in Cuba, 1952–1962*. Chapel Hill: University of North Carolina Press, 2015.

Garraway, Doris. *The Libertine Colony: Creolization in the Early French Caribbean*. Durham, NC: Duke University Press, 2005.

Guerra, Lillian. "Gender Policing, Homosexuality, and the New Patriarchy of the Cuban Revolution, 1965–70." *Social History* 35, no. 3 (2010): 268–89.

Hartman, Saidiya. *Scenes of Subjection: Terror, Slavery and Self-Making in Nineteenth-Century America*. New York: Oxford University Press, 2007.

Herzog, Dagmar. *Sex after Fascism: Memory and Morality in Twentieth-Century Germany*. Princeton, NJ: Princeton University Press, 2005.

Hollander, Harold. "Harold Hollander." In *Curaçao, 30 Mei 1969: Verhalen over de revolte*, edited by Gert Oostindie, 48–53. Amsterdam: Amsterdam University Press, 1999.

Hynson, Rachel. "'Count, Capture, and Reeducate': The Campaign to Rehabilitate Cuba's Female Sex Workers, 1959–1966." *Journal of the History of Sexuality* 24, no. 1 (2015): 125–53.

Katsiaficas, George. "Organization and Movement: The Case of the Black Panther Party and the Revolutionary People's Constitutional Convention of 1970." In *Liberation, Imagination and the Black Panther Party: A New Look at the Panthers and Their Legacy*, edited by Kathleen Cleaver and George Katsiaficas, 141–55. New York: Routledge, 2001.

Kempadoo, Kamala. *Sexing the Caribbean: Gender, Race, and Sexual Labor*. New York: Routledge, 2004.

Koot, Willen, and Anco Ringeling. *De Antillianen*. Muiderberg, NL: Dick Coutinho, 1984.

Lee, Christopher. "Between a Moment and an Era: The Origins and Afterlives of Bandung." In *Making a World after Empire: The Bandung Moment and Its Political Afterlives*, edited by Christopher Lee, 1–42. Athens: Ohio University Press, 2010.

Macpherson, Anne. *From Colony to Nation: Women Activists and the Gendering of Politics in Belize, 1912–1982*. Lincoln: University of Nebraska Press, 2007.

Matthews, Tracye. "'No One Ever Asks What a Man's Role in the Revolution Is': Gender and the Politics of the Black Panther Party." In *The Black Panther Party Reconsidered*, edited by Charles Jones, 267–304. Baltimore: Black Classic Press, 1998.

Morgan, Jennifer. *Laboring Women: Reproduction and Gender in New World Slavery*. Philadelphia: University of Pennsylvania Press, 2004.

Oostindie, Gert. "Black Power, Popular Revolt, and Decolonization in the Dutch Caribbean." In *Black Power in the Caribbean*, edited by Kate Quinn, 239–60. Gainesville: University of Florida Press, 2014.

Oostindie, Gert. "Woedend vuur: 'Trinta di mei' dertig jaar later." In *Dromen en Littekens: Dertig jaar na de Curaçaose revolte, 30 mei 1969*, edited by Gert Oostindie, 9–39. Amsterdam: Amsterdam University Press, 1999.

Quinn, Kate, ed. "Introduction: New Perspectives on Black Power in the Caribbean." In *Black Power in the Caribbean*, 1–24. Gainesville: University of Florida Press, 2014.

Reitan, Ruth. *The Rise and Decline of an Alliance: Cuba and African American Leaders in the 1960s*. East Lansing: Michigan State University Press, 1999.

Rutgers, Wim. "'Trinta di Mei a bini, Trinta di Mei a bai': De dertigste mei in de letterkunde." In *Dromen en Littekens: Dertig jaar na de Curaçaose revolte, 30 mei 1969*, edited by Gert Oostindie, 211–33. Amsterdam: Amsterdam University Press, 1999.

Schields, Chelsea. "'This Is the Soul of Aruba Speaking': The 1951 Campo Alegre Protest and Insular Identity on Aruba." *New West Indian Guide*, no. 90 (2016): 195–224.

Shepard, Todd. *Sex, France, and Arab Men, 1962–1979*. Chicago: University of Chicago Press, 2018.

Shield, Andrew D. J. *Immigrants in the Sexual Revolution: Perceptions and Participation in Northwest Europe*. London: Palgrave Macmillan, 2017.

Spencer, Robyn. *The Revolution Has Come: Black Power, Gender, and the Black Panther Party in Oakland*. Durham, NC: Duke University Press, 2016.

"Chilean! Is This How You Want to See Your Daughter?"

The Cuban Revolution and Representations of Gender and Family during Chile's 1964 Anticommunist "Campaign of Terror"

Marcelo Casals

The Chilean presidential elections of 1964 had special resonance for many who participated in them. Unlike in previous elections, the competing candidates represented comprehensive and radically incompatible political projects. All the candidates signaled a general crisis in Chile that could be remedied only by deep, ambitious reforms to the relationship between the state and society. Those options, further, mobilized the will of millions of citizens, thanks in large part to the electoral reforms of the late 1950s that had significantly broadened voting rights.

Nevertheless, the political practices and languages used in that election were not exclusively concerned with Chile. In fact, for many of the actors involved, the juncture of 1964 had a greater regional, and even global, importance. This was for a very clear reason: the elections pitted a Marxist candidate, Salvador Allende, supported by a coalition of leftist parties with strong roots in the working class, against a Social Christian candidate, Eduardo Frei, leader of the Christian Democratic Party, a reformist party that was growing rapidly. Both candidates represented the election as a critical crossroads for the future of the nation. For the Left, it was about

Radical History Review
Issue 136 (January 2020)   DOI 10.1215/01636545-7857295
© 2020 by MARHO: The Radical Historians' Organization, Inc.

overcoming the state of structural backwardness produced by Chile's peripheral capitalism through a combination of radical reforms that aimed to produce a peaceful transition to socialism. The Christian Democratic Party, for its part, proposed a "revolution in liberty" that aimed to create modernizing structural reforms explicitly meant to inhibit the outbreak of a socialist revolution.

Considering the ideological weight of the projects under debate, the political language used throughout the electoral campaign was colored by references to political events around the continent and the world. For many, Chile was simply the local expression of a global conflict. While for some, what was at stake was the possibility of constructing a democratic socialism that would emancipate the majority of people from a demeaning and dehumanizing capitalism, others feared a threat to the very existence of the nation if Chile were transformed into a socialist state. Thus anticommunism became a central issue in the electoral campaign. Fostered by conservative and reformist political actors, and resistant to critique by the Marxist Left, Chile's long tradition of anticommunism united diverse political forces around a common message: Allende was a threat to the existence of Chilean society and its socially accepted values. The nation, religion, property, and rule of law, among other things, would be abolished by the Chilean Left. Even worse, the family and conservative, naturalized gender roles would suffer intolerable modifications.

The evidence for all this was the close identification of the Chilean Left with global revolutionary actors. Socialism, in this view, operated as an intolerable dystopia; that is, as an imaginary container of fears concerning the eventual dissolution of fundamental social relationships. These fears resulted in intense coverage of revolutionary regimes by the conservative media and political actors. While in the first decades of the twentieth century, anticommunist forces had made the Soviet Union their dystopian focal point, starting in the early 1960s, they focused on Cuba as well. The urgency of stopping Allende's rise to power in 1964 was determined by the fears that the Cuban revolutionary model evoked, especially when Castro turned decidedly more socialist under the sponsorship of the Soviet Union. Socialism in power was no longer a distant reality on other continents; it now existed in Latin America, and it spoke Spanish.

This article analyzes the impact of the Cuban Revolution on Chilean anticommunist discourse during the 1964 presidential campaign. Cuba functioned as a dystopian reference point with which to accuse the Left of wanting to convert Chile into a Marxist tyranny. To this end, Cuba was used as the foundation for laying out a "moral anticommunism" that centered ideas of family and gender in its discourse. From this point of view, Allende would replicate Castro's measures aimed at weakening and ultimately annihilating family relationships and the conventional roles of men and women in society. Sons and daughters would be indoctrinated, given military training, and taken from their family homes. Women would be forced to do hard labor, supposedly incompatible with their fragile nature, while men would have to accept the ideological principles of the new regime to keep their jobs and their ability to feed their families. These ideas were systematically disseminated by anticommunist propaganda—which the Left called the "campaign of terror"—from June through September of 1964. In this campaign, local, conservative Chilean actors worked with international counterrevolutionary networks, which included the CIA and Brazilian civic organizations. All of them formulated and spread a particularly potent ideological discourse, linking concerns about gender, anticommunism, and denunciations of the Cuban revolutionary experience.

Anticommunism, Gender, and Cuba

The extraordinary potency of the propagandistic campaign against the Left was possible thanks to a combination of three factors. First, the so-called "campaign of terror" relied on topics that had a long history in Chile, and at the time were part of the political identity of the conservative and reformist sectors. Second, this was fortified by the critical reception of the Cuban Revolution in Chile, which anticommunists understood as an eminently immoral regime. And third, this "moral anticommunism" was able to take advantage of family metaphors to give meaning to political relationships. The revolution was thus seen as a threat to the nation as well as to the domestic lives of Chileans. In the articulation of these ideas into a political message, the imagined role of Cuba in Chile was central.

Anticommunism was nothing new in Chile. Its first expressions can be traced back to the conservative Chilean press at the end of the nineteenth century, especially in reaction to the organization of politicized groups of artisans and other low-income and working-class subjects, and the early local reception of socialist doctrines from Europe. The oligarchic state and its press condemned these ideas and were open to promoting and legitimizing violent actions of state repression against radicalized strikers, such as in the case of Iquique in 1907.[1] The crisis of the oligarchic state around 1920 and the foundation of the Chilean Communist Party (PCCh) in 1922, in the wake of the global impact of the Russian Revolution, exacerbated the anxieties of the dominant class. Further, the local consequences of the global economic crisis of 1929 made revolution and socialism real possibilities. The triumph of the Popular Front—an alliance of communists, socialists, and the Radical Party—in 1938 brought anticommunist anxieties to a climax, thanks especially to widespread identification in Chile with the Spanish Civil War. Communism, from the perspective of those who opposed the Chilean Popular Front, was a real destabilizing and destructive force that, supported by "Moscow gold," could lead the nation into a fratricidal war.

The bipolarity of the Cold War caused Chilean conservative sectors to reformulate their anticommunism in pro-US terms. This was expressed in 1948 in the Law of the Permanent Defense of Democracy, which made the Communist Party illegal and removed its militants from the electoral registries for a decade. By 1958, the political scenario had changed radically. The Left had managed to recover from its internal conflicts and had reunited as the Frente de Acción Popular (Front for Popular Action, FRAP) around a socialist-communist alliance. In the presidential elections of that year, their candidate, Salvador Allende, managed to come in second place, just a few thousand votes short of the winner, the conservative Jorge Alessandri.

It was in this context that the Chilean political system received the news about Cuba. The conservative press condemned the new regime for its radical approach to redistributive measures and its growing Soviet influences.[2] For its part, the Chilean Left—despite certain strategic differences with respect to the example of the Cuban *guerrillero*—acknowledged and identified with the new Cuban regime from the beginning, first as a national liberation movement, and later for its shift to socialism. In this sense, for a significant number of Chilean political actors, the Cuban model changed the local parameters for understanding revolution and counterrevolution, just as had happened with the Russian Revolution and the Spanish Civil War. Cuba became an object of internal disagreement that redefined the terms of political conflict.

Beyond the concerns about property and democracy, the conservative reception of the revolution emphasized the destructuring of socially accepted behaviors, especially those of women and young people, understood as the most vulnerable. This "moral anticommunism" saw socialism as antithetical to the structure of the family by virtue of the rapid expansion of the state that would end up dominating even the most intimate relationships within the home. This view was due in large part to the way the Cuban opposition to Castro represented the new regime. As Michelle Chase has noted, measures like the literacy campaign (which sent urban, middle-class adolescents to the countryside far from their families) fed anxieties about the deviant behavior that young people might exhibit far from parental protection, including fears about their sexual autonomy. Rumors even began to circulate that the regime aimed to eliminate *patria potestad* (parental authority and custodial rights of parents over their children) to definitively destroy the family and place children in the service of the state and communism. This growing belief motivated many parents to send their children to the United States in Operation Peter Pan, organized by the CIA from 1960 to 1962. In Chile, the interpretation of Cuban events was strongly influenced by what Chase called "transnational anti-communist narratives," which played an important role in the 1964 elections.[3]

The relationship between gender and anticommunism was not new or unique to the Chilean context. Historian Mary Brennan points out in the case of the United States that many civic anticommunist organizations of the 1950s put women and the family at the center of their discourse and political strategy. In this way, those who led these initiatives were able to present themselves as virtuous women who entered the public arena only to defend the domestic sphere, understood as the "natural" zone of female participation.[4] Something similar can be observed for the Chilean case in the 1960s and early 1970s, according to the research of Margaret Power.[5] In the 1964 elections as well as in Allende's socialist government from 1970 to 1973, women activists—with support from their male peers and the CIA—carried out anticommunist campaigns centered particularly on women. This shift was not a coincidence. Chilean women had voted for the first time in the 1952 presidential elections. In 1958, though still a minority in relation to men, the women's vote clearly favored the conservative candidate. After the electoral reforms of that year, the number of registrations grew rapidly, expanding the female electorate. In 1964, 47.6 percent of votes were cast by women. As Power demonstrated, the political Right as well as the CIA understood these implications and decided to direct an important part of their propagandistic work toward that sector to prevent Chile from becoming a "second Cuba."[6]

Nevertheless, the possibility of articulating a political message around gender had much deeper roots. As Gwynn Thomas has argued, Chilean political discourse had long used the family as a metaphor for giving meaning to the relationship between the state and civil society, in reference to both the family's implicit hierarchies and the collection of rights conferred upon "children" of the nation. At the same time, the metaphor of the family was directly related to conventional gender relations. In its conservative version, the members of a family had preestablished roles: while men must provide and children obey, women had to administer the domestic realm.[7]

The "language of family" was also used by the Left as a strategy for making proposals for social reform and the expansion of rights guaranteed by the state intelligible. As Joan Scott famously argued, gender—and, therefore, the idea of family—operates in the public sphere as a mechanism for signifying relations of power, including the possibility of subverting those relations.[8] In the Chile of the 1960s and the early 1970s, this was particularly true, given the increasingly polarized competition between opposing political projects.

The "Campaign of Terror"

To a large extent, the presidential campaign of 1964 began in the immediate aftermath of the 1958 election. While the political Right had managed to recover executive power through Jorge Alessandri, the centrist and leftist forces during the 1950s had proved themselves to be viably competitive. In 1957, the Falange Nacional merged with other social Christian groups to create the Christian Democratic Party (DC), with Eduardo Frei as its leader, joining the leftist coalition FRAP in the opposition. Both groups began to articulate projects of social reform that rested on different, and sometimes contradictory, premises. The FRAP had until then followed a line of integration in institutional democracy to gain enough strength to forge a path to socialism through the state. For its part, the Christian Democratic party followed the principles of the Social Doctrine of the Church that aimed for a path between capitalism and socialism through social reform. The reformist turn within the Catholic Church during the Second Vatican Council and US policy toward Latin America in this period both helped legitimize Christian Democracy, while also weakening the political weight of conservative Catholicism.[9]

Even so, at the beginning of 1964, the Right had the best chance of winning the election. Alessandri had been obligated to incorporate the Radical Party into his government in order to retain control of the Congress. Together, liberals and conservatives combined forces in the Democratic Front, managing to capture slightly less than half of the vote in the municipal elections of April of 1963. All of that would quickly change thanks to the surprising results of a complementary election in the province of Curicó in March of 1964, won by a leftist candidate. Conservatives and liberals were terrified by the possibility of an electoral victory by Allende in the presidential election of September, and decided to give up the Democratic Front in order to give their unconditional support to Frei.[10] The unexpected alliance between the Right and the DC determined the terms in which the electoral campaign would be understood: more than the election of a president, this was now about "saving" Chile from Marxism.

From June to September of 1964, anticommunist propaganda grew notably in both scale and impact. Through radio announcements, inserts in newspapers, posters, and public discourse, a heterogeneous message with a single goal emerged: to demonize Allende and the FRAP as representatives of totalitarianism who were incompatible with the nation, society, and the family. Many of these messages rested explicitly on a Manichaean view of the Cuban revolutionary experience, with the clear objective of warning against the apocalyptic consequences that a triumph of the Left would have in Chile. In this way a double objective was achieved: on the one hand, the Left was represented as an uncritical follower of foreign models, with little or no relation to national idiosyncrasies, and, on the other, it was represented as an eminently immoral force, given that it was ready to sacrifice national and familial unity in the name of its political project. The spread of rumors through the press was one of the preferred strategies for making these ideas clear.

First, it was necessary to establish a direct, mechanical relationship between Allende and Cuba. To do so, the conservative press presented all kinds of evidence, including a false interview with Allende by the Italian newspaper *Paese Sera*, in which he declared bluntly, "We will institute socialism like the Cubans."[11] Second, it was necessary to attribute a perverse character to Cuban socialism. Julio Durán, the candidate for the Radical Party (who maintained his candidacy in order to prevent the flight of votes from his party to Allende), began to repeat rumors that circulated in Cuba about the abolition of patria potestad, appealing to women who hoped to see their sons "converted into good men, free of the fear that one day the state would snatch them away and send them to Russia to convert them, under the pretext of education, into spies or agitators."[12] The conservative newspaper *El Mercurio* insisted on this point, reproducing the fabricated Cuban decree that supposedly sanctioned the end of patria potestad. It stipulated that all children over the age of three would come under the control of the Children's Circles (Organización de Círculos Infantiles), where they would be assigned to defense "of the highest interests of the nation."[13] In an allusive editorial, *El Mercurio* pointed out, "In ways of conceptualizing the home and relations between parents and children, one can see if we are talking about a democratic society or one of collective tyranny, if they are creating free citizens or trying to train slaves."[14] In spreading this rumor, the conservative press was not alone. Patricio Aylwin, a prominent representative of Christian Democracy, gave credibility to these accusations, asking rhetorically, "Can one conceive of a greater contempt for the very sentiments of human beings? For the natural love of mothers for their children? For the unit of the family?"[15]

The wide diffusion of these ideas was not an initiative that was exclusive to anticommunist Chileans. The CIA played a lead role in financing and creating anticommunist propaganda. As historians like Power and Kristian Gustafson have detailed, the possibility of a leftist victory in Chile led to concern in Washington over what the example of a democratically elected Marxist in Latin America and the West could mean. High-level officials organized special commissions to monitor the Chilean elections and supervise strategies of political intervention. Among other actions, the CIA produced dozens of radio spots with a markedly anticommunist tenor, as well as an undetermined number of comics, posters, pamphlets, flyers, and banners.[16] Further, many of the officials involved in US meddling in Chile acted upon ideological assumptions consistent with the propaganda they distributed. Joseph Jova, an agent of Cuban origin and a determined anticommunist, for example, warned Washington in April of 1964 that Allende "could be led by events into being harsh and ruthless with his opponents but [he will] likely use exile rather than prison or the *paredón* [firing squad wall]."[17] Beyond the differences of "temperament" between Chileans and Cubans, the danger of a regression into authoritarianism was seen as imminent.

An important part of the propaganda financed by the United States took Chilean women as both protagonist and principal audience. On the one hand, US analysts themselves were aware of the symbolic and electoral importance women had. On the other, US directives fell on fertile ground thanks to the existence of a preexisting political-cultural climate that placed special emphasis on the defense of gender roles and the family faced with the possibility of a Cuban style socialist regime. In fact, according to Jorge Rojas, it was precisely during the presidential election of 1964 that childhood became a central topic of political debate, as a symbol of the hopes of future social justice as well as of the fears of possible social changes.[18] This focus was reflected in novels that circulated widely at the time, such as *Quintral*, by the then unknown conservative writer, Isabel Letelier, in which she imagined an apocalyptic near future with the Marxist Left in power. In this representation, Chilean left-wing militants, dressed like Cuban revolutionaries, abused their new authority, attacking the stability of the family, the happiness of children, and even the sexual integrity of defenseless women.[19]

This anticommunist imagery was reproduced by political parties. The Conservative Party, in particular, reiterated these themes. In early July, they signaled to their constituents that they endorsed Frei "because no woman wants her husband to be turned into a number . . . because no father or mother wants the communists to make their children into militants, to deprive them of good judgment and destroy their concepts of morality and the home."[20] The entire social world seemed to be in mortal danger. *El Mercurio* reminded its readers that in Russia women had to undertake extremely hard labor, unsuitable for those of a fragile and delicate nature. Consequently, they would not have time to care for their children, who would learn to be loyal to the regime over their own parents. As an example, they repeated the story of Pavlik Morozov, a Soviet child who was decorated for denouncing his parents for stealing food to feed their family.[21] It is probable, according to available evidence, that several of these articles were financed or written by the CIA.[22]

The most sophisticated form of circulation of "transnational anticommunist narratives" about Cuba in Chile was the dozens of posters designed especially for the Chilean elections. In addition to invading the streets of Chilean cities, many of these posters were reproduced in daily newspapers. One of the many groups dedicated to the creation and dispersing of these kinds of images was Acción Chilena (Chilean Action), which was composed of liberal businessmen who were close to Alessandri.[23] The central idea of its propaganda was to demonstrate the radical incompatibility of Marxist leftism with the nation. One example to this end was to invoke nineteenth-century epic national figures (Bernardo O'Higgins, Arturo Prat, and José Manuel Balmaceda) to emphasize that the "Marxist threat" would put Chile's independence in danger. Similarly, Allende and the FRAP were construed as actors of direct foreign inspiration, without loyalty to the national community, whose political project would be reduced to the fight for power and domination in representation of foreign powers. To illustrate this, a dystopian image of the Cuban experience, framed in the "language of family," was used to appeal to the moral conscience of voters, irrespective of the programmatic questions of one or another candidate. In fact, of the nineteen posters created by Acción Chilena, twelve made explicit reference to Cuba, a nation in which the moral constitution of family roles would have been irretrievably deformed.

In one of the posters, the viewer was asked a dramatic question: "Chilean, is that how you want to see your children?" Under the text appeared an image of armed, militant Cuban children, with a caption that was a direct reference to the rumor of the abolition of patria potestad: "This is an authentic photograph of Cuban children, separated from their parents to receive obligatory military instruction." The supposed moral distortions of Cuban socialism were evident. Obligatory military service was an institution well known to Chileans since 1900, but it was for young men who entered into adulthood; that is, autonomous and in the physical condition to take on the work of national defense. The inclusion of children evoked the forced separation from their parents and, therefore, the dissolution of the family and intimate, emotional ties. The message was urgent: if Allende wins the elections of 1964, Chilean children will suffer the same fate.

This message was made even more dramatic in another, similar poster. The question posed was slightly different: "Chilean, is this how you want to see your daughter?" (fig. 1).[24] In the corresponding image, young Cuban women march heavily armed in military attire that repudiated feminine ideals. The caption reads, "This is an authentic photograph of Cuban women drafted into the military for militant action." The moral distortion implied here was twofold. On the one hand, the Cuban regime was being accused of exercising its power arbitrarily, obligating its citizens to exercise functions inappropriate for children and women. On the other hand, this particular situation was even more serious, considering that in the reigning imaginary of gender at the time, women were not called to carry arms or to serve in national defense. Daughters had to respect the hierarchical distribution that kept them inside the home, a place in which vigilance and disciplining of their behavior would ensure the future reproduction of domestic relations.

In addition, the fears around the destabilization of the family by socialism would take on other tones. Just as the opposition to Castro alleged in Cuba, the physical separation of daughters would put their sexual integrity at risk. From this point of view, the autonomy of young women in spaces far from parental control would put family stability in danger by facilitating spontaneous sexual contacts, with the consequent danger of pregnancy outside the institution of marriage. The direct call to Chilean men ("*Chilenos*" in Spanish implies "men") can be read in two ways. From one perspective, it indicated that it was the fathers (men) who should safeguard the sexual integrity of their daughters (women), understood as essential for the maintenance of stable family hierarchies. Acción Chilena was warning fathers about the possibility that communism would completely ruin the realm in which they had been called to exercise dominion. Seen from another perspective, it included a direct reference to the nationality of the observer, which implied that the danger had a foreign origin. The very continuity of the family and the nation, thus, depended upon the electoral defeat of "Marxism," as implied in text at the bottom of the poster: "After September 4th, Chile will continue to be Chilean." To heighten the drama, the lower-right-hand corner included a number referring to the remaining days until the election. This demanded immediate action against imminent danger.

The Left tried to counter the central issues of the "campaign of terror," emphasizing the national character of its proposals. Allende insistently presented

Figure 1. Poster published by the group "Acción Chilena" and reproduced in several conservative newspapers, such as *El Mercurio*, *El Diario Ilustrado*, and *La Nación*, between July and September, 1964.

himself as the continuation of the work of progressive presidents like José Manuel Balmaceda and Pedro Aguirre Cerda. FRAP campaign rallies were full of Chilean flags and representations of patriotic folklore, in an attempt to dispute the claims being made by the political opposition.[25] While the appeals to the national community were not new on the Left, in 1964 these arguments aimed to discredit anticommunist discourse by destabilizing the idea of a linear link between the global revolutionary experience and the political project of the FRAP. In fact, the FRAP made few allusions to Cuba and the Soviet Union, prioritizing references to local problems and redistributive and egalitarian solutions. Instead of the logic of communism/anticommunism, FRAP sought to frame the election in a Left/Right dichotomy, especially in lieu of the support of conservatives and liberals for Frei.

In the Left's reaction, the defense of family morality was prominent. The leftist press made many references to the measures that Allende's "popular government" would take to safeguard "the rights of women and children, and their well-being and happiness."[26] During the campaign, teas were organized with women from the popular sectors to bring the FRAP program to the domestic sphere, and special organisms, such as the Independent Committee of Women for Allende, were created for this purpose.[27] At the same time, massive gatherings of women on the Left were organized, particularly dedicated to responding to the anticommunist campaign.[28] In this way, FRAP also relied on the "language of family" to legitimize its position, especially in the face of the accusations made in anticommunist propaganda. While FRAP emphasized the material conditions of existence under capitalism, the fundamental assumptions around family and gender roles breached no argument: under socialism, women would be capable of carrying out their domestic roles properly, reinforcing family structures.[29]

Cuba, Brazil, and Chile: Gender and Transnational Anticommunism

Just as Cuba became a revolutionary reference for Latin America in 1959, in 1964 a counterrevolutionary reference emerged based on the overthrow of Brazilian president João Goulart on March 31 through April 1, 1964, and the establishment of a military dictatorship in Brazil, after months of intense antigovernmental political and social mobilization. Similar to what happened in Chile during the presidential campaign, anticommunism became a powerful ideological current in Brazil, with the dystopian reference of Cuba and the defense of the family and traditional gender relationships at the center of the forces for destabilizing the government of Goulart.[30] The Cuban dystopia, "moral anticommunism," and the counterrevolutionary model of mobilization in Brazil fostered networks of contact and collaboration among Chilean and Brazilian political actors, strengthening the continental circulation of "transnational anticommunist narratives." The intervention of Juanita Castro, the dissident sister of Fidel, in Chile was the most notable episode of this transnational phenomenon.

In Chile, the overthrow of Goulart was interpreted as a "lesson" with contradictory meanings. For the Left, the lesson was for those nations that "fought for liberation and independence," showing that the "oligarchy" and "imperialism" would resort to any means to defend their positions, including "slander, lies and military coups."[31] The "lesson" for the Right was the real and threatening presence of communism on a continental scale. The Brazilian military dictatorship, in this line of thinking, was the legitimate product of a massive national reaction against the threat of Marxism embodied in the figure of Goulart.[32] Both perspectives interpreted the 1964 coup d'état through universal categories ("imperialism," "democracy," and "communism"), beyond the specificities of Brazil's political conflict, making it easily transferable to the Chilean situation. Brazil, in this way, was added to Cuba as a factor of internal dispute in the tight Chilean presidential campaign of 1964.

In this context, contacts between Chilean and Brazilian anticommunist actors proliferated. The most fruitful were the links created between conservative women of both nations. Thanks to Power's research, we have a solid idea of how these ties developed.[33] The social movement that destabilized the government of Goulart and made a military intervention viable was led by organizations of conservative Brazilian women who appealed to an especially potent mix of defense of religion, family, the nation, and property. Building on this experience, the main leaders created connections for collaboration and sharing knowledge with politicians and the US government, as well as with related groups in Latin America.

In Chile, one group of conservative women saw in their Brazilian peers a source of strategic inspiration to advance a policy of social, anticommunist mobilization. To do so, they created the group Acción Mujeres por Chile (loosely, "Women's Action for Chile").[34] A few months after the coup in Brazil, in July of 1964, Bebe Nogueira, one of the most noteworthy Brazilian women leaders, called on the Chilean Sophie Eastman in a private letter to "struggle for democracy in the coming elections."[35] Chilean women responded with organization, propaganda, and bold actions to convince their fellow countrywomen of the perverse character of Allende and FRAP, such as the event they organized that included Juanita Castro, Fidel's sister.

At the end of June of 1964, Juanita Castro left Cuba bound for Mexico, denouncing her brothers Fidel and Raúl for having installed a despotic and immoral regime. For her, Cuba had become an "immense prison surrounded by water" where millions of compatriots suffered the arbitrary decisions of a regime dominated by Marxism and the Soviet Union.[36] The news of Juanita Castro's defection had a big impact in Chile, becoming a topic of debate among legislators and the press. Isauro Torres, a Radical Party senator, reiterating the central ideas of anticommunist propaganda, pointed out that the news did not surprise him in the least, given the tendency of communism to disintegrate the family.[37] A few weeks later, Juanita Castro arrived in Brazil through an invitation from her friend Virginia

Leitão da Cunha, the wife of then minister of foreign relations for the dictatorship. Those Chileans most committed to anticommunist propaganda saw this as an opportunity that they could not miss. The newspaper *El Diario Ilustrado* proposed inviting the Cuban dissident to Chile to offer her direct testimony about what would happen to the nation if Allende were to win.[38] A few days later, the same newspaper noted that a group of "democratic ladies" were organizing a "committee" to raise the resources necessary for Juanita Castro's trip to Santiago.[39]

That group of "democratic ladies" was probably linked to Acción Mujeres por Chile, since they were the ones that were ultimately able to capitalize on the figure of Juanita Castro in the Chilean electoral campaign. While they were unable to bring her to Chile, they did manage to record a powerful speech she made in Brazil and broadcast it on various radio stations on the night of September 2, even though electoral law forbade political propaganda at that point of the campaign. Elena Larraín, interviewed by Power decades later, admitted having directed this initiative. First, she financed the trip of an unidentified Chilean man with contacts in the Brazilian dictatorship to record Juanita Castro's speech. Once she had the recording, and using her influence among Chilean businessmen, she managed to convince the directors of three radio stations—*Sociedad Nacional de Minería*, *La Voz de Chile*, and *Corporación*—to play the recording three times that night.[40]

In the recording, Juanita Castro appealed to her "painful experience of those long years in the red hell of Cuba" to "awaken" the Chilean people to the possibility of an electoral triumph of the Marxist Left. Upon that election, she added, depended "a future of liberty or a future of slavery and disgrace for their children." For this reason, she called on them not to be fooled by the promises of communism, since once communists reached power they would quickly forget those promises. In the most dramatic moment of the speech, Juanita Castro once more resorted to the rumors about the repeal of patria potestad in order to present the Cuban regime as antithetical to the family. Her warning to Chileans could not have been clearer:

> Chilean mothers, I am sure that you will not let your young children be seized
> and sent to the communist bloc, as has happened in Cuba, and where, with all
> of the evil intentions that characterize the REDS as their only goal is to serve
> the interests of the Communist Party, they will begin to indoctrinate them,
> tearing from them the healthy Christian orientation that you forged in them
> with so much love.[41]

Juanita Castro's speech, played on Chilean radio stations in the final hours before the presidential elections of 1964, was the final and most powerful case of the articulation between Cuban as a dystopian reference, the local anticommunist tradition, and the language of gender and family. In this process, diverse actors came together thanks to the fluid circulation of a single "transnational anti-communist narrative."

Conclusion

On September 4, 1964, the Christian Democrat Eduardo Frei won the absolute majority of the popular vote: 56.08 percent, far more than the 38.92 percent received by Salvador Allende, the FRAP candidate. Though it is not possible to quantify the impact of the "campaign of terror" on these results, it is certain that anticommunism as an ideological stance was the main framework that gave meaning to the political conflict of that year. Unlike in previous eras, that anticommunist discourse now had a concrete, culturally close reference point: the revolutionary regime that five years early had taken power in Cuba, and that had mustered solidarity from the Chilean Left. The diverse coalition of political actors that opposed socialism and the Chilean Left saw in Cuba a dystopian mirror of what would happen in Chile if Salvador Allende and the FRAP were to take power.

The most powerful arguments had to do with the eventual destabilization of gender relations, especially within the nuclear family. In this context, the campaign insisted that a Cuban style socialism in Chile would destroy family relations and obligate women and children to undertake forms of labor unnatural for them. Children would enter the militia and be indoctrinated with official ideology far from their families, while adolescent daughters would be far from paternal monitoring, at an age interpreted as critical for their sexual development. Socialism, a modern dystopia now present in Latin American territory, would destroy the family and its accepted gender and generational hierarchies. The threat to these intimate relations also meant an attack against the very stability of the nation, as is demonstrated by the posters analyzed in this text. This message was mobilized by a coalition of conservative political actors in alliance with transnational counterrevolutionary forces, such as the CIA and civic organizations of Brazilian women. These groups provided inspiration and resources for the "campaign of terror," as is demonstrated by the broadcast of Juanita Castro's speech, which helped reinforce the centrality of Cuba in Chilean anticommunist discourse. Despite the efforts of the Marxist Left to counter the effects of the propaganda, this message constituted an urgent, dramatic, and powerful warning that aimed to transcend traditional political dividing lines.

The anticommunist campaign would not end in 1964. Conservative sectors continued to warn against the immorality of communism throughout the rest of the 1960s. When Salvador Allende finally took power in 1970, that effort redoubled. All of the threats warned of in prior years now seemed to become a reality. In fact, Allende's Popular Unity government (1970–73) was experienced by many of those who opposed his government from this framework of references, established in the 1960s. The materialization of some of the dystopian images of Marxism in power— such as the shortages of basic goods or the nationalization of medium-sized businesses—helped to confirm the rest of them. The ideological interpretations of the press and the opposition to Allende paved the way for the military coup d'état of September 11, 1973. The dictatorship of Augusto Pinochet (1973–90) elevated anticommunism to the level of state ideology, using it to justify the massive human rights violations perpetrated by the regime. During those years of military authoritarianism, calls to defend the family, under threat from a perverse global enemy, would be repeated daily.

Marcelo Casals holds a PhD in Latin American and Caribbean history from the University of Wisconsin-Madison. He is assistant professor at the Centro de Estudios de Historia Política, Universidad Adolfo Ibáñez (Chile). His most recent book, published in 2016, is *La creación de la amenaza roja. Del surgimiento del anticomunismo en Chile a la "campaña del terror" de 1964.*

Notes

1. The bibliography on these subjects is abundant. To cite just the most relevant works, see Grez Toso, *La "cuestión social" en Chile*; and Grez Toso, *Historia del comunismo en Chile: La era de Recabarren, 1912–1924*. On the Patriotic Leagues (*Ligas Patrioticas*), see González Miranda, *El dios cautivo*; and Deutsch, *Las Derechas*.
2. Castro, *La influencia de la Revolución Cubana*, 11–15.
3. Chase, *Revolution within the Revolution*, chapter 6.
4. Brennan, *Wives, Mothers, and the Red Menace*, 5–10.
5. Power, *Right-Wing Women in Chile*; and Power, "The Engendering of Anticommunism."
6. Power, "The Engendering of Anticommunism," 933–37.
7. Thomas, *Contesting Legitimacy in Chile*, chapter 2.
8. Scott, "Gender."
9. Correa, *Con las riendas del poder*, chapter 6.
10. Etchepare and Valdés, "El naranjazo y sus repercusiones."
11. *El Mercurio*, "Nosotros haremos el socialismo"; *Ercilla*, "Polémica en italiano."
12. *El Mercurio*, "Tácticas comunistas."
13. *El Mercurio*, "Para los que quieren una segunda Cuba."
14. *El Mercurio*, "Los niños, propiedad estatal."
15. *El Mercurio*, "Por primera vez en 50 años."
16. Gustafson, *Hostile Intent*; Power, "The Engendering of Anticommunism."
17. Power, "The Engendering of Anticommunism," 936; Casals Araya, *La creación de la amenaza roja*, chapter 9.
18. Rojas Flores, *Historia de la infancia en el Chile republicano*, 612–15.
19. Letelier, *Quintral*.
20. *El Mercurio*, "Votar por Frei, ¿es votar por miedo?"
21. *El Mercurio*, "Pavlik Morozov"; *El Mercurio*, "La mujer y la familia."
22. Power, "The Engendering of Anticommunism," 940.
23. Available in Acción Chilena, *Avisos de campaña "Acción Chilena."*
24. Acción Chilena, *Avisos de campaña "Acción Chilena,"* 8.
25. Veneros, *Allende*, 276–77.
26. *El Siglo*, "En el socialismo."
27. *El Siglo*, "Independientes con Allende"; *El Siglo*, "Mujeres toman té bajo lema."
28. This was the central line of the speeches in the gathering in the Caupolicán Theater in July and in the assembly in Paseo Bulnes in August. *El Siglo*, "Madurez de las mujeres"; *El Siglo*, "La más grande concentración femenina de la historia."
29. Power, "The Engendering of Anticommunism," 950.

30. On the centrality of anticommunism in Brazil during 1964, see Motta, *Em guarda contra o perigo vermelho*, chapter 8.
31. *El Siglo*, "'La reacción no respeta los estatutos jurídicos de ninguna patria.'"
32. *El Mercurio*, "Lecciones del caso brasileño."
33. Power, "Who but a Woman?"
34. Power, *Right-Wing Women in Chile*, 102–16.
35. Power, "Who but a Woman?" 107.
36. *El Diario Ilustrado*, "Cuba dirige la subversión comunista en Latinoamérica"; *El Diario Ilustrado*, "Las denuncias de hermana de Castro."
37. *El Mercurio*, "Efectos en el campo político nacional."
38. *El Diario Ilustrado*, "Invitación a Juana Castro."
39. *El Diario Ilustrado*, "Juana Castro será invitada a Chile."
40. Power, *Right-Wing Women in Chile*, 109–10.
41. *El Diario Ilustrado*, "Juana Castro leyó un mensaje radial advirtiendo los peligros del comunismo."

References

Acción Chilena. *Avisos de campaña "Acción Chilena."* Santiago: Imprenta Sopech, 1964.

Brennan, Mary C. *Wives, Mothers, and the Red Menace: Conservative Women and the Crusade against Communism*. Boulder: University Press of Colorado, 2008.

Casals Araya, Marcelo. *La creación de la amenaza roja: Del surgimiento del anticomunismo en Chile a la "campaña del terror" de 1964*. Santiago: LOM Ediciones, 2016.

Castro, Javiera. *La influencia de la Revolución Cubana en el imaginario de las derechas política y mediática, 1958–1962*. Vol. Serie Documentos de Trabajo no. 5. Santiago: Programa de Historia de las Ideas Políticas en Chile - Universidad Diego Portales, 2014.

Chase, Michelle. *Revolution within the Revolution: Women and Gender Politics in Cuba, 1952–1962*. Chapel Hill: University of North Carolina Press, 2015.

Correa, Sofía. *Con las riendas del poder: La derecha chilena en el siglo XX*. Santiago: Editorial Sudamericana, 2005.

Del Pero, Mario. "The United States and 'Psychological Warfare' in Italy, 1948–1955." *Journal of American History* 87, no. 4 (2000): 1304–1334.

Deutsch, Sandra McGee. *Las Derechas: The Extreme Right in Argentina, Brazil, and Chile, 1890–1939*. Stanford, CA: Stanford University Press, 1999.

El Diario Ilustrado. "Cuba dirige la subversión comunista en Latinoamérica." July 1, 1964, 12.

El Diario Ilustrado. "Invitación a Juana Castro." August 20, 1964, 3.

El Diario Ilustrado. "Juana Castro leyó un mensaje radial advirtiendo los peligros del comunismo." September 3, 1964, 3.

El Diario Ilustrado. "Juana Castro será invitada a Chile." August, 22, 1964, 9.

El Diario Ilustrado. "Las denuncias de hermana de Castro afectan el prestigio del 'Frap.'" July 1, 1964, 1–2.

El Mercurio. "Efectos en el campo político nacional de revelaciones que hizo hermana de Fidel Castro." July 1, 1964, 43.

El Mercurio. "La mujer y la familia en el mundo comunista." July 19, 1964, 45.

El Mercurio. "Lecciones del caso brasileño." April 3, 1964, 3.

El Mercurio. "Nosotros haremos el socialismo como los Cubanos." August 19, 1964, 27.

El Mercurio. "Para los que quieren una segunda Cuba." August 5, 1964, 29.

El Mercurio. "Pavlik Morozov." July 5, 1964, 5.

El Mercurio. "Tácticas comunistas denunció candidato Don Julio Durán en concentración de San Antonio." July 9, 1964, 23.

El Mercurio. "Votar por Frei, ¿es votar por miedo?" July 5, 1964, 43.

El Mercurio. "Los niños, propiedad estatal." August 6, 1964, 29.

El Mercurio. "Por primera vez en 50 años el país tiene conciencia de una resuelta e intransigente 'voluntad de cambio.'" August 23, 1964, 29.

El Siglo. "En el socialismo la familia se funda en una moral real, no hipócrita." April 5, 1964, 8.

El Siglo. "Independientes con Allende." July 3, 1964, 2.

El Siglo. "La más grande concentración femenina de la historia." August 1, 1964, 5.

El Siglo. "'La reacción no respeta los estatutos jurídicos de ninguna patria.'" April 4, 1964, 3.

El Siglo. "Madurez de las mujeres." July 21, 1964, 2.

El Siglo. "Mujeres toman té bajo lema: 'Allende en nuestros hogares.'" June 2, 1964, 5.

Etchepare, Jaime Antonio, and Mario Eduardo Valdés. "El naranjazo y sus repercusiones en la elección presidencial de 1964." *Política,* no. 7 (1985), 117–53.

Ercilla. "Polémica en italiano." August 5, 1964, 8.

González Miranda, Sergio. *El dios cautivo: Las Ligas Patrióticas en la chilenización compulsiva de Tarapacá (1910–1922).* Santiago: LOM Ediciones, 2004.

Grez Toso, Sergio. *Historia del comunismo en Chile: La era de Recabarren, 1912–1924.* Santiago: LOM Ediciones, 2011.

Grez Toso, Sergio. *La "cuestión social" en Chile: Ideas y debates precursores, 1804–1902.* Santiago: Dirección de Bibliotecas, Archivo y Museos—Centro de Investigaciones Diego Barros Arana, 1995.

Gustafson, Kristian. *Hostile Intent: U.S. Covert Operations in Chile, 1964–1974.* Washington, DC: Potomac Books, 2007.

Letelier, Isabel. *Quintral.* Santiago: Ediciones Andes, 1963.

Motta, Rodrigo Patto Sá. *Em guarda contra o perigo vermelho: O anticomunismo no Brasil, 1917–1964.* São Paulo, SP, Brasil: Editora Perspectiva: FAPESP, 2002.

Power, Margaret. *Right-Wing Women in Chile: Feminine Power and the Struggle against Allende, 1964–1973.* University Park: Pennsylvania State University Press, 2002.

Power, Margaret. "The Engendering of Anticommunism and Fear in Chile's 1964 Presidential Election." *Diplomatic History* 32, no. 5 (2008): 931–53.

Power, Margaret. "Who but a Woman? The Transnational Diffusion of Anti-Communism among Conservative Women in Brazil, Chile, and the United States during the Cold War." *Journal of Latin American Studies* 47, no. 1 (2015): 93–119.

Rojas Flores, Jorge. *Historia de la infancia en el Chile republicano: 1810–2010.* Santiago: Junta Nacional de Jardines Infantiles, 2010.

Scott, Joan W. "Gender: A Useful Category of Historical Analysis." *American Historical Review* 91, no. 5 (1986): 1053–75.

Thomas, Gwynn. *Contesting Legitimacy in Chile: Familial Ideals, Citizenship, and Political Struggle, 1970–1990.* University Park: Pennsylvania State University Press, 2011.

Veneros, Diana. *Allende: Un ensayo psicobiográfico.* Santiago: Editorial Sudamericana, 2003.

Between Emotion and Calculation

Press Coverage of Operation Truth (1959)

Ximena Espeche

On January 2, 1959, Fidel Castro declared, "The revolution begins now."[1] That day, forces led by Che Guevara and Camilo Cienfuegos entered Havana. Just six days later, Castro himself marched triumphantly into the capital. The use of *now* indicated a watershed moment that divided the past of fighting from the present of victory. But it also pointed to the continuum of the wheel of history and signified an era of unstoppable change. The revolution marked the beginning of a revolutionary time and space.

The new forces in power carried out a global press intervention under the name *Operación Verdad* (Operation Truth), which would turn out to be a key episode in that foundational moment. On January 21 and 22, the revolutionary government invited journalists and politicians from various countries around the world to attend the trials and executions of individuals accused of committing human rights abuses during the Fulgencio Batista dictatorship. This global news operation furthered the construction of the revolution as a new kind of order and justice, radically different from the Batista regime. As previous studies have shown, it exalted the figure of Fidel and thus helped shape *Fidelismo*. It was one of the threads woven into the "narrative of the revolution," helping to consolidate the military victory of the July 26 Movement (M-26-7) and legitimize the monopoly of the use of force. Operation Truth was also an early step in the founding of Cuba's prorevolutionary

Radical History Review
Issue 136 (January 2020)   DOI 10.1215/01636545-7857307
© 2020 by MARHO: The Radical Historians' Organization, Inc.

news agency *Prensa Latina*. Despite these gains, it was a partly failed operation due to the criticism it drew.[2]

In contrast to those studies, I am interested in understanding the many voices and interpretations prompted by the press coverage of Operation Truth. This approach introduces a variable that is key for analyzing the support and criticism the revolution received. I argue that the coverage of Operation Truth was an information battle waged to define the legitimacy of emotion and calculation as a way of supporting political action in Cuba. By characterizing the revolutionaries as bearers of a "true masculinity," and positively or negatively judging their "Latin" identity, Operation Truth coverage granted or denied something "extra"—namely, the ability to order and control the emotions unleashed by the revolution and, consequently, the revolutionaries' suitability as calculating government officials.

Given that this was a press operation, my analysis will follow the interventions of a range of different actors who disputed the meaning of the events covered. I will take into account the discursive threads that drew on long-established images to refer to Cuba and the revolutionaries. I distinguish between the statements made by revolutionary leaders as part of the government project that sought to produce and convey a specific message regarding the revolution, on the one hand, and the articles and views of certain news correspondents and politicians in the days leading up to Operation Truth and as a corollary of the coverage. I will focus on the global scale and transnational flows of information and interpretations, in particular, on material produced by certain renowned correspondents and politicians from the Southern Cone and the United States, including some who supported the revolution and the trials or tried to understand them, and who would play a major role in the future communication policies of the revolutionary government, as well as some who opposed the trials and the revolution or viewed them with unease and skepticism.[3]

The *Now* of the Revolution: Emotions and Time

The victors structured the narrative of the revolution around a series of milestones that were typical of the bid for political leadership and ultimately led to the establishment of a new order. In this way they placed the revolution firmly within a regional democratic movement that fought against dictatorships in Latin America.[4] On January 13, in an interview conducted by Argentine journalist Jorge Ricardo Masetti, founder of *Prensa Latina* and its director as of June 1959, Castro confirmed that revolutionary timeline: "This is an event, a historical process." In another interview conducted that same day by Carlos María Gutiérrez, a left-wing intellectual from Uruguay who wrote for that country's weekly *Marcha* and would also become a prominent member of the *Prensa Latina* staff, Castro announced that the "impact of the revolution will cross borders" and "spread to countries that are still suffering under tyrannies or oppressive regimes." He added, "We have nothing to fear from political parties. We only have public opinion to fear." His words were part of a specific narrative, one that calculated the drawbacks and benefits associated with public opinion and leading the masses. In the context of the Cultural Cold War, having power over how information was handled was decisive. The revolutionary government needed to quickly and actively come up with its own agenda to address that global public opinion, an agenda that would allow it to influence the political concert of nations. Castro placed the revolution within the sphere of democracies that were opposing dictatorships. To do so, he approached two Southern Cone journalists who had already contributed to spread the message of the revolution in Latin America: Gutiérrez and Masetti, both of whom had interviewed him, in 1957 and 1958, respectively. Along with US journalist Herbert Matthews, both were members of what Che Guevara dubbed the "Press Club" of the Sierra Maestra, before the triumph of the revolution.[5]

The interviews by Masetti and Gutiérrez are steps in the construction of a single message, through which Castro sought to convey a common story to the world. The "crossing borders" reference in the revolutionaries' discourse directly evoked José Martí and his "Nuestra América" ("Our America") essay, in which the nineteenth-century Cuban poet, journalist, and revolutionary stressed the importance of Latin American unity and recognition. "Spreading" the revolution thus entailed solidarity with countries in the region, such as Guatemala and the Dominican Republic, which were suffering under dictatorships. The foundational tone of this initial moment was celebrated in news articles and interviews with unquestionably democratic politicians, such as Venezuelan president Rómulo Betancourt and former Costa Rican president José Figueres. In such pieces, the restoration of Cuba's tarnished honor was contrasted with the immorality of dictatorships and the affront to Latin America. As Figueres said, "severity can be a lesser evil than impunity."[6]

Several studies have noted that in visual, literary, commercial, and government representations—in particular in the United States—Cuba was depicted as a younger sister, a lover, with potential for modernization, and as a territory for the establishment of hotels, casinos, and brothels. The island was characterized as a woman, an object of desire. It had been a US protectorate, and as a tourist destination it was considered a paradise of relaxation, but also of pleasure and debauchery. In 1941, a travel guidebook described the island as a woman in love, thus appealing to tourists by highlighting the supposedly intimate nature of the relationship between the two countries: "Eager to give pleasure, she will be anything you want her to be." In 1958, for many, Havana was still "the brothel of the New World." The revolutionaries co-opted these images and used them to their advantage. In the Sierra Maestra they presented themselves as embodying the fight against the "immorality" of the dictatorship and its ties to the Mafia. If the former oppressed the people of Cuba and brought shame on it, the latter debased it in casinos and through the exploitation of Cuban women in brothels. The journalists spread this idea. "He spoke of Cuba as a bride and of Batista as her rapist," Masetti said of one combatant. According to its leaders, the revolution had come to reverse these roles. One of the measures adopted by the revolutionaries when they came to power was closing down all brothels and casinos (later reopened under different conditions), a move they presented as the founding of a new moral order against impunity, based on the rejection of economic, social, and sexual exploitation.[7]

The great unknown in those initial moments was how far the revolution would go and what limits it would meet, because the promise of a new moral order coexisted with the fear of excess. As has been demonstrated, this uncertainty was present in the global press and in US officials involved in foreign affairs. The Dwight Eisenhower administration had to figure out as quickly as possible whether or not Castro was a leader who supported the American way of life and US democracy or if he was a communist.[8]

There were reasons for that sense of threat, namely, revolutionary radicalism and its concrete measures. These included the announcements of land reform, the expropriation of companies, many of them with majority US shareholders, the summary trials and deaths by capital punishment that had been taking place in the territories controlled by the revolutionaries, and the unleashed force of the people of Havana. But, according to Castro and Che Guevara, the critics of the revolution had not raised their voices against the persecution, torture, and murders committed under the dictatorial regime, or against the sale of arms and the training of Cuban troops facilitated by the United States. The two leaders accused the Associated Press (AP) and other news agencies of conducting a campaign to discredit the revolution. As historian Michelle Chase explains, Operation Truth brought to the fore a battle of information that entailed recalling the intimate relationship between the United States and Cuba, and also the connection with Latin America and the Caribbean: a common, anti-imperialist, and democratic destiny.[9]

Before Operation Truth was organized, the press picked up stories of trials that were being held throughout the country. According to AP correspondent Larry Allen, "newspapers in Brazil, Peru, Ecuador, Argentina, and Costa Rica have called for the killing to stop." Allen and other AP correspondents claimed to have been victims of violence in Havana in the early days of the triumph of the revolution, so they were wary of Castro and his supporters. In contrast, Rogelio García Lupo, an Argentine journalist and one of the first to denounce the news campaigns that he saw as US imperialist attacks, declared that "all repression—however legitimate, and we believe Cuba's is legitimate—carries a dangerous burden, which is that of the injustice into which it can erupt." He thus provided a more nuanced analysis of the news, as Castro and Guevara had requested, to counter the coverage of agencies such as the AP. In August of that year, García Lupo joined the information offensive that followed Operation Truth. The experience and knowledge of journalists such as

Masetti, Gutiérrez, and García Lupo would become key in the founding and implementation of *Prensa Latina*.[10]

García Lupo's analysis countered statements by US Democratic senator Wayne Morse, who had been invited to participate in Operation Truth but had declined the invitation. Morse criticized the revolutionary violence. How each assessed the time in which that violence was processed determined whether they were supportive or critical. For García Lupo, the violence was necessary to prevent excesses of injustice, and he approved of the rapidity with which the executions were carried out. Morse, instead, saw manipulation in how the revolutionaries decided on the timing of the trials and executions: the illegitimate use of time involved in the process of justice evidenced a desire for revenge. García Lupo argued that the actions of the revolution, and therefore the trials, had to be defended against representatives of the United States such as Morse. And he believed the revolutionary leaders were capable of containing the "excesses."

The revolutionary leaders saw that uncertainty as an opportunity and devised a strategy to seduce global public opinion through Operation Truth. Perhaps the greatest challenge to the success of that seduction was posed by "revolutionary justice." To understand that strategy, we need to look at how news correspondents showcased the revolutionaries' ability to handle their own emotions, the emotions of the people, power, and time itself.

Controlling the Trials: Hysteria and Restoration

On January 17, Fidel Castro announced to ten thousand spectators in Havana's Presidential Palace that the executions would come to about 450 in all. In that same event, he called for a rally to be held the following Wednesday, January 21. The agenda of activities also included a five-hour press conference for January 22 and trials open to the public, as proof that the government was complying with procedural guarantees (a prosecutor, the right to counsel, the right to submit evidence, etc.). The first trial was held at the Sports Palace, which had a capacity for seventeen thousand people. Some days earlier, Castro had given journalists an idea of why they had received the invitation, which had also been extended to representatives of the US government in particular: they were meant to be witnesses to those events.

For Uruguayan lawyer, writer, and journalist Carlos Martínez Moreno, Operation Truth served as a way for Castro to communicate with "a single global audience." Martínez Moreno's account encapsulates the revolution's need for capable *translators*—in the words of Rafael Rojas—who would know how to explain its particularities. It also shows that revolutionary emotionality was considered a virtue. The revolution was an "emotional state"—in other words, a prerational state, associated with the body. A sensation capable of being explained and experienced through its discursive significance. When one entered this state, feelings were altered and actions were governed by passion.[11] As we will see, this characterization is present in other coverage: the revolution triggered emotions and was in turn triggered by them, and it needed individuals who could guide. In this framework, the revolution was subjected to a rational calculation, of which Operation Truth was one example.

In his articles, Martínez Moreno did not hide his unease. Coming as he did from a democratic country like Uruguay, considered by many to be an oasis of economic and social stability in South America, the decision of the revolutionaries forced him to explain the nature of those trials. As he had done with the 1952 revolution in Bolivia, he highlighted as positive the connection between the revolutionary leaders and the people. Castro had "an innocent, youthful knack for gatherings, fraternizing, and joy"; he was brave, spontaneous, and a skillful communicator. He showed pure fearlessness and emotionality without the "restraints of inhibition" or the "ponderings of calculation, the silences of interest." Batista, in contrast, was the distorting mirror that reflected a manliness without its mainstays: courage and will. To govern himself and Cuba he drew on a "compensating, pathological sensuality of power." Martínez Moreno also saw that sensuality in Ernesto de la Fe, who was part of the dictatorial apparatus that persecuted dissidents, accusing them of being communists. He stressed de la Fe's "physical vanity" and "erotic conceit," documented in some photographs that were found of him posing with a bow and arrow to "show off his biceps." Both revealed or hid too much and were the object of unhealthy attractions. In contrast, Castro awakened a healthy attraction and fascination, hiding nothing, "more the executing arm than the guiding head of this emotional state." The "emotional state" that was the revolution had a body with healthy masculine attributes through which it could materialize.[12]

Martínez Moreno repeated terms already codified in the media: the "love affair" between the revolutionaries and the global media. Representatives of the revolution sought and gained support from the press. It had been a way of combating the censorship of the dictatorship in Cuba and of spreading the message of the revolution beyond borders. In that "romance," the stress on the *barbudos* (or "bearded ones," as the revolutionaries were known) fed the characterization of "true manhood." As others have argued, Castro's bearded image touched the minds and hearts of global public opinion. *New York Times* correspondent Matthews was one of the reporters that successfully communicated these images, and he contributed to furthering the revolutionary seduction strategy outside Cuba, particularly in the United States, during the "incubation period." What had been a military and defensive tactical decision—growing a beard so the army would not blame rural laborers—became a publicity strategy. Castro and his barbudos were attractive because they were rebels with a cause in the face of the disturbing, and tempting, models of a dissipated and unruly youth portrayed with mistrust and fascination in the press or the movies.

Another quality attributed to the revolutionaries was their Latin identity. Christine Skwiot has shown how Latinos could be seen as "sufficiently white," in the sense of a "Pan-American whiteness." According to Van Gosse, this ambiguity of racial status was connected with an admiration toward "not entirely" white heroes: "a way of talking about race (and flirting with racial difference) without confronting it."[13] But, as we will see, that Latin identity could be a problem, because it presumably carried with it an emotionality that had no boundaries and was, therefore, equivocal.

The use of the term *Latin*, in cultural and racial contexts, or as an anti-value when compared to "Saxon," is a constant in US sociology and the history of ideas, but also in the summaries produced by diplomatic reports. Latin America and its inhabitants were viewed by part of the US people and government officials as "lazy, quick tempered and dark-skinned." There were doubts as to whether Latin Americans were capable of having a democracy like that of the United States, or stable governments and reliable economies. Racial prejudices can also be found throughout Latin America, namely toward native peoples and descendants of slaves. In particular, Argentina and Uruguay have a long intellectual and political tradition of seeing themselves as "exceptional," among other reasons due to the intermixing of the native population with white European immigrants. This image is not unambiguous. Depending on the discipline and the political and ideological tendency, Latin identity could be considered either a good or a bad thing, in both Latin America and the United States.[14]

We need to look at how the coverage of Operation Truth in the US media regarded the actions of the revolutionary leaders and the Cuban people. For the most part, critics of the revolution echoed the characterization of unleashed emotions that could not be controlled. At the same time, they discredited Castro and Operation Truth because the former would prove he could be calculating and the latter would be revealed as a calculated publicity move. In the prorevolutionary press coverage analyzed here, there is no explicit mention of a Latin identity. Moreover, in these news accounts the revolutionary leaders were considered morally upright, and that view conditioned the assessment of the "calculation" component. There were, thus, other possible combinations.

These combinations were summarized in an account featured in *Time*, one of the magazines launched by Henry R. Luce, the publishing magnate who played such an influential role in journalism and mass culture. In that article, Castro was described as "egotistic, impulsive, immature, disorganized. A spellbinding romantic." He was also portrayed as someone who could display "confidence, physical courage, shrewdness, generosity and luck." The reporter concluded that if Castro "can summon maturity and seriousness, the bloody events of last week may yet turn out to be what Puerto Rico's Muñoz Marín thinks they are: 'A bad thing

happening in the midst of a great thing.'" In contrast to Martínez Moreno's assertion, *Time*'s reporter cast Castro in the same light as his combatants who were bringing order to Havana: they had will, but were too fearless. The virtuous combination
of "maturity and seriousness" coexisted with the revengeful nature of the visionary.
For *Time* magazine, Operation Truth posed a concrete threat: the transition from an
idealist Cuba to "the Latin capacity for brooding revenge and blood purges."[15]

Among those who believed in the revolutionaries' capacity for restraint was
US Democratic representative Charles O. Porter. According to an account in the
Uruguayan press, Porter expressed his concern for the situation of Latin America's
democracies and their ties to the United States, and he described the Cuban revolutionaries as devout, but not fanatical or arrogant; angry, but not bloodthirsty, and
Castro's men as moderate, disciplined, and dedicated to their task, not a mob in
arms. The violence was legitimate, because it was not mob violence (as had been
the case in 1933 when dictator Gerardo Machado was toppled and the streets of
Havana were inundated by the masses).

Life, another publication of the Luce empire that weighed in on the romance
between the media and the Cuban Revolution, photographed the masses, with cap-
tions written by Joe Scherschel and Andrew St. George. One caption read, "A man in
the dock quailing under the hatred and orgiastic show trial last week reflected the
hysteria that held all Cuba." Here the "emotional state" of the revolution was
depicted as dangerously unhinged.[16]

According to *Time*, "overwhelming public opinion, especially among women,
urged the firing squads on." This was followed by a description of Castro's interaction with the public at the January 21 press conference: "Castro stopped to talk with
two old women, who blubbered a request that their murdered sons be avenged. 'It is
because of people like you,' said Castro, hugging the pair, 'that I am determined to
show no mercy.'" *Time* highlighted an association that had not been articulated by
the revolutionary leader himself: the pressure from that "feminine" public opinion
as justification for the trials. The "woman" reference is so strong that it goes beyond a
universal concept such as public opinion and is particularized as a "thirst for
revenge." The above anecdote could represent several things, including Castro as
a demagogue leader using that pressure as an excuse to justify capital punishment
in a country that had opposed it in its most recent constitution (1940). Also, in contrast to Martínez Moreno, *Life* and *Time* portrayed Castro as seized by the Cuban
"hysteria" into which the revolution had turned. He was indeed the executing arm,
but of a collective hysteria. He was the head of a calculated move that had simmered
slowly: revenge.[17]

Another use of the adjective *Latin* can be found in Al Newman's article in the
Reporter, a typical publication of the Cultural Cold War. In his account of the trial of
Jesús Sosa Blanco, a commander in Batista's rural guard, Newman noted that a

witness, Juana Bautista Castillo, "breaks into the screaming hysteria of the Latin woman and tries to fly at him. She is led away." While he did not elaborate on the relationship between "hysteria" and the "Latin woman," Newman expressed his skepticism regarding revolutionary justice: Operation Truth was a synthesis of the dangerous, and clumsy, nature of emotion and calculation. Castro had to realize that a "bad mistake" had been made—while it had been essential for the trials to be public, they had been turned into a circus. As an English colleague said to him, the Latin and Anglo-Saxon legal systems were different "and the press should have been briefed on the difference." But the misunderstanding was more than just an error in calculation, because Newman and his colleague presented the spectacular trial of Sosa Blanco as an example of how the court acted: "A bear beating!"[18]

To grasp the scope of the image of an "orgiastic show," and of the "hysteria" that overtook all of Cuba, we need to understand the pervasiveness of a certain tradition of analysis of social behavior. That tradition linked hysteria to a form of collective pathology where irrationality and violence prevailed, and thus explained the biological or psychological confusion, which was considered as a feminine trait. This allows us to read between the lines to see what the *Time* and *Life* articles omit when they speak of "hysteria": the "true masculinity" of the barbudos and their seductiveness was affected by a condition determined by their Latin temperament, and by a commonsense notion that associated hysteria with manipulation, in a behavior considered feminine. This made it difficult to distinguish calculation from emotion, because the two were too similar. Calculation was as fascinating as it was dangerous, as visionary as it was revengeful. Thus its value was diminished; it was reduced to a "bad mistake."[19]

In his account of the January 22 press conference, Newman analyzed the interaction between his Latin American colleagues and the revolutionary leader: "They have bought Castro sight unseen, and one can imagine what kind of high-flown stuff they are sending to their papers." He presented himself to his fellow reporters as a professional who knew how to keep his distance, and who could resist seduction. Martínez Moreno was also critical of other journalists, noting "the belligerent novelty of many correspondents dazzled by the Sierra Maestra feat or stunned by the martial justice of the revolution." But he did not lay the blame for the lack of professionalism on Castro's power of seduction or on the Latin temperament. Martínez Moreno did not see Castro as a threat, but as a guarantee for the future: he connected Cuba's past struggles with those it faced in the present, and in doing so revitalized a political tradition. In this way, Castro was linked to Martí and "political romanticism," an emotion that was channeled historically.[20]

Newman, instead, associated Castro with a different political tradition. He wondered if Castro could be considered a "Cuban Cromwell," in reference to the English military and political leader who was the central figure of the English

Revolution in the seventeenth century (1958 had marked the three-hundred-year anniversary of his death). His ironic portrait of the revolutionary leader replicated the image of the moral hero: "I have yet to see one of the Beards drunk or even taking a drink. Come to think of it, bawdy Havana is remarkably quiet and sober. Where are all the prostitutes?"[21] This allows us to look at another meaning of the revolution, which was also present and which we can better understand by tracing the tension between calculation and emotion as legitimate or illegitimate underpinnings of political actions. Before the French Revolution crystallized *revolution* as a concept that denotes a complete transformation, the term described the path of a star, a return to the origin. In political terms, it expressed the restoration of order.

Conclusion

The Operation Truth coverage reveals the shards of a battle to stabilize information. The analyses regarding the legitimacy of emotion and calculation in revolutionary actions were key in determining the suitability or unsuitability of the revolutionaries as heads of government.

We have seen the different views of correspondents and politicians who were invited and covered the events. Some, like Martínez Moreno, Figueres, Matthews, and García Lupo, supported the revolution and tried to understand the reasons for the trials and executions (whether they approved or disapproved of the decision to carry them out). In their coverage, Castro was a healthy seducer, an apostle who guaranteed that violence would be contained and there would be no "excesses" of injustice. Castro was the representative of a shared, and thus legitimate, emotion: the healthy struggle for democracy, the confirmation that the only danger was in misinterpreting calculation as "sensuality" of power.

We have also read accounts by *Time*, *Life*, and Newman that questioned Operation Truth, as it was seen as representing the dangers opened by the revolution and its main leader. These reports confirmed concerns over the "hysteria" of Castro and the Cuban people. The characterization of calculation as the opposite of emotion went from being something positive to something negative. In the description of Castro in the coverage of *Life* and *Time*, the identification of the "hysteria" of the Cuban people as the epitome of Latin temperament highlighted the leader's ability for manipulation, also feminized. This coverage called into question that the new order could be any different from the violence that had preceded it. In these critical reports, the reference to Latin character was effective: the passage from *Cuban* to *Latin* undermined the legitimacy of the new order. In contrast, those who supported the revolution, and in particular those who did so from the Southern Cone, did not dwell on that distinction. They either refrained from appealing to the Latin stereotype or inverted its value, presenting emotion as a positive quality.

Instability was the norm, and the struggle to stabilize the meanings of the revolution, its leaders, the Cuban people, and, in particular, Operation Truth, provides a map for understanding the extent to which the coverage examined the very legitimacy of Cuba's political events, defined around emotion and calculation.

Translated by Laura Pérez Carrara

Ximena Espeche is a researcher at the Consejo Nacional de Investigaciones Científicas y Técnicas (CONICET) and is affiliated with the Centro de Historia Intelectual (Universidad Nacional de Quilmes) and the Centro de Estudios Latinoamericanos (Universidad Nacional de San Martín). She teaches at the Universidad de Buenos Aires. She was a member of the feminist collective Ni Una Menos until 2018 and is author of *La paradoja uruguaya: Intelectuales, latinoamericanismo y nación a mediados de siglo XX* (2016).

Notes

I thank the editors of the issue and Laura Ehrlich for reading the article and providing feedback.

1. *La Prensa*, "Difundióse una entrevista con Fidel Castro," January 2, 1959.
2. Chase, "The Trials," 178–83; Pérez-Stable, *The Cuban Revolution*, 79; Woodard, "Intimate Enemies," 53; Guerra, *Visions of Power in Cuba*, 37–74.
3. In the first case, I will look at Uruguayan journalists Carlos M. Gutiérrez (*La Mañana*) and Carlos Martínez Moreno (*El Diario*), Argentine journalists Jorge Ricardo Masetti (radio and *El Mundo*) and Rogelio García Lupo (Radio Argentina). In the second case, I will focus on the texts by Joel Scherschel and Andrew St. George (*Life*), Al Newman (*The Reporter*), Larry Allen (*AP*), and US politicians Wayne Morse and Charles O. Porter (both Democrats). Martínez Moreno, Allen, Scherschel, St. George, Porter, and Morse were among the more than three hundred correspondents and politicians who were invited.
4. On this periodization, see Chase, *Revolution within the Revolution*. On democracy, see Rojas, *Historia mínima de la Revolución Cubana*, 97.
5. *La Prensa*, "Difundiose una entrevista con Fidel Castro"; Gutiérrez, "Aquí se pelea tanto como en la Sierra"; Iber, *Neither Peace nor Freedom*; Calvo González, "La Sierra Maestra en las rotativas"; Vaca Narvaja, *Masetti*.
6. *La Nación*, "Juicio del ex Presidente Figueres."
7. Pérez, *Cuba in the American Imagination*, 235. Here I draw on Schoultz, *The Infernal Little Cuban Republic*; Woodward, *Intimate Enemies*, 20–191; Anderson, *Che Guevara*, 366; Skwiot, *The Purpose of Paradise*; Masetti, *Los que luchan*. For a study on "feminine" and "feminized" roles, see Chase, *Revolution within the Revolution*.
8. Gosse, "'We Are All Highly Adventurous,'" 1957–58.
9. Chase, "The Trials."
10. Allen, "Las ejecuciones llegarán." On the AP, see Dell'Orto, *American Journalism and International Relations*, 121–27; and García Lupo, "Comentario transmitido por LR2 Radio Argentina" (opinion broadcast on Argentine radio).
11. Martínez Moreno, "La revolución como estado emocional"; Hogget and Thomson, *Politics and the Emotions*; Rojas, *Traductores de la utopía*.

12. Martínez Moreno, "Teoría y práctica"; "El 26 de julio y el Anti-comunismo"; "El tema del traidor y del héroe"; Espeche, "Traducir Bolivia."

13. On "true manhood" and "true romance," see Woodard, "Intimate Enemies," 95; and Gosse, "'We Are All Highly Adventurous,'" 238–56. On racism, see Skwiot, *The Purposes of Paradise*, 108 and 169, and Gosse, *Where the Boys Are*, 212. On the "incubation period," see Gosse, *Where the Boys Are*, 4.

14. On the Latin/Saxon distinction, see Schoultz, *The Infernal Little Cuban Republic*, 38–39; Palti, "La historia intelectual latinoamericana," 238–39; and Gosse, *Where the Boys Are*, 212.

15. *Time*, "The Vengeful Visionary."

16. *El Diario*, "Opinión de Ch. O. Porter"; Scherschel and St. George, "Castro's Roman Circus."

17. *Time*, "The Vengeful Visionary."

18. Newman, "Operation Truth."

19. Gilman, King, Porter, Rousseau, and Showalter, *Hysteria beyond Freud*.

20. Newman, "Operation Truth"; Martínez Moreno, "La revolución como estado emocional."

21. Newman, "Operation Truth"; Sewell, *Logics of History*.

References

Allen, Larry. "Las ejecuciones llegarán a 450 según un cálculo expresado por Fidel Castro." *El Diario* (Montevideo), January 17, 1959.

Anderson, Jon Lee. *Che Guevara: A Revolutionary Life*. New York: Grove Press, 2010.

Calvo González, Patricia. "La Sierra Maestra en las rotativas. El papel de la dimensión pública en la etapa insurreccional cubana (1953–1958)." PhD diss., Universidad de Santiago de Compostela, 2014.

Chase, Michelle. *Revolution within the Revolution: Women and Gender Politics in Cuba, 1952–1962*. Chapel Hill: University of North Carolina Press, 2015.

Chase, Michelle. "The Trials: Violence and Justice in the Aftermath of the Cuban Revolution." In *A Century of Revolution: Insurgent and Counter-Insurgent Violence during Latin America's Long Cold War*, edited by Gilbert M. Joseph and Greg Grandin, 178–83. Durham, NC: Duke University Press, 2010.

Dell'Orto, Giovanna. *American Journalism and International Relations: Foreign Correspondence from the Early Republic to the Digital Era*. Cambridge, MA: Cambridge University Press, 2013.

El Diario (Montevideo). "Opinión de Ch. O. Porter." January 27, 1959.

Espeche, Ximena. "Traducir Bolivia: Carlos Martínez Moreno y la revolución del 52." *A Contracorriente* 14, no. 1 (2016): 200–25.

García Lupo, Rogelio. "Comentario transmitido por LR2 Radio Argentina" (Buenos Aires), January 14, 1959. Fondo Rogelio García Lupo, caja RGL no. 53, Cuba, 59–66. Biblioteca Nacional, Buenos Aires, Argentina.

Gilman, Sander L., Helen King, Roy Porter, G. S. Rousseau, and Elaine Showalter. *Hysteria beyond Freud*. Berkeley: University of California Press, 1993.

Gosse, Van. "'We Are All Highly Adventurous': Fidel Castro and the Romance of the White Guerilla, 1957–1958." In *Cold War Constructions: The Political Culture of United States Imperialism, 1945–1966*, edited by Christian G. Appy, 238–56. Boston: University of Massachusetts, 2000.

Gosse, Van. *Where the Boys Are: Cuba, Cold War America, and the Making of the New Left.* New York: Verso, 1993.

Guerra, Lillian. *Visions of Power in Cuba: Revolution, Redemption, and Resistance, 1959–1971.* Chapel Hill: University of Carolina Press, 2012.

Gutiérrez, Carlos M. "Aquí se pelea tanto como en la Sierra, pero morimos más." *La Mañana* (Montevideo), March 16, 1958.

Hogget, Paul, and Simon Thomson. *Politics and the Emotions: The Affective Turn in Contemporary Political Studies.* New York: Continuum, 2012.

Iber, Patrick. *Neither Peace nor Freedom: The Cultural Cold War in Latin America.* Cambridge, MA: Harvard University Press, 2015.

La Nación. "Juicio del ex Presidente Figueres." January 21, 1959.

La Prensa. "Difundiose una entrevista con Fidel Castro." January 13, 1959.

Martínez Moreno, Carlos. "El 26 de julio y el Anti-comunismo." *El Diario* (Montevideo), January 30, 1959.

Martínez Moreno, Carlos. "El tema del traidor y del héroe." *El Diario* (Montevideo), January 31, 1959.

Martínez Moreno, Carlos. "La revolución como estado emocional." *El Diario* (Montevideo), March 28, 1959.

Martínez Moreno, Carlos. "Teoría y práctica de los procesos revolucionarios." *El Diario* (Montevideo), January 29, 1959.

Masetti, J. R. *Los que luchan y los que lloran: El Fidel Castro que yo vi.* Buenos Aires: Editorial Freeland, 1958.

Newman, Al. "Operation Truth: A Diary." *Reporter*, February 19, 1959.

Palti, Elías. "La historia intelectual latinoamericana y el mal de nuestro tiempo."*Anuario IEHS*, no. 18 (2003): 238–39.

Pérez Jr., Louis. *Cuba in the American Imagination: Metaphor and the Imperial Ethos.* Chapel Hill: University of North Carolina Press, 2010.

Pérez-Stable, Marifeli. *The Cuban Revolution: Origins, Course and Legacy*, 2nd ed. New York: Oxford University Press, 1999.

Rojas, Rafael. *Historia mínima de la Revolución Cubana.* Mexico City: Colegio de México, 2015.

Rojas, Rafael. *Traductores de la utopia: La revolución cubana y la nueva izquierda de Nueva York.* Mexico: Fondo de Cultura Económica, 2016.

Scherschel, Joel, and Andrew St. George. "Castro's Roman Circus for His Public: Hate Holds Court in Cuba." *Life*, February 2, 1959.

Schoultz, Lars. *The Infernal Little Cuban Republic: The United States and the Cuban Revolution.* Chapel Hill: University of North Carolina Press, 2009.

Sewell Jr., William H., *Logics of History: Social Theory and Social Transformation.* Chicago: University of Chicago Press, 2005.

Skwiot, Christine. *The Purposes of Paradise: U.S. Tourism and Empire in Cuba and Hawai'i.* Philadelphia: University of Pennsylvania Press, 2010.

Time. "The Vengeful Visionary." January 26, 1959.

Vaca Narvaja, Hernán. *Masetti: El periodista de la revolución.* Buenos Aires: Sudamericana, 2017.

Woodard, Blair D. "Intimate Enemies: Visual Culture and U.S.-Cuba Relations, 1945–2000." PhD diss., University of New Mexico, 2010.

Rewriting Gender in the New Revolutionary Song

Cuba's Nueva Trova and Beyond

Aviva Chomsky

This essay examines the meanings of gender in the music of Cuba's Nueva Trova, an important expression of what came to be known as the Nueva Canción (New Song) that flourished throughout Latin America between the 1960s and the 1980s. The continent-wide movement sought to challenge the commercialization of the airwaves by raising profound, revolutionary, and deeply Latin American themes while revaluing traditional instruments and styles. Socially and politically engaged, Cuban *trovadores* engaged with their own musical traditions and revolution. Revolutionary Latin American musicians and movements from Chile and Argentina to the Andes and Nicaragua likewise interwove local artistic roots with pan-Latin American political realities and struggles.

The revolutionary wave passing through Latin America in the second half of the twentieth century was at once political, social, and cultural. Music played an important role in articulating a rejection of capitalist and colonial values, a turn to popular and indigenous roots, a commitment to continent-wide revolution, and a vision of a better world. Through festivals, gatherings, and conferences; mass concerts and radio; international travel; and, under dictatorship, clandestinely circulated cassette tapes, the Nueva Canción exemplified a generation's search for multiple meanings of liberation.

Radical History Review

Issue 136 (January 2020)   DOI 10.1215/01636545-7857319

© 2020 by MARHO: The Radical Historians' Organization, Inc.

In participating in radical critiques of Latin America's social order, the Nueva Canción rewrote gender norms embedded in society and its music. The meanings of gender in Latin America were shaped by Spanish Catholic and colonial, and US imperial and capitalist, contexts. Overturning the oppressions of the past and creating a new, liberated society meant creating an *hombre nuevo* or New (Revolutionary) Man. Revolutionary singer-songwriters explored the meanings of human emancipation in ways that challenged traditional gender roles and ideologies. Political, personal, and love songs upended gender stereotypes to offer new, revolutionary meanings to romantic love. Songwriters linked the Cuban Revolution to other Latin American revolutionary processes and imagined how the new society would liberate the human spirit and human potential, "hombre y mujer todos juntos" ("men and women, all together"). Socially committed art reflected, explored, and contributed to imagining the new world, and reimagining gender played a role in the process and in its music.

The Emergence of Cuba's Nueva Trova

Latin America's late twentieth-century musical revolutions had intensely local roots and styles, but also a strong connection to a continent-wide struggle for liberation. In Chile, Violeta Parra and her two children founded a *peña* (a political/cultural/musical gathering spot) in 1965 to create a space for radical artists and to encourage explorations in Chile's musical traditions. The trio Quilapayún, formed in 1965, and singer-songwriter Víctor Jara collaborated with the Parras and explored internationalist and Andean themes. In Argentina, folk musician and Communist Party member Atahualpa Yupanqui spent decades immersed in the country's indigenous communities, gaining national and international recognition as part of the rise of the Nueva Canción in that country. Mercedes Sosa too linked Argentine indigenous and folk music to global revolutionary trends. In the ferment of revolutionary change in Cuba in the 1960s, the young singers Silvio Rodríguez, Pablo Milanés, and Noel Nicola joined in the movement for a musical "expression of the times." As Rodríguez reflects, "I began to write songs because what I wanted to listen to didn't exist. So I said, 'then I'll have to write them.'"[1]

The Cuban Revolution contributed to the cultural innovations of 1960s Latin America through the work of its artists, through the ideas and questions its revolution raised, and through its leadership role in creating alternative political and cultural institutions. Cuba, wrote music critic Fidel Díaz Castro, was "the heart of the new America."[2] The revolution's premier cultural institution, the Casa de las Américas, is best known for its prestigious literary journals and prizes, but its mission of building Latin American cultural relations took it into all cultural spheres including music.

In 1967 the Casa brought together some fifty artists of the new generation of singer-songwriters from across the Americas in the first Encuentro Internacional de la Canción Protesta (International Protest Song Gathering). Cuban musicologist

Clara Díaz explains, "Over the course of three days they held work sessions in which the delegates analyzed the defining aspects of this type of music, and its links with the liberation struggles of oppressed peoples, against racial discrimination, and in support of the Cuban Revolution. The delegates described the trajectories of political song in their countries, and brought together the topics they discussed in a combative and militant Final Resolution of the Encuentro."[3]

"Song," the Encuentro proclaims, "is an arm at the service of the people, not an object for consumption used by capitalism to alienate the people. . . . Protest Song workers must take a clear position on the side of the people as they confront the problems of the society in which they live."[4] The double album "Canción Protesta" ("Protest Song") that the Casa produced out of the Encuentro declares, "Coming from all of the continents, singing in many languages, bringing their voices of protest and hope to this Island of the Caribbean, they showed their solidarity with the humble and the heroes of the earth, and they showed once again that it is not just possible, but desirable or even necessary, that art come together with people's urgent needs."[5]

Some participants found the term *protest song* too narrow, especially in the context of the Cuban Revolution. "Yes, the event [the Primer Encuentro] united them in an act of protest against imperialism," explains one critic, "but they were popular singers who addressed the realities, the dreams, and the loves of their people . . . . Their songs were not limited to protest." In most of Latin America, the term *Nueva Canción* or *New Song* took hold, while Cuban singer-songwriters adopted the particularly local term *Nueva Trova*. These terms, writes Díaz Castro, "more accurately encompassed this poetic song descended from local folklores but bringing new aspects, fusing different sounds and taking a more committed stance in solidarity with the social causes of their people, defined both as those closest to home, and as humanity in general."[6]

The Nueva Canción flourished in Chile under Allende (1970–73) and in Nicaragua under the Sandinistas (1979–90). Under Pinochet and other right-wing dictatorships, it was at best officially ignored, and at worst repressed with exile, violence, and murder. Even in Cuba the government was wary. Certain sectors and individuals, especially an older generation from the prerevolutionary Communist Party, held a rigid view of the nature of acceptable cultural production. The Centro de la Canción Protesta, established in the Casa de las Américas after the Encuentro to serve as a meeting point, sponsor public events, and host a monthly television show, was closed in 1969. Many practitioners found refuge in the Cuban Film Institute (ICAIC), where they formed the Grupo de Experimentación Sonora. Although the ICAIC too struggled with the contradictions of making revolutionary, socially critical art in the context of a revolutionary society, the film institute proved to be a welcoming home for the movement. Numerous albums, festivals, and international events resulted during the following decades.

Silvio Rodríguez described some of the contradictions of making revolutionary music in a society where the revolution has become institutionalized:

The group of trovadores I belonged to had led hundreds of guitar presentations
in schools, universities, factories, hospitals, agricultural centers, and military
units. The youth identified us among the myths and controversies that our
polysemic existence generated: that of a generation that defined itself as
revolutionary and for that reason was self-critical; patriotic and thus rebellious,
questioning our society—which we defended even though it didn't always make
us proud. . . . I knew, or believed, that I didn't need to be formed [trained],
that what was deformed was the bureaucracy and opportunism, the leaders
who said one thing and did another, the conformists, those who mistrusted
youth, those who were comfortable, the enemies of culture, the yes-men and
the timid who spoiled the Revolution that was inside me, that I dreamed, that
I was trying furiously to carry out.[7]

Gender Themes in Revolution and Song

The continent's revolutionary struggles drew on long-standing male, *machista*, and
patriarchal ideologies even as they questioned and challenged them. Singer-
songwriter contributions ranged from rewriting stereotypical romantic themes to
exploring a humanistic vision of revolutionary society and liberation, to exploring
the meanings of the "hombre nuevo," to explicitly challenging gender roles and
examining the colonial underpinnings of *machismo*. Silvio Rodríguez's work frequently probed the ways that the struggle for a new social order intersected with
the transformation of intimate relations. The resonance of his music inside and outside of Cuba has made him, for many in the Spanish-speaking world and beyond, the
face of the Cuban Revolution.

The Nueva Canción explicitly rejected the glorification of machismo and the
objectification and stereotyping of women common in Latin American popular
music. On the songs' novel treatment of gender, Cuban musicologist Leonardo
Acosta wrote that

in these songs love appears in all of its manifestations and subtleties, from
love for the homeland, for heroes and martyrs, for parents, and also the
traditional theme of love between a man and a woman. But in the latter, the
traditional focus has been transcended, and the topic has come to acquire a
new richness of shades. These songs reflect relations between partners in all of
their complexity and depth, with their contradictory aspects and from the
perspective of an evolving society in which patriarchal and 'machista' values are
giving way to more authentically human values. This approach means an
inevitable break with the whole repertoire of images so dear to the love songs
and "romantic" songs of the past. . . . This rupture brings with it a more direct,

more audacious, and richer language with all kinds of nuances. The old
rhetoric that objectified women physically has been blown to pieces. . . .
Likewise the worn-out trope of the 'lost woman' has been exploded.[8]

According to Díaz, early songs of what would become Cuba's Nueva Trova "engaged
with the dynamic and changing reality in all spheres, and meant assuming even a
new ethic with respect to romantic love, which necessarily required a change in
both artistic content and in form."[9]

One of Rodríguez's compositions delved specifically into the contradictions
between popular romantic songs and the ways that the Nueva Canción sought
to engage more meaningfully with social questions. In "Debo partirme en dos"
("I Should Split Myself in Two," 1969), Rodríguez intersperses conventional lyrics:
"I love you, my love, don't leave me alone, I can't be without you, look at how I'm
crying"—with reflections on his own musical career: "But I started getting mixed up
in other issues, and themes about this world appeared [in my music]." The chorus
affirms the need to make art that is meaningful, rather than to please the market:
"Some say here, some say there, but I just want to say, I just want to sing, and it
doesn't matter what happens to the song. . . . It doesn't matter if they cancel my
concert." Yet Rodríguez discovered that his more critical, topical songs also "became
fashionable," and wondered if that acclaim compromised the social and artistic value
of the songs.

Addressing Gender, Colonialism, and the Church

Latin America's Catholic Church played a complicated role in its revolutions, supporting, variously, the old order, reform, and radical social change, the latter especially after Vatican II and the growth of liberation theology. It shaped gender
assumptions and laws, and even at its most revolutionary, limited change in areas
like divorce, contraception, and sexuality. In Cuba, the relative weakness of the
Church and its rootedness among white elites made it easier for the revolution to
directly attack its dominance. Church control over marriage, sexuality, and reproductive health was dismantled, with profound implications for women's rights and
status. Civil marriage, widespread sex education, a free and comprehensive public
health system, and, by the 1970s, easy access to birth control and abortion accompanied other revolutionary changes like the massive entry of women into the workforce, free daycare and education, and an open embrace of women's rights and gender equality from the first days of the revolution. But, as the 1979 Cuban film
Portrait of Teresa suggested, personal relations and consciousness didn't always
transform in smooth tandem with structural changes. "Men will always be men,
and women will always be women; even Fidel can't change that," an older woman
in the film counsels her daughter, who is struggling to reconcile the complexities of
her own life with the values and demands of the revolution.

Rodríguez's "La familia, la propiedad privada, y el amor" (1969) directly confronted the historical construction of gender in Cuban culture. The title drew on Friedrich Engels's 1884 *The Origins of the Family, Private Property, and the State*, which linked the sexual repression of women to the development of capitalism. Just as Cuban Marxism inflected European analysis with Caribbean culture, Rodríguez replaced "the state" with "love" in his title, and the song relates Engels's theory to specifically Spanish and Caribbean realities.

The song begins with the fragile potentiality of love: two beings encounter each other, and they happen to be "you" and "me." But the (female) "you" is held back:

Your skin was tied with white bonds.
Your price had been set since yesterday.
The law valued you at four stamps.
You were settled [stuck] in the fear of running.

From there the song launches into the myriad of religious, social, cultural, and economic strictures on women:

A good girl from a decent home can't go out.
What would people say at Sunday mass if they knew about you?
What would the friends, the old neighbors who come here, say?
What would the windows say?
Your mother and her sister,
And all of those centuries of Spanish colonialism that not in vain have made
    you a coward?
What would God say, If you loved without the church and the law?
God, to whom you gave yourself in communion?
God, who makes the souls of the children eternal?
The children, who will be destroyed by bombs and napalm?

As is common in Rodríguez's lyrics, images and references tumble over each other. The stanza begins with the cultural value of women's purity ("a good girl from a decent home can't go out") and moves to the ways this purity is enforced, through the permanent and multiple gazes women are subject to that enforce social control ("the friends, the old neighbors . . . the windows . . . your mother and her sister"). But culture is quickly historicized and politicized—these cultural values are attributed to "all those centuries of Spanish colonialism" that impose deference to authority. The gaze of the neighbors channels the gaze of the Spanish church, state, and God, as the language and rituals of Christianity that are imposed from above ("the church and the law") come to infuse the culture. Moral codes that enforce women's purity are an element of colonial oppression.

The last line of the stanza rips away the veil covering the hypocrisy of the institutions that preach morality. The very same entities that claim to love and protect children promote war and violence. While self-righteous church ritual and conservative social values emphasize the protection of women's purity, the same institutions enable a war in which children are destroyed by bombs and napalm. The song was written in 1969, two years after Che Guevara called for "two, three, many Vietnams" at the Tricontinental Congress and at the height of international protest against the US war there; the evocation of napalm clearly refers to Vietnam.

Romantic Love and Revolutionary Love

Numerous Nueva Canción compositions from Cuba and elsewhere probed the identity of the "New Man" and the possibility of liberation based on human values without directly addressing the politics of gender. Others explored how intimate and family relationships could express new notions of human liberation and solidarity.

Rodríguez's songs frequently imagine a new, liberated kind of relationship and society by overlaying romantic love with revolutionary love. Similarly, Cuban poet Roberto Fernández Retamar writes, "with the same hands that I use to caress you, I am building a school."[10] This imagining flows through Rodríguez's songs from his early classic "Te doy una canción" (1970) through the pensive "Madre" (1972) to a darker, but ultimately optimistic "Juego que me regaló un 6 de enero" (1991). Rodríguez's continued ability to fill performance venues to capacity from Madrid to New York and throughout Latin America attests to the ongoing resonance of his voice and music, and the questions and dreams raised by his lyrics.

"Te doy una canción" ("I give you a song") became one of Rodríguez's signature songs. Originally released on the album *Días y Flores* by EGREM in Cuba in 1975 (and in Spain the same year by Movieplay [later Fonomusic] with the album title *Te doy una canción*), the lyrics express romantic love as artistic and revolutionary commitment. In longing for an absent love, the poem recreates it:

How I waste paper remembering you.
How you make me speak in the silence.
How I never stop wanting you.

All that remains is for the speaker to give the song promised in the title. But then both the song and love become something bigger:

I give you a song and I make a speech about my right to speak.
I give you a song with my two hands, the same that I use to kill.
I give you a song and I say 'homeland,' and I keep speaking for you.
I give you a song like a shot, like a book, a word, a guerrilla. . . .
Like I give love.

Romantic love becomes revolutionary love, and dreams of happiness transcend the individual to encompass liberation of society and of the human spirit.

Rodríguez's "Madre" plays on traditional themes of the Latin American veneration of motherhood, known as the cult of *marianismo*, but with a revolutionary twist. The song is a Mother's Day paean, sung to a mother by her absent children. Their absence is not selfish but political, and the children explain that they are expressing their love for their mother by building the society that she too dreams of:

Mother, on your day, we don't stop sending you our love.
Mother, on your day, we are building your song with our lives. . . .
Mother, your nostalgia becomes the fiercest hatred. . . .
Mother, do not be sad, for spring will return
Mother, with the word freedom.
Mother, those of us who are not here to sing you this song
Mother, remember that it is for your love.
Mother, on your day, Mother Homeland and Mother Revolution
Mother, on your day, your kids are sweeping the [US] mines from Haiphong
    [harbor].

As in "Te doy una canción," individual love here becomes revolutionary love: the children's fight for freedom for Vietnam expresses their love for their mother.

Nueva Trova and Chile

As in Cuba, Chile's revolutions in art, culture, and politics were intertwined, and immersed in local politics and local roots while reaching for larger solidarities. Chilean Nueva Canción singer-songwriters were deeply involved in Salvador Allende's Popular Unity project and campaign in 1970, and Cuba was a touchstone. A year after Cuba's Primer Encuentro, Chile's Instituto Chileno-Cubano de Cultura organized the first Festival de la Canción Comprometida, followed in 1969, weeks before the election, by the Primer Festival de la Nueva Canción Chilena.[11] During the campaign Allende took the stage alongside the Parras, Quilapayún, and Víctor Jara beneath a banner proclaiming "No hay revolución sin canciones," and his speech reiterated the message that "there can't be revolution without songs."[12]

Groups and artists like Quilapayún, Inti Illimani, Jara, and Parras participated enthusiastically in the "Chilean Road to Socialism" in the early 1970s, suffering exile and—in the case of Jara—torture and death at the hands of the Pinochet dictatorship that overthrew Salvador Allende in 1973. As Jan Fairley explains, "Music became the lifeblood of the solidarity movement established outside the country after the coup, with Inti Illimani and Quilapayún marooned in Europe, joined in exile by Isabel and Ángel Parra."[13] Human rights organizations began to spring up in Chilean exile communities. La Peña in Berkeley, founded by Chilean exiles and modeled on the peñas shut down in Chile, became a center of progressive and revolutionary music and solidarity that continues to this day.

Robin Moore argues that Allende's election in 1970 and the flourishing of
Nueva Canción there contributed to Cuban authorities' "official reevaluation of
the Nueva Trova" in their own country.[14] Thus internationalist solidarity helped
shape domestic musical developments in Cuba. Certainly in the early 1970s the
Trova became more officially adopted and promoted by state and Party institutions.[15] Cuban trovadores' first major international tour was to Chile under Allende
in 1972, when Noel Nicola, Pablo Milanés, and Silvio Rodríguez performed in
Chile's national stadium and collaborated with Chilean singer-songwriters. "They
shared experiences with the most important musicians of the Chilean movement,"
and "the strong attendance and heavy publicity surrounding these events demonstrated a high level of enthusiasm among Chilean leftists for musicians affiliated
with the Cuban Revolution."[16] In 1974 the ICAIC produced "La canción, una
arma de la Revolución" ("The Song, a Weapon of the Revolution"), echoing
Allende's proclamation.

A year after the military coup that overthrew the Allende government, Rodríguez finished "Santiago de Chile," evoking his impressions of his 1972 visit to revolutionary Chile. The song begins with romantic love—"There I loved a terrible
[incredible] woman"—but moves quickly into the multiple impressions of the experience, from nature to politics: the cold, the rain and the fog, the monumental
nature of the challenges facing Allende's government, and the premonition that
the Chilean Road could be overthrown by the powerful forces bent on undermining
the economy and the attempt to build socialism:

There our song became small, among the desperate crowd, a powerful song of
    the earth was what sang the most. . . .
There I felt a hatred, a shame, children begging at dawn, and the desire to
    exchange every string for a bag of bullets.

But despite his recollection of the impending sense of doom, Rodríguez sings his
chorus with a ferocious nostalgia. Despite the death of Allende and of the Chilean
Road, "That [experience] is not dead! They did not kill it! Not through distance, nor
with the vile soldier [Pinochet]."

The Casa de las Américas released an album dedicated to Salvador Allende,
Compañero Presidente, in 1975.[17] The album included two songs by Pablo Milanés:
"A Salvador Allende en su combate por la vida," sung by Venezuelan Soledad Bravo,
and "Yo pisaré las calles nuevamente," sung by Milanés himself. The latter dreamed
of returning to the "bloodstained streets of Santiago" in an aspirational future, when
the books and songs that had been burned by the assassin [Pinochet] could return:

A child will play in an *alameda* [tree-lined boulevard],
and will sing with its new friends,
and this song will be the song of the soil,

to a life snuffed out in La Moneda [Chile's National Palace, a reference to the
    bombing of the palace in the 1973 coup and the death of Allende].

The song evokes nationalism and international solidarity, as well as the humanistic
understanding of socialism and resistance to imperialism.

Rodríguez's voice contributed to keeping the dream alive among Chilean
exiles, on alternative radio, and through clandestine cassettes circulated in underground circles in Chile that became, Nancy Morris shows, "extraordinarily popular"
in the early 1980s even as the Nueva Canción was officially banned under the dictatorship.[18] When he returned to Chile in 1990, just after the restoration of democratic rule, eighty thousand people filled the National Stadium to hear him perform.
As Richard Elliott notes, "His return . . . signified, for many, a return to the promise
of the Allende years and an end to the official silencing of his and others' music."[19]

Nicaragua, 1979

After the coup in Chile, Cuba remained the lone revolutionary experiment in Latin
America until the Sandinista victory in Nicaragua in 1979. In Chile, socialism came
through popular organizing and through the ballot box. Although women played key
roles at the grassroots level, the faces of leadership remained male. Nicaragua's
armed struggle was also male-led, but highlighted women's role in the guerrilla
struggle. A key image of the revolution, Orlando Valenzuela's 1984 photograph "Miliciana de Waswalita, Matagalpa," painted on a mural in Managua (later painted over
after the Sandinista electoral loss in 1990) and featured in innumerable solidarity
posters, campaigns, and other media, showed a beaming woman in civilian dress
standing facing the camera, AK-47 slung over one shoulder, her baby nursing at
her breast. The image emphasized an expansive and humanistic understanding of
revolution as it fused traditional and nontraditional women's roles.

Cuba played multiple roles in Nicaragua's revolution, although never the way
US policymakers claimed. The Cuban Revolution was inspirational to Nicaraguans
who dreamed of overthrowing their own US-supported dictator and creating a new
Nicaragua founded on principles of independence, social justice, and equality. Sandinista theoretician Carlos Fonseca studied in Cuba and reconstructed there the history of Nicaraguan nationalist leader Augusto Cesar Sandino.

Nicaragua's Nueva Canción has received less scholarly attention than that of
Cuba and Chile. It is a much smaller country, and it did not experience the dramatic
blow that scattered Chile's Nueva Canción protagonists worldwide. But Nicaraguan
protest and revolutionary music played a huge role both domestically and in terms of
international solidarity.

As the United States moved quickly to undermine the Nicaraguan Revolution, the 1980s brought an outpouring of revolutionary optimism and solidarity rem-
iniscent of the 1960s in Cuba. In 1983, Nicaraguan troubadours, the brothers Carlos

and Luis Enrique Mejía Godoy, hosted a historic "Concierto por la Paz" in the capital's Plaza de la Revolución that perhaps represented the high point of international solidarity expressed through song. The concert, and the double album released by the Spanish label Fonoplay as *Abril en Managua: Concierto de la Paz en Centroamérica*, brought together luminaries of the Nueva Canción movement from Cuba (Silvio Rodríguez), Argentina (Mercedes Sosa), Mexico (Amparo Ochoa and Gabino Palomares), Venezuela (Alí Primera), Puerto Rico (Silverio Pérez), Uruguay (Daniel Viglietti), Brazil (Chico Buarque), and Bolivia (Luis Rico).[20]

The songs highlighted the revolutionary ideologies sweeping the continent: a rejection of the social and economic orders and racism of Spanish colonialism, US imperialism, and capitalism; Third World revolutionary nationalism; Latin American solidarity; the struggle for a new social and economic order; and the protagonism of the dispossessed. Rodríguez sang "Canción Urgente para Nicaragua," which eulogized male, military heroes—Simón Bolívar, Che Guevara, and Augusto Cesar Sandino—who exemplified anti-imperialism and the internationalist nature of Latin American nationalisms. But it also turned to the intimate, humanistic nature of revolution in constructing a better world, and to explain the US opposition to Latin American liberation struggles:

Now the eagle [i.e., US imperialism] has its greatest pain.
Nicaragua hurts it because love hurts it.
It's hurt by a child going to school, healthy,
because out of that wood made of justice and tenderness,
it cannot sharpen its spurs.

Luis Enrique Mejía Godoy's "Yo soy de un pueblo sencillo" contained similar themes:

I am from a small country. . . .
With half a century of dreams, of shame, of courage. . . .
I am from a people born between a gun and a song,
Who because we have suffered so much, have a lot to teach.
The brother of so many peoples that they have wanted to separate
because they know that even though we are small, together we are a volcano!
I am from a new country, but its pain is ancient.
My people are illiterate, and in rebellion for half a century.

Carlos Mejía Godoy's "Nicaragua, Nicaragüita" described his love for his country in popular, rural language (using the diminutive of the country's name), ending the chorus with the lines "But now that you are free, Nicaragüita, I love you even more." Amparo Ochoa and Gabino Palomares sang "La Maldición de Malinche" ("The Curse of La Malinche"), tying Mexicans' adulation of things foreign to the figure of the indigenous woman who translated for Spanish conquistador Hernán

Cortés. Mercedes Sosa sang of the peasant's deep longing for land in "Cuando tenga la tierra." Ideas about freeing the human spirit through revolution suffused the event.

In Central America in the 1970s, the strength of the popular church and liberation theology enabled religion to become a vehicle for revolutionary claims in ways very different from in Cuba in the 1960s. Nicaraguan Nueva Canción's longings for a better world challenged gender norms by reinterpreting Catholicism itself. Carlos Mejía Godoy's "Cristo de Palacagüina" brought the story of Christ's birth into poor, rural Nicaragua. His poor father, José, was a carpenter who worked his fingers to the bone, while his mother María humbly ironed the wealthy landlord's clothes, dreaming that her son would grow up to be a carpenter like his father. But then in "the philosophical part of the song," the *cipotillo* (Nicaraguan slang for a small child) thinks that no, when he grows up he wants to be a guerrilla. Mejía Godoy's Misa Campesina (Peasant Mass), which was celebrated clandestinely during the last years of the Somoza dictatorship and openly throughout the country after the revolutionary triumph, featured Christ as a peasant who struggled against exploitation and for liberation. The prominence of the popular liberation church in Central American revolutions contributed to a rapprochement between the Cuban revolutionary government and the church in the 1980s and 1990s.

Meanwhile, the youth and promise of these new revolutions inspired Cuban artists. One of Rodríguez's signature songs, "Unicornio," is suffused with a terrible nostalgia for a lost magical creature, a blue unicorn (perhaps referring to the giddy sense of potential of the early days of the revolution). In the album notes, Rodríguez explains that somewhere in the hills of El Salvador, among the guerrilla fighters, the creature has been spotted.

Conclusion

The Nueva Canción of the 1960s to the 1980s recalls a moment of intense solidarity and hope in Latin America and worldwide. Chile's revolutionary experiment was killed in 1973; the neoliberal tide of the 1990s saw the Sandinistas' electoral loss (in 1990) and the crash of the Cuban economy. Even as Rodríguez returned triumphantly to a newly democratic Chile in 1991, Cuba was entering the economically devastating "Special Period" following the fall of the Soviet Union. Rodríguez's 1992 composition "Juego que me regaló un 6 de enero" reflected on the new realities, in particular the opening of a market economy, in his typically poetic and multilayered way. Rodríguez related the song to his debate with a third-grade classmate over the existence of the Reyes Magos (the Three Kings, comparable to US children arguing over the reality of Santa Claus). Although Rodríguez's atheist parents had removed him from the required catechism class, he was the one who insisted that the Kings were real, while his classmate claimed the gifts came from their parents. The song speaks to the ability to continue to believe in revolutionary ideals, even when everyday realities would seem to thoroughly undermine them.

"I am a citizen of love," the song begins, immediately highlighting universalistic longings (love) and nationalist realities (citizenship) of the continent's revolutions. The song contrasts the promises of religion with its disappointments, intertwining these with similar contradictions in the revolution itself:

Martí spoke to me of friendship, and I believe in him every day,
even though the crude economy has given birth to a different truth.
The world has its logic, based on bread, on the newspaper [or, the everyday],
on that rudimentary gentleman [the priest, or the party bureaucrat] who gives
    us absolution.

Despite the harshness of the bleak realities of the Special Period, Rodríguez does not succumb to cynicism. "Neither the bitterness nor the disillusion" is reason to give up. "Blind, the new life is like a backwards verse," the chorus offers, "like a love to decode, like a god in an age of playing [gambling]." "Sing," the chorus concludes, "that even without the Three Kings, I am still standing." Though the song does not explicitly invoke gender, its harking to Martí, to friendship, and especially to the "love to decode" as antidotes to the crude (capitalist) realities of the day continue to explore the connections between revolution and the human spirit and human relationships. The Nueva Canción's dreams of a better world may have suffered devastating defeats in the realities of the end of the twentieth century, but the dreams themselves continue to animate both the music and the social movements of Latin America today.

Aviva Chomsky is professor of history at Salem State University in Massachusetts. Her books include *Undocumented: How Immigration Became Illegal*; *A History of the Cuban Revolution*; *Linked Labor Histories: New England, Colombia, and the Making of a Global Working Class*; *They Take Our Jobs! And Twenty Other Myths about Immigration*; and *West Indian Workers and the United Fruit Company in Costa Rica, 1870-1940.*

Notes

I thank the editors of the issue and Laura Ehrlich for reading the article and providing feedback.

1. Díaz, *Silvio Rodríguez*, 22.
2. Díaz Castro, "Primer Encuentro."
3. Díaz, *La Nueva Trova*, 22.
4. Díaz, *La Nueva Trova*, 22.
5. Díaz Castro, "Primer encuentro."
6. Díaz Castro, "Primer encuentro."
7. Rodríguez, *Canciones del mar*, 10, 12.
8. Acosta, "Prólogo," 21–22.
9. Díaz, *Silvio Rodríguez*, 21.
10. Díaz, *La Nueva Trova*, 14.
11. González, "Chile y los festivales," 10; Fairley, "La Nueva Canción Latinoamericana," 109.

12. Alonso, "'No hay revolución sin canciones.'"
13. Fairley, "La Nueva Canción Latinoamericana," 108.
14. Moore, "Transformations in Cuban Nueva Trova," 21.
15. See Díaz, *La Nueva Trova*, 28–30.
16. Memoria Chilena, "Nueva Trova Cubana"; Mularski, *Music, Politics, and Nationalism*. For further discussion of these connections, see González, "Chile y los festivales," 10; Fairley, "La Nueva Canción Latinoamericana," 109.
17. Recording information for *Compañero Presidente* is available at www.discogs.com /Various-Compa%C3%B1ero-Presidente/release/6511959.
18. Morris, "Canto Porque es Necesario Cantar," 129.
19. Elliott, "Public Consciousness," 335. See also McSherry, *Chilean New Song*, 177; and Mularski, *Music, Politics, and Nationalism*.
20. Recording information for *Concierto de la Paz en Centroamerica* is available at www .discogs.com/Various-Abril-En-Managua-Concierto-De-La-Paz-En-Centroamerica /release/6974196.

References

Acosta, Leonardo. "Prólogo." In *Canciones de la Nueva Trova*, edited by Jorge Gómez, 5–27. Havana: Letras Cubanas, 1981.

Alonso, Jimena. "'No hay revolución sin canciones': El arte y la música en la revolución chilena." Paper presented at VII Jornada de Historia Reciente, Universidad Nacional de La Plata, Buenos Aires, Argentina, August 6–7, 2014.

Díaz, Clara. *La Nueva Trova*. Havana: Editorial Letras Cubanas, 1994.

Díaz, Clara. *Silvio Rodríguez*. Havana: Editorial Letras Cubanas, 1993.

Díaz Castro, Felipe. "Primer encuentro de la canción protesta: Peleando aprendió a cantar." *La Jiribilla*, August 9–15, 2014. www.epoca2.lajiribilla.cu/articulo/8316/primer-encuentro-de -la-cancion-protesta-peleando-aprendio-a-cantar.

Elliott, Richard. "Public Consciousness, Political Conscience, and Memory in Latin American *Nueva Canción*." In *Music and Consciousness: Philosophical, Psychological, and Cultural Perspectives*, edited by David Clarke and Eric Clarke, 343–74. New York: Oxford University Press, 2011.

Fairley, Jan. "La Nueva Canción Latinoamericana." *Bulletin of Latin American Research* 3, no. 2 (1984): 107–15.

González, R. Juan Pablo. "Chile y los festivales de la canción comprometida." *Boletín Música*, no. 45 (2017): 5–23.

McSherry, Patrice. *Chilean New Song: The Political Power of Music, 1960s–1973*. Philadelphia: Temple University Press, 2015.

Memoria Chilena. "Nueva Trova Cubana." Biblioteca Nacional de Chile. www.memoriachilena .cl/602/w3-article-96427.html.

Moore, Robin. "Transformations in Cuban Nueva Trova, 1965–95." *Ethnomusicology* 47, no. 1 (2003): 1–41.

Morris, Nancy. "Canto porque es necesario cantar: The New Song movement in Chile, 1973– 1983." *Latin American Research Review* 21, no. 2 (1986): 117–36.

Mularski, Jedrek. *Music, Politics, and Nationalism in Latin America: Chile during the Cold War*. Amherst, NY: Cambria Press, 2014.

Rodríguez, Silvio. *Canciones del mar*. Madrid: Ojalá Ediciones, 1994.

Between Politics and Desire

Fresa y Chocolate, Homosexuality,
and Democratization in 1990s Brazil

Paula Halperin

Introduction

On February 12, 1994, renowned Brazilian philosopher and political scientist Emir Sader interviewed Cuban writer Senel Paz for the Rio de Janeiro daily *Jornal do Brasil*.[1] Paz was promoting the 1993 box office success *Fresa y Chocolate* (*Strawberry and Chocolate*, directed by Tomás Gutiérrez Alea and Juan Carlos Tabío). The film premiered to high acclaim and several awards during the 22nd Gramado Film Festival in early August 1994 and was released commercially later that month throughout Brazil. *Fresa* was based on Paz's short story "The Wolf, the Forest, and the New Man," which tells the story of the close friendship between David (played by Vladimir Cruz in the film), an idealistic young revolutionary college student, and Diego (played by Jorge Perugorría), a witty, cultured, and sensitive gay man.

Fresa's significance was multifold. First, it was created by Tomás Gutiérrez Alea (1928–96), the outstanding director who had been closely committed to Cuba's revolutionary process since the beginning of his career. Alea's brilliance as a filmmaker and his critical support of the revolution made him a renowned intellectual figure worldwide. He was also seen as a representative director of the New Latin American Cinema. His reputation spread internationally following the superb 1968 *Memorias del subdesarrollo* (*Memories of Underdevelopment*), which was

Radical History Review
Issue 136 (January 2020)   DOI 10.1215/01636545-7857332
© 2020 by MARHO: The Radical Historians' Organization, Inc.

ranked by the *New York Times* as one of the year's ten best films in 1973, the year of its release in the United States. In 1995, Alea received global recognition once again with *Fresa y Chocolate*, the first Cuban film to be nominated for an Oscar for Best Foreign Film.[2]

Fresa was the first Cuban film to address homosexuality openly. In a departure from the hypermasculine revolutionary characters of the 1960s and 1970s, it portrayed an overtly gay character sympathetically, a remarkable feat among both Cuban and Brazilian audiences in the 1990s. The film was widely exhibited and discussed in Brazil; no other film made during Fidel Castro's regime had received so much publicity. The military dictatorship that ruled Brazil from 1964 to 1985 had prevented the commercial exhibition of Cuban films produced by the highly influential Cuban Institute of Cinematographic Art and Industry (ICAIC), created in 1959 by the new revolutionary government. Thus Brazilian audiences were exposed to Cuban films comparatively later than their Latin American counterparts.

Despite some sporadic commercial releases during the 1980s, Cuban films had not circulated widely in Brazil.[3] ICAIC films, however, had been instrumental politically and aesthetically to several generations of Brazilian filmmakers, particularly those associated with the Cinema Novo movement beginning in the late 1960s.[4] By the time *Fresa* was released in Brazil, Cuban cinema had undergone innumerous political and artistic transformations and had lost the influence it had enjoyed internationally for decades.

In this essay, I explore the wide debate *Fresa y Chocolate* aroused in the Brazilian press at the time of its release. In *Fresa*, Brazilian publics perceived Cuba as a mirror for Brazil's slow (re)democratization process after the end of Brazil's long period of military rule less than a decade prior. Journalists and intellectuals recognized Brazil's journey in the cinematic portrayal of a suffering but dignified Cuba submerged in the throes of the so-called Special Period.

The Brazilian press trod a line between open debate and things left unsaid. Despite the parallels on which the press liked to comment, some issues of grave concern for Cuba at the time were barely mentioned by journalists, as they were deemed too sensitive. This included the economic embargo imposed on the island by the United States, which was one of the causes of the severe economic crisis that punished the island in the 1990s. The Cuban crisis, vaguely defined, was adjusted and analogized to the Brazilian situation.

One remarkable aspect of *Fresa* is its rendering of (homo)sexuality. The film's novel depiction of same-sex relations reminds us how sexual difference has been historically packaged to enforce heteronormativity and cultural homogeneity. Much like race, sexuality has been presented as a particularly important issue in the range of representations used simultaneously to distinguish and exclude.[5] As David Foster has shown, there is a wide Brazilian cinema production that, along with popular film criticism, used images of sexual difference to condemn and pathologize it.[6] Unlike several of those films, particularly those made from the 1960s to 1990s, *Fresa* established a complex narrative about homosexuality that transcended mere abnormality.

Sporadically addressed by the Brazilian press, Diego's sexual preference is outweighed by a much more powerful, hypervisible narrative that inserts him in a universal and humanist life experience. At a time when the global gay experience was overwhelmingly conflated with the devastation of AIDS, the reception of *Fresa* in Brazil became a quintessential test case for the limits of representation and interpretation of sexual difference that challenged the production and repro-duction of the dominant regime of sexual life in contemporary Western society.[7]

"Cuba Is not an Island Anymore"

Both Cuban cinema and Tomás Gutierrez Alea enjoyed a very modest popular dif-fusion in Brazil before the release of *Fresa*. Cinephiles and festivalgoers had had few opportunities to see the critically acclaimed Cuban films, even those that had been celebrated in previous decades all over Latin America. In 1977, film critic and essay-ist Leon Cakoff organized the first Mostra Internacional de Cinema em São Paulo (International Cinema Festival of São Paulo), which aimed to contribute to the "knowledge and friendship among peoples." In the second edition of the festival in 1978, Alea's *La última cena* (*The Last Supper*, 1976) was awarded best film and praised by the audience. Comparisons with Brazil's Cinema Novo became de rigueur, and the film was given a modest national release in 1980.[8]

Gutiérrez Alea's previous film *Memories of Underdevelopment* was exhibited in the third edition of the Mostra Internacional in 1979, along with documentarian Santiago Álvarez's *79 Primaveras* (*79 Springs*, 1969), a reflection on Ho Chi Minh's life and anti-imperialist struggle, and Jesús Díaz' *55 Hermanos* (1978), about a group of exiles returning to the island. At the time of its original 1968 release, showings of *Memories* had been prevented by fierce Brazilian censorship and repression, which had hardened significantly in the late 1960s. The few critics who had the opportu-nity to see the film abroad wrote about its brilliance and Alea's accomplished work.[9]

Before the commercial release of *Fresa*, the Brazilian press had already seized on the success achieved by the film in the 44th Berlin International Film Fes-tival (Berlinale) in February 1994, where it received the Silver Bear award. On August 7 of that same year, at the Gramado Film Festival (an annual showcase of Brazilian and Latin American films that has taken place in the state of Rio Grande do Sul since 1973), *Fresa* was shown to a full house, receiving several minutes of enthusiastic applause after its screening. Journalists praised the beauty of the film, the friendship between the two men, the happy ending, and the call for a more open and democratic society that would foster dialogue about universal issues.[10]

The ensuing coverage of *Fresa* after the festival provided the Brazilian press with an opportunity to settle the score on a Cuba that had not had any commercial or political ties with Brazil since the coup of 1964. On June 25, 1986, diplomatic relations had resumed, and embassies were opened in both countries.[11] The film thus opened a window onto a culture and people that had been little more than a chimera for more than two decades, a specter of a time that was never fully grasped by the Brazilian public.

Fresa obliquely approached another difficult subject: the resounding fall of film production in Brazil and the extinction of EMBRAFILME (Empresa Brasileira de Filmes/National Film Production Enterprise), which was closed in March 1990 during President Collor de Mello's neoliberal turn. His policy toward the film industry significantly deepened the crisis in film production that had been dragging on for years. The state-owned company EMBRAFILME, created by military decree in 1969, had been responsible for many of the biggest box-office successes in Brazilian cinema history. The Brazilian press had already reflected in the early 1990s on the crisis in Cuban cinema. In a 1994 interview with Alea regarding the delayed commercial release of *The Last Supper*, which was screened in a reduced number of indie theaters throughout Brazil in 1982, the journalist used Cuba's cinematic crisis to criticize not only the lack of resources available to Brazilian film production, but also the lack of official support. Unlike Brazil, the journalist emphasized, Cuba "has plenty of it."[12] The press understood *Fresa* as a symptom of an artistic art-house rebirth in Cuba, drawing parallels with the path of Brazilian film production, which began to recover only in the mid-1990s.[13]

Once *Fresa* was distributed and exhibited nationwide in Brazil, the tone of the critics around the political questions they believed the film presented deepened significantly. Renowned film critic Ely Azeredo praised Cuba's effort to escape its ideological and cultural isolation, writing, "Cuba is not an island anymore."[14] An honest film, he continued, *Fresa* "did not hide the lack of freedom and bread (*pão e liberdade*) that ravaged the country for so long." Repeating what had been said before (and would be retold several times over the subsequent months), Fidel Castro praised the film, in what was seen as symbolizing, in Brazil and elsewhere, Cuba's political openness. *Fresa* had gathered more than a million spectators in the first weeks of exhibition on the island the previous year, a box office record in Cuba.[15]

The Brazilian political monthly *Veja*, in its article "Real Cuba," established a line of debate—concurring with other publications—that envisioned Diego and David's friendship as a metaphor that led to the discussion of real social problems other than Diego's sexuality "without falling into neoliberal hysteria."[16] By the same token, in the interview referred to in the opening paragraph of this article, Paz alluded to the exercise of freedom of expression (Diego's constructive criticism of the revolution) as the reason for the film's success. For him, it was not Diego's identity as a gay man and his sexuality, which we hardly see displayed in the film, that makes him a marginalized character in Cuba, but his fierce position toward Cuba's closed cultural policies, especially the official stance on religion. The gay character, Paz continued, served "a function of exorcism in the film." For him, "audiences are highly attracted to *Fresa*, as [it shows] the student, the prostitute, and the gay man [who] are common, simple folk; [they are] street corner guys."[17]

The aforementioned metaphor was thus established. The friendship between the two men and the existing prejudice the film displayed was seen "as a vehicle to criticize, in a constructive and caring way, any kind of intolerance."[18] Tolerance became the common trait both nations were finally learning to develop. Another critic thought of *Fresa* as an "allegory in favor of humanism, the understanding of difference and respect for individual will," themes he saw as pertinent to a Brazil looking to deepen its democracy. *Allegory* as a term was not neutral in Brazilian cinema, which had made an extended use of that aesthetic strategy as a way to avoid the censorship imposed by the military regime on film production.[19]

Deeming the film allegorical meant overlooking the realism of its narrative and aesthetics. A dramatic comedy, *Fresa* did not display elements of magical realism, nor did it make use of the varying repertoire of popular cultural expressions such as the carnival or folkloric features that had characterized so many of the so-called allegorical films of Latin America for decades. Allegory became an interpretative key for Brazilian critics, an element that crew members frequently remarked on in interviews.

Alea's references to his second-to-last film were significant for understanding the allegorical meaning attributed to *Fresa y Chocolate* in Brazil. In an interview following his receipt of the award at the Berlinale, the director asserted that "the main intention of the film is to remind us that beyond the issues caused by Castro, there is a strong national culture in Cuba. . . . The cultured gay character loves his country, and it is through him that it's possible to talk about its music, its culture, and the city (Havana)."[20] Diego's identity is important, as it communicates a truer image of the island, "Neither a communist hell nor a paradise."[21]

Regarding the issue of homophobia and the pathologization of homosexuality in Cuba that had led to so many cases of imprisonment and exile, Alea had had a major confrontation with exiled and openly gay filmmaker Nestor Almendros in the pages of the *Village Voice* in 1984 (a popular weekly that covered much of Manhattan's gay community at that time). That year, Almendros had released *Improper Conduct*, his shocking documentary on the systematic oppression of gays in Cuba, opening wide controversy and political debate. Both directors published articles attacking each other in the paper. Almendros implied that Alea was obliged by the Cuban government to criticize his work, and Alea responded that Almendro's film was "part of an official current of the US policy toward Cuba. The film feeds that current of opinion, which is well orchestrated and well backed by the official [US] media."[22]

For Alea, Almendros's denunciation of Cuba's patent homophobia sullied Cuba's international reputation. Alea's work at that time, however, recognized the very real problems of misogyny and *machismo* present on the island. His movie

Hasta cierto punto (*Up to a Certain Point*, 1983) explored those issues with delicacy. Released in Brazil in 1986, this important piece in Alea's career, one that was certainly in dialogue with the issues presented in *Fresa*, went unnoticed in the country.[23]

Reflecting on the controversy with Almendros in 1995 (in a posthumous gesture of goodwill toward his fellow filmmaker), Alea declared that Paz's short story, which formed the basis of *Fresa*, had been written in the 1980s, when prejudice against gays on the island had been at its worst. His 1994 film, however, "was not about homosexuality," but about the reconciliation of all Cubans at a moment of deep economic and cultural crisis.[24] In a reference to the central theme of the film, one critic declared, echoing Alea's words, "a history of reconciliation between Cubans fills the theaters around the world."[25]

The Brazilian press did not acknowledge *Improper Conduct* in 1984. Years after its release, prompted by both *Fresa's* success and the popularity of Alea's last film, *Guantanamera* (1995), film critic, essayist, and curator Amir Labaki found the documentary manipulative: "The information may be right, but it's manipulated. The way it is presented. . . . It is too broad, too extended. To me, it seems a dishonest operation in the first place."[26]

Fresa y Chocolate Satisfies a Tropical Dream

In several interviews with the Brazilian press, actors Victor Cruz and Jorge Perugorría discussed Diego's sexual orientation. The actor's heterosexuality was reasserted multiple times by both men. The day *Fresa* was released, Perugorría explained how difficult it was for him to play the character, stating that Diego "lives in a world I don't know."[27] Cruz, who thought the film preached tolerance against a world still full of prejudice, clarified that Perugorría was not gay. "People in the street (in Cuba) do not make fun of him; they do not see him as a *maricón*."[28]

I have claimed from the outset that the Brazilian press created an intricate and contradictory interpretation of this film. Diego's homosexuality and his manifest desire for David became elusive, and was mostly read as a friendship between the two men. This relationship was seen variously as a symbol, metaphor, or allegory of David's tolerance; fraternal coexistence; or sheer humanism. Both the crew of the film and an overwhelming number of critics and journalists who reviewed it constructed such a narrative, which ultimately desexualized and neutralized the threat that an alternative sexuality could pose to heteronormativity, as I established in the introduction.

In that vein, Arnaldo Jabor, Cinema Novo's filmmaker, journalist, and known polemicist, wrote in a review titled "Morango e Chocolate vinga sonho tropical" ("Fresa y Chocolate Satisfies a Tropical Dream") that he viewed the film as "doing so much more than defending faggots (*veados*). . . . It is a film for a democratic socialism, about the loss of kindess (*gentileza*) the blockage caused."[29] Considering

Cuba "a Bahia that floats in the Caribbean," very similar to Brazil in its popular religion and its effusive tropical culture, Jabor's article's affected coolness in fact reinstated *Fresa*'s depiction of sexual difference as a transposition of something more "elevated" and "universal" ("democratic socialism," "anti-imperialism"). Burdened with prejudice, he called gays *bichas* and *veados*, fully derogatory labels at that time, in a pseudo-unbiased gesture.

Bicha or not, in the film Diego gives up hope of having sex with David, a necessary sacrifice in exchange for Diego's friendship. Going even further, he facilitates Diego's sexual encounter with his neighbor Nancy (Mirta Ibarra), an older former prostitute who was barely noticed by the Brazilian critics, despite Ibarra's superb performance in the film. What begins with David's sexual frustration (he was still a virgin) and Diego's comical pseudo-predatory pursuit of the young college student, concludes with Diego's lack of visible sexual desire as a trade-off for the men's physical and emotional proximity.

Sader's line of questioning to Paz about homosexuality, as I showed above, reaffirmed that homosexuality had a particularly harmless function in the film. In the words of the writer, the fact that Diego was a socially marginal character made him "a Trojan Horse" that posed all the difficult issues. For Paz, "People do not build defenses at the individual or political level because they expect nothing from such a character. This facilitates his entry."[30] Surprisingly, a solitary harsh critic of Cuba's regime ("Fidel is a dissolute dictator") detected some of the film's complacency. The journalist R. E. Filho declared *Fresa* to be a conventional film that "delivers an old message, at least 30 years late, that homosexuals are human and if the hero behaves properly, he can even get a hug at the end."[31]

Fresa y Chocolate was certainly not the first film seen in Brazil that had a gay character as a protagonist. The visual record of homosexuality was increasingly robust in Brazilian film production during those years. From the 1960s onward, gay characters were seen more often in national productions, not only in films, but also in plays and soap operas. In the more than seventy films made during the 1970s, the homosexual was a presence not only in the so-called *pornochanchadas* (low-budget erotic comedies), but also in fiction films of various genres.

Particularly in pornochanchadas, which were popular during the 1970s and early 1980s, these characters were not well rounded, and their toneless depiction contributed to a stereotype of representation that emphasized camp and flamboyant comportment. Often, Brazilian cinema presented these characters as carnival freaks—sometimes mischievous, energetic but ridiculous, and lacking humanity.[32]

In the mid-1980s and before the press completely conflated the AIDS epidemic with the gay experience, a new film established a slightly more complex narrative about homosexual subjectivity and sociability: *O beijo da mulher aranha* (*Kiss of the Spider Woman*, dir. Hector Babenco, 1985). Released in April 1986 and based on the 1976 Manuel Puig novel, it tells a story that takes place in a prison cell of an unnamed Latin American country immersed in the violence of a harsh dictatorship, especially vicious toward its political opponents. Valentin Arregui (Raúl Julia), a revolutionary fighting against the dictatorship, finds consolation in his cellmate Luis Molina (William Hurt), a gay man incarcerated for molesting a minor. Molina loves cinema passionately and spends countless hours recounting his favorite romantic films. The hostility Valentin feels toward Molina at the beginning (the revolutionary is a macho man, after all) gives way to an increasing proximity, a brief, unseen sexual encounter, and eventually friendship between the two.

The temporal proximity of the military dictatorship (which had ended only a year before the film's release) accentuated the tension provoked by some of the sensitive issues represented in *Kiss of the Spider Woman*. Torture, repression, homosexuality, and the national origin of the film (it is spoken in English and has American actors) were the most common topics in the press. In a similar path followed by *Fresa* years after, Molina was often seen as a metaphor and the film as a call for tolerance and (re)democratization.[33] Hurt's character was either read as feminine and nurturing or not considered at all, as the main topic of discussion was the Oscar nomination and award, and the Brazilian origin of the film.[34] Babenco finally characterized *Kiss* as a "film about love," giving the gay story a universal dimension, taking the story out of the "gay ghetto" associated with the original novel.[35]

Comparisons to *Kiss* were on the agenda of some of the journalists and critics who reviewed *Fresa* in Brazil. Perugorría's Diego was often described as a more sophisticated version of Molina's character, and the friendship between the men in both films was seen as similar. (While unlike Diego and David, Molina and Valentin have a sexual encounter, it happens in the dark and is therefore unseen.)[36] Others found the roots of *Fresa* already present in Babenco's film, but *Fresa* was distinct in its depiction of what Cuba could have been if the United States and the Cold War had not crushed its dream of a democratic society.[37]

Conclusion

On August 23, 1996, Alea's and Tabío's *Guantanamera* was commercially released in Brazil, after winning many major Kikito awards during the twenty-third Gramado Film Festival earlier that month.[38] Starring the same main actors that worked in *Fresa*, the film was awaited with great anticipation. *Guantanamera* tells the story of an old woman who dies in Guantánamo, and because she wants to be buried in Havana, a quasi-military vehicle is improvised to carry the corpse across the island. The film shows all the issues the vehicle and the funeral procession face, such as gasoline rationing and bureaucratic obstructionism. The film received a less enthusiastic reception than *Fresa* and was read as being of a lesser quality than the previous film. Seen as either a comedy or a road movie, *Guantanamera* was interpreted as an inferior, humoristic version of Alea's more caustic film, *Muerte de un burócrata* (*Death of a Bureaucrat*, 1966).[39]

Fresa had been seen through a positive lens as the press projected certain ideas about people's coexistence in society, the value of democratic practices, and the significance of individual subjectivity. *Guantanamera*, however, was measured against a completely different set of expectations. Rather than searching the film for an active humanism, critics and viewers expected an inexorable criticism of Castro's regime.[40] This expectation was also propelled by Alea's death on April 16 of that year and the obituaries written about his work and his life throughout Brazil. He was praised as a great filmmaker, but especially as someone who had been "a fierce critic of Castro's regime" and the revolutionary process, especially during the final years of his life—characterizations that were not completely accurate.[41]

Both *Fresa y Chocolate* and *Guantanamera* revolved around themes that Alea had addressed throughout all of his work. He approached situations by emphasizing his characters' subjectivity, and this approach, even if sometimes limited, always raised more questions than definite answers. The fact that his earlier films had not been released commercially and extensively in Brazil led to the hasty conclusion that Alea's late work criticized Castro and the Cuban Revolution. Instead, the filmmaker had been a supporter of and major actor within the revolutionary process, even though he had at times been a harsh critic of it.

In *Guantanamera*, the Brazilian press focused less on the subjectivity of the characters and more on the economic crisis that was believed to be the engine of the drama in the film. That same generalizing and universalizing reading had been present when *Fresa y Chocolate* was exhibited in Brazil in 1994. Beyond the problems the film may have had constructing the gay character, the approach chosen by the critics led, ultimately, to the veiling of Diego's homosexuality in its specificity within an heteronormative society that had trouble naming sexualities it considered to be disturbing and challenging.

Diego, the sensitive character who appears somewhat edgy and suspicious in the beginning of the film, was transformed into a luminous being by both the film's narrative arc and the film's critical reception in Brazil. He came to represent an overall humanism and an ongoing process of broadly defined social tolerance. This repositioning allowed the character to be integrated into the "normal" world of both the film and the Brazilian public sphere as long as his "volatile" sexuality was rendered invisible.

Paula Halperin is associate professor of cinema studies and history at SUNY Purchase. Her research focuses on media, history, and the public sphere in Brazil during the twentieth century. She has published a range of essays on cinema, television, race, gender, and the process of "being Brazilian." Her articles have appeared in academic journals in the United States, Brazil, and Argentina. She also writes film criticism for websites and blogs.

Notes

I would like to thank the editors of this issue, Isabella Cosse and Michelle Chase. I would also like to thank Leandro Benmergui for his support and invaluable insights.

1. Sader, "A crítica é um direito e um saber."
2. See García Borrero, *El primer Titón*.
3. One of the few and key exceptions is Fernando Morais's beautifully crafted book *A Ilha* (1976), a work of in-depth journalism about Cuban society and culture that circulated in Brazil at the time.
4. Villaça, *Cinema Cubano*; García Borrero, *Otras maneras de pensar el cine cubano*.
5. See Parker, *Beneath the Equator*.
6. Foster, *Gender and Society*.
7. Sedgwick, *Epistemology of the Closet*.
8. Filho, "Próximo ao Cinema Novo."
9. Teixeira, "Obra cubana de bela encenação."
10. *Jornal do Brasil*, "A morte accidental"; *O Globo*, "Filme sobre os gays de Cuba arrebata Gramado"; *Jornal do Brasil*, "Obra cubana é ovacionada."
11. Vasconcelos, "Um repasse," 187–203.
12. Caetano, "Câmera Lenta."
13. "Cinema cubano ilhado pela crise econômica;" for the recovery of Brazilian film industry in the mid-1990s, see Ikeda, *O cinema brasileiro*; and Naguib, *O cinema da retomada*.
14. Azeredo, "Um é premiado."
15. Azeredo, "Um é premiado."
16. *Veja*, "Cuba de verdade."
17. *Jornal do Brasil*, "Entrevista a Senel Paz."
18. *Diario Popular* (São Paulo), "Amizade entre gay e hetero fisga o público."
19. Xavier, *Allegories of Underdevelopment*.
20. *Jornal do Brasil*, "Filme cubano premiado é o retrato do país."
21. *Jornal do Brasil*, "Filme cubano premiado é o retrato do país."
22. Almendros, "Cuba Sí! Macho No!"; Alea, "Cuba Sí! Almendros No!"
23. *Tribuna da Imprensa*, August 15, 1986.
24. *Jornal do Brasil*, "Alea dá estocadas no regime comunista."
25. Alamida, "O suave critico de Cuba."
26. Labaki, *Folha de São Paulo*, April 28, 1996.
27. *Jornal do Brasil*, August 19, 1994.
28. Caetano, "Morango ou Chocolate?"
29. Jabor, "Morango e Chocolate."
30. Sader, "A crítica é um direito e um saber."
31. Filho, "Um tabú mostrado com humor."
32. Moreno, *Personagem homossexual*; Lekitsch, *Cine arco-iris*.
33. *Jornal do Brasil*, "Um filme latino e universal."
34. de Almeida, *Folha de São Paulo*; *O Globo*, "Um decreto."
35. *O Globo*, "Diretor diz que seu filme extrapola universo gay."
36. *Veja*, "Cuba de verdade."
37. Jabor, "Morango e Chocolate."
38. *A crítica* (Manaus), "Guantanamera"; *O Estado de São Paulo*, "Guantanamera."
39. Rezende, "Morrer em Cuba."
40. *O Liberal* (Belem), "Guantanamera"; *Diario do Grande ABC* (Santo André), "Dupla de Morango e Chocolate."
41. *Jornal do Brasil*, "Aliado e crítico de Fidel"; *O Globo*, "Tomás Gutierrez Alea cineasta, 69 anos."

References

A crítica (Manaus). "Guantanamera faz sucesso em Gramado." August 13, 1996.

Alamida, Sol. "O suave critico de Cuba." *Jornal do Brasil*, April 3, 1995.

Alea, Tomás Gutierrez. "Cuba Sí! Almendros No!" *Village Voice*, October 2, 1984.

Almendros, Nestor. "Cuba Sí! Macho No!" *Village Voice*, July 24, 1984.

Azeredo, Ely. "Um é premiado, o outro é polemico." *O Globo*, August 19, 1994.

Caetano, Maria do Rosário. "Câmera Lenta." *Jornal de Brasília*, February 11, 1992.

Caetano, Maria do Rosário. "Morango ou Chocolate?" *Jornal de Brasília*, August 14, 1994.

De Almeida, Miguel. *Folha de São Paulo*, March 22, 1985.

Diario do Grande ABC (Santo André). "Dupla de Morango e Chocolate retorna com road movie fúnebre." August 26, 1996.

Diario Popular (São Paulo). "Amizade entre gay e hetero fisga o público." August 19, 1994.

Filho, Rubens Ewald. "Próximo ao Cinema Novo." *O Estado de São Paulo*, August 28, 1980.

Filho, Rubens Ewald. "Um tabú mostrado com humor." *A Tribuna* (Santos), March 3, 1995.

Foster, David. *Gender and Society in Contemporary Brazilian Cinema*. Austin: University of Texas Press, 1999.

García Borrero, Juan Antonio. *El primer Titón: Los años de juventud*. Havana: Oriente, 2016.

García Borrero, Juan Antonio. *Otras maneras de pensar el cine Cubano*. Santiago de Cuba: Instituto Cubano del libro, 2009.

Ikeda, Marcelo. *O cinema brasileiro apartir da retomada: Aspectos econômicos e politicos*. São Paulo: Summus, 2015.

Jabor, Arnaldo. "Morango e Chocolate vinga sonho tropical." *Folha Ilustrada*, August 23, 1994.

Jornal da Tarde. "Cinema cubano ilhado pela crise econômica." August 25, 1980.

Jornal do Brasil. "A morte accidental." August 7, 1994.

Jornal do Brasil. "Alea dá estocadas no regime comunista." August 19, 1994.

Jornal do Brasil. "Aliado y crítico de Fidel." April 17, 1996.

Jornal do Brasil. "Entrevista a Senel Paz." December 2, 1994.

Jornal do Brasil. "Filme cubano premiado é o retrato do país." March 5, 1994.

Jornal do Brasil. "Obra cubana é ovacionada." August 9, 1994.

Jornal do Brasil. "Um filme latino e universal." March 16, 1986.

Labaki, Amir. *Folha de São Paulo*. April 28, 1996.

Lekitsch, Stevan. *Cine arco-iris: 100 anos de cinema LGBT nas telas brasileiras*. São Paulo: GLS, 2011.

Moreno, Antônio do Nascimento. *Personagem homossexual no cinema brasileiro*. MA diss., University of Campinas (UNICAMP), São Paulo, 1995.

Morais, Fernando. *A ilha: Um reporter brasileiro no país de Fidel Castro*. Rio de Janeiro: Companhia das Letras, 2001.

Naguib, Lúcia. *O cinema da retomada: Depoimento de 90 cineastas dos anos 90*. São Paulo: Editora 34, 2002.

O Estado de São Paulo, "Guantanamera: Critica Cuba con amor." August 23, 1996.

O Globo. "Tomás Gutierrez Alea, cineasta, 69 anos." April 17, 1996.

O Globo. "Diretor diz que seu filme extrapola universo gay." July 25, 1996.

O Globo. "Filme sobre os gays de Cuba arrebata Gramado." August 9, 1994.

O Globo. "Um decreto, o beijo e sua nacionalidade." March 26, 1986.

O Liberal (Belem), "Guantanamera." August 23, 1996.

Parker, Richard. *Beneath the Equator: Cultures of Desire, Male Homosexuality, and Emerging Gay Communities in Brazil*. London: Routledge, 1998.

Rezende, J. "Morrer em Cuba." *Correio Brasiliense*. November 18, 1996.

Sader, Emir. "A crítica é um direito e um saber." *Jornal do Brasil*, February 12, 1994.

Sedgwick, Eve Kosofsky. *Epistemology of the Closet*. Los Angeles: University of California Press, 2008.

Teixeira, Novais. "Obra cubana de bela encenação." *O Estado de São Paulo*, April 6, 1969.

Tribuna da Imprensa. August 15, 1986.

Vasconcelos, Luiz L. "Um repasse sobre as relações Brasil-Cuba contexto internacional." *Rio de Janeiro* 13, no. 2 (1991): 187–203.

Veja. "Cuba de verdade." August 24, 1994.

Villaça, Mariana. *Cinema Cubano: Revolução e política cultural*. São Paulo: Alameda, 2010.

Xavier, Ismail. *Allegories of Underdevelopment: Aesthetics and Politics in Modern Brazilian Cinema*. Minneapolis: University of Minnesota Press, 1997.

Tricontinental's International Solidarity

Emotion in OSPAAAL as Tactic to Catalyze Support of Revolution

Lani Hanna

Talking about revolutionary values in the abstract, without being historically specific, is superficial. In Cuba, one of the most powerful revolutionary values is internationalism. The promotion of internationalist consciousness plays almost as large a role in Cuba as the promotion of nationalist consciousness plays in most other left-revolutionary societies (like North Vietnam, North Korea, and China) and insurgent movements. The revolutionary élan of Cuba is profoundly rooted in its not settling for the achievements of a nationalist revolution, but being passionately committed to the cause of revolution at the global scale.
—Susan Sontag, "Posters: Advertisement, Art, Political Artifact, Commodity."

The 1966 Tricontinental Conference held in Havana marked a moment of particular import for the development of an internationalism grounded in anti-imperialist and decolonial solidarity. A crucial gathering for global socialist, communist, nationalist, and anticolonial leaders to strategize anti-imperial tactics and continue to organize coalitional work, the Tricontinental Conference took place at the height of crisis for many nations fighting for independence.[1] In a press conference leading up to the 1966 conference, the Moroccan revolutionary theorist Mehdi Ben Barka, an integral figure to the development of the Tricontinental movement, stressed the need for dialogue and solidarity across Asia, Africa, and Latin America

Radical History Review
Issue 136 (January 2020)   DOI 10.1215/01636545-7857344
© 2020 by MARHO: The Radical Historians' Organization, Inc.

in light of the new imperial strategy of neocolonialism.[2] The conference came about as a result of ongoing relationships of international solidarity, in this case a political project referred to as Tricontinentalism.

Developing out of this conference was the Organization of Solidarity of the People of Africa, Asia, and Latin America (OSPAAAL), a graphic design and publishing organization based in Havana, Cuba. OSPAAAL published *Tricontinental Bulletin*, which became a central form of communication across movements in the 1960s and 1970s.[3] In Spanish, English, French, and occasionally Italian or Arabic, the *Tricontinental Bulletin* offered a wide selection of writing from the perspectives of revolutionary leaders who were concerned with struggles for decolonization and national liberation. It combined theoretical writing with personal contributions about various revolutionary events to build an effective, affective relationship with each political project. Folded inside the magazine were vividly designed, brightly colored posters with designs aimed at aestheticizing political events, solidarities, and revolutionary tactics. OSPAAAL posters consistently pointed out US imperialist actions and connected anti-imperial and decolonial movements and struggles for power. Tricontinentalism promoted intellectual, aesthetic, and symbolic forms of international solidarity. This essay offers an analysis of the political and aesthetic meanings of OSPAAAL's graphic work, grounded in its historical context.

In an attempt to decenter the commonly celebrated images of revolutionary front men, I highlight examples of work by women, as well as the image of women as revolutionaries within OSPAAAL. As Lincoln Cushing notes, only eight women worked as artists with OSPAAAL, producing only twenty-two of the over three hundred posters.[4] However, images of revolutionary women were regularly depicted within the designs. In this essay, I focus on two affective aesthetic tactics: the mobilization of images of women represented as actors in armed struggle, and more commonly gendered representations of motherhood. These images were used to garner support for internationalism and expand the imaginary of revolutionary possibility.

OSPAAAL posters are regularly shown in galleries and museums. These posters are often celebrated for their design and aesthetic merit. This focus on design, while warranted, can decontextualize the posters from the political formations and solidarities they aimed to propagate. I appreciate the work of Susan Sontag and Lincoln Cushing, whose writing about these posters centers the role of the poster in political solidarity. As Sontag has noted, OSPAAAL's primary goal was to communicate international solidarity. Through their focus on the posters, both Sontag and Cushing expand on the way these politics influenced Cuban identity, moving beyond purely aesthetic appreciations of the images. Drawing on Antonio Gramsci's writings on cultural revolution, Sontag develops her own critical engagement with Cuban political poster art. Whereas Gramsci suggested that cultural revolution requires the dismantling of all aspects of bourgeois culture, Sontag saw the appropriation of bourgeois aesthetics by the artists of OSPAAAL as a revolutionary act.

For her, the use of these aesthetics allowed the artists to build internationalism as "Cuba's indigenous path to cultural revolution."[5] In other words, for Sontag, the posters were indicative of a particularly Cuban revolutionary strategy.

Engaging with Sontag's writing about these posters, I seek to build on her appreciation of their political work while proposing an alternative view of their ripple effects. Regarding the range of influence of these posters, I ask, how did this print project catalyze solidarity and inform revolutionary languages, practices, and aesthetics globally? Furthermore, how did the image of revolutionary women play into this global aesthetic? In this essay, I consider the design work of OSPAAAL as part of a *tactic* of internationalist political education. Here I differentiate political strategy that takes place within particular communities or nations—among groups fighting against power structures from shared histories of subjugation—from tactics of political communication and solidarity building. Tactics differ from political strategy in their transmissibility across varying political and geographic terrain. In the case of OSPAAAL, such tactics required a graphic lexicon to support, inform, and relate broadly to diverse audiences.

OSPAAAL attempted to weave emotion into the cultural narrative of revolution through their design and publications, and through the political instrumentalization of emotion and intimacy. Methodologically I am inspired in this by sociologist Deborah Gould, who examines emotion as an important aspect of political life.[6] I take seriously the tactical aspirations of this intellectual project for communicating between struggles against imperialism across myriad cultural histories. In doing so, I suggest that mobilization of affective narratives dilutes differences among movements, thereby increasing solidarity. In what follows I present a few of OSPAAAL's many tactics deployed to circulate and inspire broad support for internationalism, beginning with propagation of political affinity.

Propagating Political Affinity through OSPAAAL Graphics

OSPAAAL created an affective design language that has influenced political graphics since the 1960s. Graphics of the hand-held gun, featured prevalently across the organization's posters and publications, associated revolution with the history, future possibility, and support of ongoing armed struggle. OSPAAAL also used imagery, such as bombs and airplanes, in association with imperialist oppression, in what Cushing describes as "visual shorthand."[7] OSPAAAL's representation of international solidarity celebrates pivotal events, movement leaders, and martyrs as part of its work to represent successful revolutions and drum up support for anti-imperialist and decolonial movements.

It was not uncommon to see the sharing of graphics and writing among *Tricontinental* and many other publications from this time. Shared political affinity allowed for the use of the work of other political artists, photographers, and designers. OSPAAAL followed a long tradition of posters and graphics as a form of

Figure 1. Poster by Lazaro Abreu, 1968, silkscreen. Original illustrations by Emory Douglas 1966 and 1967. Durant, *Black Panther: The Revolutionary Art of Emory Douglas*, 18. Poster image courtesy Lincoln Cushing / Docs Populi.

propagating revolutionary ideals. Many of the artists had formal training as artists and brought distinct styles to their work.[8] For example, Lazaro Abreu's 1968 poster (fig. 1) is a composite of two designs by artist Emory Douglas, former Black Panther Party Minister of Culture and editor of the *Black Panther* newspaper, whose designs were featured prominently in the newspaper.

   In this powerful illustration, Abreu shows two women holding their babies in one arm while guns are slung over their opposite shoulders. Abreu's composite graphic draws the viewer's attention in two directions. The gun, as noted earlier, points the viewer toward the revolutionary image of armed struggle. The image of the children, common in OSPAAAL posters, signals a more typically gendered representation of women as mothers, referencing their role in reproduction and raising and nurturing the next generation of revolutionaries.[9] Placing the guns opposite the children, with the mothers in between, heads held high, the poster depicts the women acting not as passive defenders but as actors within a revolutionary futurity. Abreu used bright and complementary colors to create the poster, which both draws the attention of the viewer and softens the militant aspects. Tactically, the proliferation of such images of the armed revolutionary woman expanded the vision of the role of women in revolution. As Colette Gaiter has explained, images of revolutionary women—such as Vietnamese women—in the *Black Panther* newspaper signified solidarity with an international revolutionary imaginary.[10]

   Women came to symbolically represent the future of revolution, through the reproduction of images of women holding children and firsthand narratives by women published in *Tricontinental Bulletin*. As Michelle Chase notes, the heavily circulated narratives of the Cuban Revolution were hypermasculine: "This theater of war was predominantly a man's world, as was the inner circle of revolutionary leadership that emerged after the 1959 triumph."[11] Taking a cue from Chase's approach to decenter narratives of heroic male leadership, I focus primarily on visual representation and briefly on narrative accounts by women revolutionaries. These pieces exemplify the affective tone asserted through these images and narratives. They touch on discussions of gender inequality within the cadres of the Cuban Revolution and the hope in revolutionary futurity. While strategies vary across geography, revolutionary futurity within internationalist solidarity networks was created through shared visions of mutual aid, reduced poverty, access to education and resources, and peace from war and capitalist exploitation.

   Within OSPAAAL's design the future became a place of hope, creating a better life for subsequent generations, and lent value to the necessary sacrifices of armed revolution. Through the design of the poster "For Youth and the Future" (fig. 2), we can see that for OSPAAAL, the goals of revolutionary armed struggle and internationalism were in service of the eventual end of violence. The image of the dove represented the same hopes Fernández expressed when she wrote, "You must learn to value that paradise of peace and freedom you will have."[12] In the imaginary of Tricontinentalism, this teleology of revolutionary success is inevitable.

Figure 2. Poster by Rene
Portocarrero, 1978, offset.
Poster image courtesy
Lincoln Cushing / Docs
Populi.

Posters frequently offered ideas of revolutionary temporality, depicting
genealogies of resistance, and drawing attention to the roots of revolutionary struggle. This is exemplified in figure 3, designed by Daysi García, graphic designer in the
Central Committee of the Communist Party of Cuba's Department of Revolutionary Orientation.[13] This 1968 poster dedicated August 18 as a "day of solidarity with
the Afro-American People." In this graphic is the similar figure of a mother, fighting
to defend the child she carries on her back, again pointing toward the future of revolutionary movements. This design represents a revolutionary temporality. It
depicts a genealogy of resistance within African American communities through
a variation of weaponry and style of dress; the young woman in front is dressed in
more modern attire compared to the man behind her and she is carrying a gun

Figure 3. Poster by Daysi García, 1968, offset. Poster image courtesy Lincoln Cushing / Docs Populi.

while the man in the background fights with historical weaponry, a bow and arrow.[14] The tree growing along the right side of the image can be seen to point to the ways in which knowledge is both grounded in historical resistance and passed along through generations. In a final look at the details of this poster, this genealogical narrative was held again within the profile of a person, ambiguously gendered but presumably a woman. This oriented the viewer to the ways in which the revolutionary imaginary was rooted consecutively in armed struggle, histories of resistance, and futurity.

    Poster designs often featured the figure of the female guerilla fighter, an image that subverted dominant narratives that centered young men as the primary

Figure 4. Poster by Rafael
Enríquez, 1978, offset.
Poster image courtesy
Lincoln Cushing / Docs
Populi.

actors in armed struggle. Young and fierce, these women are shown as affectively serious, proud, and joyful. They carry guns, emphasizing their role as participants in armed struggle for the freedom of their nations (see figs. 4 and 5). Their attire, such as the Converse sneakers pictured in figure 4 and the white T-shirt in figure 5, place them temporally within the contemporary revolutionary moment, while the clothing in figure 6, although militant, could be read more ambiguously for its historical moment. The weaponry in all three images similarly places them in the decades within which they are fighting. Their youth speaks simultaneously to futurity and to a celebratory depiction of the changing roles for women within these movements. While similarities exist between these three women, they are connected

Figure 5. Poster by Rafael Enríquez, 1984, offset. Poster image courtesy Lincoln Cushing / Docs Populi.

through an intellectual project meant to tie together the global processes of capital and imperial exploitation. They are fighting revolutions that are geographically diverse yet ideologically united. OSPAAAL's internationalist vision sought to connect global struggles for liberation across all forms of imperial oppression and violence.

OSPAAAL often used the image of women guerrillas to draw attention to international liberation movements while also celebrating women's roles in militant forms of labor.[15] Territorial claims assisted with efforts to build support for decolonial movements, particularly within the context of the political nationalisms with which OSPAAAL expressed solidarity. These claims of self-determination and territoriality were critical for those involved in the intellectual project of making visible forms of belonging that countered the logic and violence of colonialism. Berta Abelénda's 1968 poster captures these ideas (see fig. 7). It shows a stylishly modern

Figure 6. Poster by Rafael
Morante, 1973, offset.
Poster image courtesy
Lincoln Cushing / Docs
Populi.

Figure 6. Poster by Rafael Morante, 1973, offset. Poster image courtesy Lincoln Cushing / Docs Populi.

armed fighter, flanked by the images of two figures that seem to broadly connote indigeneity.[16] This combination of a contemporary fighter and an indigenous past again referenced a genealogy of resistance, but in this case it operationalized ideas about the place-based relationship of indigeneity to territory, which tied those fighting for liberation to the land.[17] OSPAAAL sought to promote an internationalist political perspective that interrelated global revolutionary movements through their collective opposition to imperial and colonial governance and resource extraction.

This also meant solidarity with anti-imperialist and antiracist movements and organizations within the United States. *Tricontinental Bulletin* regularly published

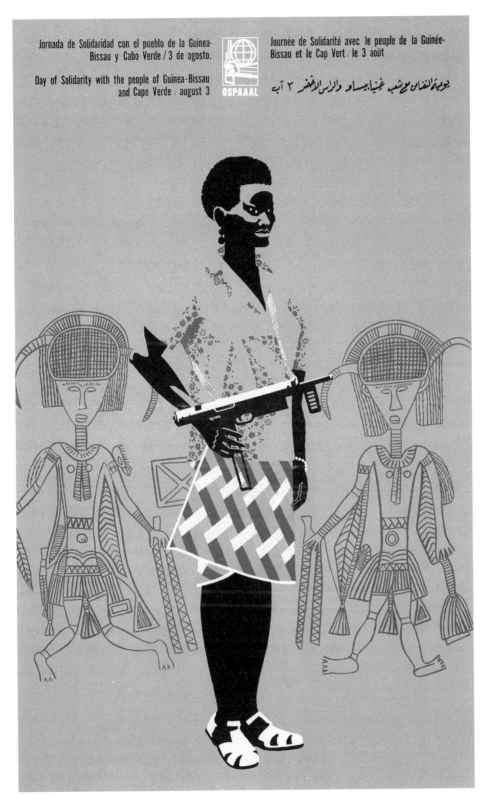

Jornada de Solidaridad con el pueblo de la Guinea-Bissau y Cabo Verde / 3 de agosto.

Day of Solidarity with the people of Guinea-Bissau and Cape Verde / august 3

OSPAAAL

Journée de Solidarité avec le peuple de la Guinée-Bissau et le Cap Vert / le 3 août

يومية التضامن مع شعب غينيا بيساو والراس الأخضر ٣ آب

Figure 7. Poster by Berta Abelénda, 1968, offset. Poster image courtesy Lincoln Cushing / Docs Populi.

articles by revolutionary figures in the United States, including one of the founders of the Black Panther Party, Huey P. Newton.[18] It also featured pieces by US-based Black liberation activists Stokely Carmichael and Angela Davis.[19] *Tricontinental Bulletin* and *Tricontinental Magazine* had extensive influence among Left movements and intellectuals abroad; at their height in 1968, their combined global circulation reached fifty thousand.[20] The impact of those copies in circulation would have been amplified by the practice of sharing graphics and articles, common among Left political movements at the time.[21] The bulletin's diverse contributors, broad circulation, and internationalist vision all contributed to imagining a united global revolutionary movement.

Emotional narratives of revolution written by women also pepper the pages of *Tricontinental Bulletin*, sandwiched between works of anti-imperialist theory and dispatches from revolutionary movements abroad. Their contributions show that attention to women as revolutionary actors went beyond their inclusion as iconic subjects in posters. These essays occasionally addressed gender relations within revolutionary movements. In one article, Cuban revolutionary Melba Hernández reflected on the historic attack on Moncada Barracks.[22] Hernandez described an argument between herself, Haydée Santamaría, and Fidel Castro about whether the women should stay behind. Hernández's account of these internal debates is a personal and compelling narrative that suggests that debate over gender equality was at the heart of the Cuban revolutionary movement.[23]

In 1973, *Tricontinental Bulletin* published a piece by Margaret Randall, a poet, writer, and editor from the United States who lived in Cuba for much of the mid-century.[24] Her essay focused on the American Indian Movement and the massacre at Wounded Knee.[25] In 1971, the cover of *Tricontinental Bulletin* 60 featured images of Denise Oliver and Gloria Fontanez of the Young Lords Party. Inside they published the "13 Point Program and Platform of the Young Lords Party," as well as the "Young Lords Party Position Paper on Women,"[26] the latter of which was originally printed in the independent newspaper of the Young Lords Party, *Palante*.[27] This paper concisely described the layers of oppression faced by Puerto Rican, African American, and Third World women, and it developed an analysis that saw the Third World woman as "the most oppressed person in the world today."[28] It raised the intersection of violence against women, aspects of capitalism, imperialism, interpersonal relationships, family and women's reproductive rights, and culture. Women of the Young Lords similarly invoked internationalism, drawing comparison, solidarity, and inspiration from the women of Vietnam, particularly the women's brigade of the National Liberation Front of the North Vietnamese Army.[29]

Tricontinental Bulletin's sharing of the Young Lords Party's position paper on women, in addition to the articles by women mentioned above, demonstrated an engagement with the broad articulations of political organizing taking place across the movements, and drew readers' attention to organizations that were actively addressing gendered power relationships. These examples exemplify OSPAAAL's affective invocation of revolutionary women and their own accounts of participation in their respective revolutions.

Conclusion

This discussion of the posters of OSPAAAL and writings in the *Tricontinental Bulletin* draws from a very small segment of OSPAAAL's output. The aesthetic languages and allure of Cuban graphic design, particularly in its posters, have captivated global art audiences for decades. In addition, *Tricontinental Bulletin* offered insight from global vanguard movements so that those fighting on their own front lines could learn from and engage with one another. This process included building a revolutionary aesthetic that captured the imagination of those organizing their own movements. As Cushing notes, OSPAAAL artists expertly represented abstract concepts such as anti-imperialism through minimalist design.[30] While the design aesthetics of OSPAAAL have continually been the focus of this essay, I also situate design choices as part of a tactics of political education and outreach. By invoking emotional involvement with the inclusion of images of women and children and pointing to genealogical forms of revolutionary imaginary and practice, the artists of OSPAAAL created a tactic of political education and outreach that built international support of revolutionary movements. OSPAAAL's images can be found throughout the pages of various publications during the 1960s, 1970s, and 1980s. These circulated images intermingled aesthetics from different schools of design and nourished the sensibility of the Left on a transnational scale, transcending the limits of OSPAAAL's own publications.

CURATED SPACES provides a focus on visual culture in relation to social, historical, or political subject matter.

Lani Hanna is a doctoral student in feminist studies at University of California Santa Cruz. She lives in Oakland and is involved in community archiving in New York and San Francisco. As a volunteer at Interference Archive, she has co-organized several exhibitions, including *Armed by Design: Posters and Publications of the Organization of Solidarity of the Peoples of Africa, Asia, and Latin America*. She is active in community organizing and practices Danzan-ryū jujutsu.

Notes

I want to express my immense gratitude to several colleagues who helped me find archival material, edited, and co-conspired in the process of writing this piece. Neel, Ahuja, Louise Barry, Kevin Capliki, Dylan Cooke, Lincoln Cushing, Gabriel Evans, Lisa Floyd-Hanna, Debbie Gould, Jen Hoyer, Noya Kansky, Josh MacPhee, Claude Marks, Nathaniel Moore, Jane Norling, Vero Ordaz, Sarah Seidman, Delio Vasquez, Taylor Wondergem, Vivian Underhill, and archivists at Interference Archive, Freedom Archives, and the International Institute of Social History.

1. Mahler, "Beyond the Color Curtain," 102. For more details about the Tricontinental Conference and its global impact see Mahler, *From the Tricontinental to the Global South*.
2. Ben Barka, *Ben Barka Tricontinental Leader*, 7.
3. OSPAAAL is currently active in Havana; see Seidman, "On Tricontinentalism," 16.
4. Cushing, *¡Revolución!*, 12.
5. Sontag, "Posters: Advertisement, Art, Political Artifact, Commodity," xix. Sontag is clear to delineate the major differences in Cuba's aesthetic practice and ideology of cultural revolution from the more commonly associated use of the phrase which refers to fascist strategies that employ cultural revolution as a form of building national pride. I agree with Sontag in her assessment that Cuba's internationalist ideology offers inspiration for Left revolutionary movements to move toward shared understandings of imperial oppression.
6. Gould, *Moving Politics*, 3. There is an immense body of literature on the relationship between emotion and affect. My invocation here approximates Gould's use of the terms. I am drawn to Gould's work for the same reason I was drawn to OSPAAAL and the *Tricontinental Bulletins*—they help me explore what forms of political possibilities become imaginable and which do not.
7. Cushing, *¡Revolución!*, 14–15.
8. Cushing, *¡Revolución!*, 16.
9. Contemporary feminist scholarship has found inspiration in revisiting the revolutionary role of motherhood, centering a politics of care in conjunction with the radical futurity offered in raising new generations of revolutionary actors. See Gumbs, Marten, and Williams, *Revolutionary Mothering*.
10. Gaiter, "What Revolution Looks Like," 98.
11. Chase, *Revolution within the Revolution*, 2.
12. Fernández, "If I Have the Privilege of Seeing You Again," 45.
13. See *Cuban Poster Art*.
14. Hanna, "A Short Archival Survey," 43.
15. Militancy and armed struggle was not the only form of organizing in which women were involved during revolutionary periods. The various roles they played both operationalized and destabilized notions of motherhood or reproduction as a singular form of revolutionary involvement. For an important example of this in the Cuban context, see Chase, *Revolution within the Revolution*.
16. If the artists were drawing specific indigenous and past figures from the Guinea Bissau and Cape Verde struggle, this was not clarified in the poster.
17. Hanna, "A Short Archival Survey," 43.
18. Newton, "Culture and Liberation," Freedom Archives, San Francisco, 101–4. Newton, a founder of the Black Panther Party, wrote extensively on theories of internationalism. His term for this is *intercommunalism*. For more about Newton's theory and a glimpse at the archive of intercommunalism, see Vasquez, "Intercommunalism."
19. For more information on the relationship between Carmichael and Tricontinentalism, see Seidman, "Tricontinental Routes of Solidarity." On Davis, see Davis, "Angela Davis Speaks from Jail," 17.
20. Seidman, "On Tricontinentalism."
21. For example, in 1972 and 1973, San Francisco–based political press People's Press collaborated with OSPAAAL to put out a North American version. See Norling, "As Big as the World."

22. Hernández was General secretary of OSPAAAL in the 1980s. The exact dates are unknown. *Tricontinental News Service 1*.
23. Hernández, *Tricontinental News Service 1*, 17.
24. See the interview with Margaret Randall featured in this issue.
25. Randall, "Two, Three, Many Wounded Knees," 25–40.
26. "Young Lords Party Position Paper," 25–31; "13 Point Program," 18–24; Hanna, "A Short Archival Survey," 44.
27. Hanna, "A Short Archival Survey," 44.
28. "13 Point Program," 19.
29. "Young Lords Party Position Paper," 31.
30. Cushing, *¡Revolucion!*, 14.

References

Ben Barka, Mehdi. *Ben Barka Tricontinental Leader*. Pamphlet. Havana: OSPAAAL, n.d.

Chase, Michelle. *Revolution within the Revolution: Women and Gender Politics in Cuba, 1952–1962*. Chapel Hill: University of North Carolina Press, 2015.

Cuban Poster Art: A Retrospective, 1961–1982. Exhibition. Westbeth Gallery, Center for Cuban Studies, and Cuba Ministerio de Cultura. January 16–February 9, 1983, Westbeth Gallery, 463 West St. New York, New York: The Center, 1983. Translations by Geoffrey Fox. Sponsored by the Center for Cuban Studies in Collaboration with the Ministry of Culture, Havana, Cuba.

Cushing, Lincoln. *¡Revolucion! Cuban Poster Art*. San Francisco: Chronicle Books, 2003.

Davis, Angela. "Angela Davis Speaks from Jail." *Tricontinental Bulletin 63*, 17–23. Havana: OSPAAAL, 1971.

Douglas, Emory, Bobby Seale, and Sam Durant. *Black Panther: The Revolutionary Art of Emory Douglas*. New York: Rizzoli International Publications, 2007.

Fernández, Idania. "If I Have the Privilege of Seeing You Again." *Tricontinental Bulletin* Special Edition XIII. Havana: OSPAAAL, 1979.

Gaiter, Colette. "What Revolution Looks Like." In *Black Panther: The Revolutionary Art of Emory Douglas*, edited by Emory Douglas, Bobby Seale, and Sam Durant, 93–128. New York: Rizzoli International Publications, 2007.

Gould, Deborah B. *Moving Politics: Emotion and ACT UP's fight against AIDS*. Chicago: University of Chicago Press, 2009.

Gumbs, Alexis Pauline, China Marten, and Mai'a Williams. *Revolutionary Mothering: Love on the Front Lines*. Toronto: Between the Lines, 2016.

Hanna, Lani. "A Short Archival Survey of the Representation of Women in OSPAAAL." In *Armed by Design: Posters and Publications of the Organization of Solidarity of the Peoples of Africa, Asia, and Latin America*, edited by Jen Hoyer, Lani Hanna, Vero Ordaz, and Josh MacPhee, 40–45. New York: Interference Archive, 2015.

Hernández, Melba. *Tricontinental News Service 1*, no. 13, 15–19. Havana: OSPAAAL, 1973.

Mahler, Anne Garland. "Beyond the Color Curtain: The Metonymic Color Politics of the Tricontinental and the (New) Global South." In *The Global South Atlantic*, edited by Kerry Bystrom and Joseph R. Slaughter, 99–123. New York: Fordham University Press, 2017.

Mahler, Anne Garland. *From the Tricontinental to the Global South: Race, Radicalism, and Transnational Solidarity*. Durham, NC: Duke University Press, 2018.

Newton, Huey P. "Culture and Liberation." *Tricontinental Bulletin 11*. Havana: OSPAAAL. 1969.

Norling, Jane. "As Big as the World: An Interview with Jane Norling." In *Armed by Design: Posters and Publications of the Organization of Solidarity of the Peoples of Africa, Asia, and Latin America*, edited by Jen Hoyer, Lani Hanna, Vero Ordaz, and Josh MacPhee, 67–80. New York: Interference Archive, 2015.

Randall, Margaret. "Two, Three, Many Wounded Knees." *Tricontinental Bulletin 85*. Havana: OSPAAAL, 1973, 25–40.

Seidman, Sarah. "Tricontinental Routes of Solidarity: Stokely Carmichael in Cuba." *Journal of Transnational American Studies* 4, no. 2 (2012). n.p.

Seidman, Sarah. "On Tricontinentalism." In *Armed by Design: Posters and Publications of the Organization of Solidarity of the Peoples of Africa, Asia, and Latin America*, edited by Jen Hoyer, Lani Hanna, Vero Ordaz, and Josh MacPhee, 13–23. New York: Interference Archive, 2015.

Sontag, Susan. "Posters: Advertisement, Art, Political Artifact, Commodity." In *The Art of Revolution: Castro's Cuba: 1959–1970*, by Stermer Dugald and Susan Sontag. New York: McGraw-Hill, 1970.

Vasquez, Delio. "Intercommunalism: The Late Theorizations of Huey P. Newton, 'Chief Theoretician' of the Black Panther Party." *Viewpoint Magazine*, June 11, 2018.

"Young Lords Party Position Paper on Women." *Tricontinental Bulletin 60*, 25–31. Havana: OSPAAAL, 1971.

"13 Point Program and Platform of the Young Lords Party." *Tricontinental Bulletin 60*, 18–24. Havana: OSPAAAL, 1971.

Women, Gender, and Sexuality in the Cuban Revolution

Conversations with Margaret Randall

Elizabeth Quay Hutchison

Among those who have gathered, translated, and disseminated the stories of Cuban women, Margaret Randall holds pride of place: the US-born lesbian feminist artist, activist, and scholar published some of the very first interviews with Cuban women in the 1970s, discussed women's issues with Latin American revolutionaries in the 1980s, and has since produced a raft of creative and scholarly work about Cuba, with a particular focus on women and gender relations. As a corpus, these works trace a vital history of women's activism within Latin American revolutionary movements, in which Randall actively participated for over three decades. Born in New York, she grew up in New Mexico and at the age of twenty-four moved to Mexico City, where she founded and for eight years coedited the iconic bilingual literary magazine *El Corno Emplumado / The Plumed Horn*. In 1969, forced into hiding as a result of her participation in the Mexican student movement, she moved to Cuba with her four children, where she lived for almost eleven years, working as an editor and writer at the Cuban Book Institute and as a freelance journalist and writer. During this time, Randall also attended important meetings of the international women's movement, including those sponsored by the Popular Unity government in Chile (1972) and by United Nations International Women's Year in Venezuela (1975). By 1980 she had moved on to Nicaragua, where she served as publicist for

Radical History Review
Issue 136 (January 2020)   DOI 10.1215/01636545-7857356
© 2020 by MARHO: The Radical Historians' Organization, Inc.

the Ministry of Culture and helped shape a new journalism in the fledgling Sandinista government. Randall then moved home to New Mexico in 1984, which has served as her home base for teaching in women's studies and English and continuing to produce new creative and scholarly works at an impressive clip for over three decades. Randall's manuscripts and photographs are now held at the University of New Mexico's Center for Southwest Research.[1]

Out of Randall's Latin American travels arose an uncompromising socialist activism, which allowed her both to influence revolutionary policies (particularly toward women) and to transmit those views to a wider audience. As a participant-observer in these movements, Randall was uniquely positioned to assess the progress and limitations of socialist revolution from a feminist perspective, even as her own notions of revolution and feminism changed over time. Resident in Cuba between 1969 and 1980, and a constant artistic and scholarly collaborator with Latin American revolutionary leaders thereafter, Randall has remained an important observer of the Cuban Revolution, bringing an insider's view to the origins, impact, and limitations of the "revolution within the revolution" announced by Castro in 1966. By the time she moved to Nicaragua in 1980, Randall's expertise on the subject of women and revolution allowed her to provide informal advising to Sandinista colleagues and women's organizations during a critical period in the development of Sandinista policies on women, gender, and sexuality.

Randall's work has been instrumental in the politics of North-South transmission, which is manifest in her work on tasks of oral history and translation of Latin American voices for a North American public. The longest trajectory within Randall's scholarly work began with oral history: in *Cuban Women Now*, the English-language edition of a 1972 Cuban publication, Randall told the stories of women in the Cuban Revolution and allowed readers to glimpse the nuance and complexity of that government's commitment to gender equality.[2] Randall continued to develop her feminist perspective on gender and revolution in later works,[3] taking readers inside women's experience of revolution through her series of English-language publications on Nicaragua, which provided urgent testimony for solidarity movements as well as Latin American and women's studies programs in the United States.[4] The fact that many of Randall's books have also been published in Spanish also means that her works have also been widely appreciated among Latin American readers, and her most recent monographs have opened new windows onto Cuban histories of gender, art, and internationalism.[5]

As I sat with Randall in the heat of Albuquerque's summer of 2018, the task of understanding women's role in revolution, particularly through the lens of Cuba's long struggle, seemed ever more urgent. In oral and written exchanges, we discussed a variety of questions: What have women and sexual minorities contributed to Cuba's experiment in radical equality, and what remains to be done? How has feminism—in all its variety—shaped the aspirations of Cuban men and women, and what have US feminists learned from their efforts? What makes gender justice happen, and who or what constitutes barriers to change? As always, the Cuban people show us some of the ways that these changes can come about.

Elizabeth Quay Hutchison: *As I prepared for our conversation, I was again struck by the remarkable nature of your journey through Cold War Latin America. As you have recounted elsewhere, these moves were driven by a mixture of curiosity, repression, and family, as well as your evolving political and professional commitments. How did your experience as a young translator, artist, and ethnographer in Cuba shape your later experiences in Sandinista Nicaragua?*

Margaret Randall: I've often been asked how I happened to live and work in such interesting places, and I've usually responded that I was lucky enough to have "found myself in the right place at the right time": in New York City as the abstract expressionist movement came to prominence, in Mexico during a particularly vibrant period brought to its dramatic end by government repression against the student movement of 1968, in Cuba during the revolution's exciting second decade, in North Vietnam six months before the end of the war, and in Nicaragua immediately following the Sandinista victory of 1979. But I didn't just "find myself" in any of these places at those times. Some of my moves were driven by repression or family considerations, but I actively sought out places where important changes were taking place, and—as much as possible—threw my lot in with the people making those changes. I wanted to experience social change, to understand and be part of it. As a poet, I quite naturally became a translator. As a woman discovering the power of feminism, I wanted to know about women's lives in these places. And so I asked. I developed projects that would allow me to speak with women, listen to their stories. I became an ethnographer through my own on-the-ground experience.

I made mistakes, but I also learned and grew. So, my experiences in one place very naturally led to working better in the next. And, of course I wasn't working in a vacuum; I was interested in what others in the field were doing, and had ongoing conversations about ethical implications and methods. The twenty years separating the Cuban and Nicaraguan revolutions were also important: the decades when what we now call the second wave of feminism swept the Western world and liberation theology became an important force within the Catholic Church. Both movements freed Nicaraguan women in ways that the Cuban Revolution had not. By the time I did the field work for *Sandino's Daughters*, in 1979, and went to live in Nicaragua at the end of 1980, my thinking was quite a bit more advanced. After eleven years in Cuba I could see that a gender analysis was needed there, that without such an analysis, profound change was not likely to come to that country. Women in Nicaragua's revolutionary leadership were considerably more advanced than their Cuban counterparts in terms of how they envisioned women's roles. I was becoming a better

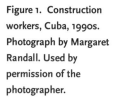

Figure 1. Construction workers, Cuba, 1990s. Photograph by Margaret Randall. Used by permission of the photographer.

feminist and better ethnographer, and I was also interviewing women who were more advanced in their thinking and social participation.

And I brought my own artistic vision to my work. I became a photographer by apprenticing to a Cuban photographer in 1978–79, and this also enabled me to develop a particular practice that I think made my oral history work deeper: I began photographing my informants *as I interviewed them*. People often wondered how I could make pictures and record interviews at the same time, but I never felt I was neglecting one for the other. Later, I would develop and print those images— gestures, expressions—as I was transcribing the words. One practice fed the other. My later oral history books, those with Nicaraguan women and others, benefited from this merging of two skills. The faces emerging from the developer fluid in my darkroom influenced how I edited our conversations, and vice versa. In all sorts of ways, from simple professional growth through the march of history and because of my own artistic practices, I simply became better at what I was doing.

In your memoir, To Change the World, *you talk about the ambivalence you felt about continuing discrimination against women when you lived in Cuba in the 1970s. How did you handle this, especially when—as you write in that memoir—"feminism redirected me"? How did this awareness shape your political work at the time?*

I went to live in Cuba in the late summer of 1969, fresh out of several months in hiding as a result of paramilitary repression because of my involvement in the Mexican student movement of the year before. Fearing for their safety, I had been forced to send my four children on ahead. I was seriously ill—I had to have a kidney removed shortly after my arrival—so I was both physically and emotionally vulnerable. This, along with the fact that my incipient feminism wasn't yet solidly grounded historically and culturally, made me expect too much from a revolution just ending its first decade and seriously threatened by the United States. My discovery of feminism *had* redirected me, professionally as well as in my personal life. So, when I encountered contradictions between the revolution's stated aims and residual attitudes, it surprised, sometimes even shocked me. But I believed in the revolution and thought that, once consolidated, these other issues would be addressed. We are talking about half a century ago, and I should also say that back then I too considered the class contradiction to be the more important.

I remember a scene in a toy store where I was helping each of my three older children pick out their one big and two smaller toys before International Children's Day in January of 1970. My daughter Ximena, then five, wanted a cowboy outfit, and became irate when she saw that the girl's version didn't include the gun or lasso included in the boy's. Ximena sat down on the floor of that store and threatened to throw a tantrum. I gave a "feminist speech" trying to convince the saleswoman to alter the toy's contents. She finally consented, probably more out of an effort to appease the foreigner than because my argument had convinced her. I had to learn the hard way that Cubans had other priorities in those days: consolidating the revolution, defense, jobs, food, and housing. Women saw issues such as equal pay for equal work and childcare as the main achievements that would bring them equality. I was considered irrationally feminist by many. I remember writing an article addressing women's double shift; I suggested housecleaning brigades that might lighten their task. Cubans were indignant at the thought of outsiders invading the privacy of their homes!

I've written in several places about being asked, in 1970, to help judge Cuba's annual Carnival Queen contest. The person who asked me was Haydée Santamaría, revolutionary heroine, president of the country's preeminent arts institution, and someone I deeply admired. I was horrified but didn't feel I could say no. I judged the contest but wrote an article about how beauty contests have no place in a revolutionary society, and my article appeared the next day on the front page of the most important newspaper. Several years later I was able to ask Haydée why she had asked me, someone she knew was a feminist, to participate on that jury. She replied that she chose me precisely because she knew it would make me uncomfortable, and that I would find a way to help rid the country of the sexist tradition. It was only then that I realized those contests had ceased to exist.

I think it was a few years later that the government issued a list of jobs considered inappropriate for women because they would presumably harm our reproductive systems. It was quite a long list. I struggled with that one and spoke out against it. My opinion was considered "too feminist." They did shorten the list, but I don't believe it was ever eliminated. Despite decades in which women have fought alongside men on internationalist missions and done a great deal of heavy lifting at home, the revolution has maintained an analysis of the woman's role that is very much rooted in biological determinism.

In the early 1970s, you published the edited collection of feminist writings in Spanish translation and your first collection of interviews with Cuban women. What motivated you to focus your attention on questions of women and gender, and how did your colleagues and friends respond to what you wrote about women in revolutionary Cuba?

Las mujeres came out in Mexico in 1970 and the Cuban edition of *Cuban Women Now* was published in 1972, although its English edition didn't appear until 1974. I worked on the first book while I still lived in Mexico. I had begun reading texts from the women's liberation movement surging in the United States at the end of the 1960s, and my world changed. Perhaps because I lacked the disciplinary direction university studies might have provided, my personal and professional lives tended to move as one: when I became passionate about a subject, that subject claimed my professional attention as well as influencing how I was living my life. It was personally illuminating to realize that the problems in my relationships with men hadn't necessarily been "my fault" but had social roots. At the same time, I wanted to know how other women dealt with misogyny and sexism, and it seemed logical to me to ask them. Being in Cuba also made me curious as to whether or not a socialist revolution really brought equality for women. So shortly after my arrival, I decided to interview women about their lives. I had no training in ethnography, simply charged ahead with the passion and discipline that has always characterized my work. That was the project that became *Cuban Women Now*, the first of more than a dozen books of oral history, most with women.

It's important to remember that because I left the US in 1961, I hadn't really been part of the women's movement in my country of origin. I was an outsider in some ways, an insider in others; perhaps this is what allowed me to become a bridge. My colleagues and friends at the time weren't necessarily feminists; most were artists or others involved in trying to bring about social change, revolutionaries and leftists of various stripes. So, I think most responded gratefully to my transmitting the stories of Cuban women. There was very little available in the United States back then about what was really happening on that island so close to our shores but so distant ideologically. It wasn't until a bit later that some of the important feminist theoreticians—Maxine Molyneux, Isabel Larguía, etc.—began to question the ways in which a gender analysis was largely absent from Cuban revolutionary discourse.

Cuban film, poetry, and other artistic production has offered other ways for us to understand how gender and sexuality changed after the revolution. Based on your long experience with Cuban and other revolutions, do you believe that there are some things that even a radical social revolution cannot change?

My idea of what constitutes a radical social revolution has changed. My own experiences—in Mexico, Cuba, Vietnam, Peru, and Nicaragua—and my connections to other revolutionary projects throughout the 1970s and 1980s have taught me that unless a revolution considers and changes a society's power dynamics, long-term change is impossible. Profound and lasting change can't be made by a political party acting on behalf of the population. And unless all social sectors feel truly represented, it isn't likely they will defend the revolution in hard times. Forms must be developed so that all sectors can orchestrate the changes they need. The Leninist model failed, although I don't yet see a successful alternative (the Zapatistas in southern Mexico notwithstanding). Power itself—who wields it, how it is wielded, and to what ends—is key. And feminist theory gives us the best tools I know of to analyze power. This is why I have stopped thinking of feminism simply as necessary for women. It is necessary to changing society overall. Nowhere is that more obvious than right here in the United States today.

As for Cuban film, poetry, and other artistic production, these are all very powerful, both as reflections of the status quo and as agents for change within the Cuban Revolution. Cuban theater groups have a long history of showcasing social problems; Teatro Escambray and other groups are brilliant examples. Cuban cartoonists have been incisive in their social critique. The New Song Movement (Silvio Rodríguez, Pablo Milanés, Sara González, and others) pinpointed important social issues in their lyrics, and successive generations of singer-songwriters have continued the tradition—including today's exponents of rap and hip hop. Some of these are all-women groups and specifically target sexist attitudes. Poetry and other literary manifestations provide the arena in which social issues are exposed, a task that in other countries might be taken on by the press (which is notoriously one-sided on the island). Poets were those who first came out publicly against the repressive period known as *El quinquenio gris*, demanding public forums and open discussion to safeguard against such repression repeating itself in the future. As a scholar of Cuban culture and recent translator of a great deal of Cuban poetry, I have examined the immense role that art has in shaping the Cuban consciousness; it continues to surprise and impress. And, unlike the elitism that surrounds art and culture in many countries, in Cuba these are national pastimes. The 1961 literacy campaign gave almost all Cubans access to literature. The cost of books is subsidized and so they are extremely easy for people to buy. Entrance to most cultural events is free. It's also true that Cubans freely and loudly express diverse opinions about anything and everything. Even with Cuba's considerable restrictions on the internet, people there have found ingenious ways to share access to social media.

In your 2009 memoir, you reflect on your early defense of the revolution from the critical gaze of certain European and North American feminists, writing that you had become "blindly defensive of poor little David" (104). How do you now see revolutionary leaders and institutions, gender and family policy, and the treatment of women and sexual minorities?

My thought process in this respect has followed a broad arc, mostly related to personal experience. I had never lived in a socialist country before Cuba. I was awed by a society that seemed to be working for real equality, that was spending its resources on health and education. I was also influenced by the great social benefits my family and I enjoyed. The Cuban Revolution had rescued my four children from a situation that could easily have claimed their lives. And it cared for them with generosity and sensitivity until I could get to the island. Thousands of children whose parents were involved in revolutionary struggle at the time were in Cuba in similar circumstances. And there was more: free healthcare, including preventative care; living quarters assigned to us by the number of people in our family, not by how much rent we could afford; free daycare for my youngest and free education for my older children; and a job in line with my skills and interests. And there were less tangible things: the extraordinary feeling one gets from participating in a society intent on creating equality—however imperfect that equality may seem in retrospect, or whatever social groups may have been devalued at the time. It would be difficult to overemphasize the differences I experienced in comparison with my years in the US or Mexico. A single example is illustrative. In Mexico my daughter Ximena needed an ear operation to save her life. It was prohibitive, and when the repression hit we were still saving for it. In Cuba, soon after our arrival, she received that operation without cost.

Having said all this, my years in Cuba and since have taught me that profound social change is only wrought by changing the power dynamics. When a small group of (mostly) men govern a country, they are unlikely to admit the need to look at how power is being exercised. The Latin American revolutionary experiences of the past century were all led by powerful men who, to varying degrees, became authoritarian figures who held on to power far too long. In Cuba there were a number of women in the inner circle, some of them exceptional. Haydée Santamaría was an innate feminist long before that word was used. Yet a male-dominated political party held unquestioned power. My generation does have examples of great male leaders, such as Ho Chi Minh and Nelson Mandela, whose modesty and disinterest in personal power helped them avoid the patriarchal stance. They have been the exception to the rule.

The FMC [Federación de Mujeres Cubanas/Federation of Cuban Women] was a huge mass organization, at one point representing 80 percent of all Cuban girls and women over the age of fourteen. Its stated goal was to mobilize women in support of the revolution and to bring women's needs to the attention of the revolutionary leadership. It was always more successful at the former than the latter. Thus, gender issues and also race were present in the discourse; but when power was threatened, the unity required to confront US aggression was used as an excuse for postponing real change.

Recognition of the rights of sexual minorities wasn't on the official radar when I lived in Cuba. On the contrary, moments of extreme denigration and repression came and went. Early on there were the infamous UMAP [Unidades Militares de Ayuda a la Producción/Military Units to Aid Production] camps, where homosexuals and others deemed "different" were sent for "reeducation." The "New Man" was still a macho man, and a warped idea of masculinity ruled. Then there was the 1971 Education and Culture Conference, at which homosexuals were judged unfit to be teachers. The quinquenio gris in general targeted gay men and lesbians. During my last years in Cuba I argued against these attitudes and policies. Since then, however, respect for the LGBTQ community has improved considerably. Cuba's National Center for Sex Education (CENESEX), founded in 1989 and headed by Mariela Castro, Raúl Castro's daughter, has centralized efforts to organize and educate around sexual difference. At the moment, Cuba's National Assembly is considering a major overhaul of the country's constitution, and CENESEX and others are pushing hard for marriage equality.[6] It is much more comfortable to be openly gay in Cuba today than when I lived there. I see positive changes each time I visit. There is also still a long way to go.

At the same time, I think it's important to point out that Cuba is traveling its own journey to full equality for LGBTQ people, and that journey is different from the one we are traveling in the US. There are ways in which the country lags behind and others in which it has outpaced us. One example of this different journey can be seen in Cuba's response to the AIDS crisis in the 1980s, which Cuba dealt with as a health crisis. Cuba established a community outside Havana where those who were HIV positive were required to live for a time, with their families if they chose, until they learned how to handle the disease. Outsiders protested, but when a group of gay visitors from San Francisco was taken to the community they found the inhabitants wanted to live there. In another example, sex reassignment surgery is carried out free of cost under the country's universal healthcare program. And marriage equality, while important, doesn't carry the same weight as it does here, because in Cuba the taxation, inheritance, adoption, and other laws affecting people's lives are more egalitarian.

I believe that until power is understood as a political category, and exercised differently, long-term social change is impossible. This means every social group must be seen, listened to, taken into account: Women. Those of all races and ethnicities. Every sexual identity. The differently abled. Young people and children. People of different ideologies. Believers and nonbelievers. Pacifists and others who understand that wars only provoke more wars. Cuba is making progress toward this goal. As for criticizing that which one believes is wrong, it is always important to speak truth to power, respectfully and taking into consideration that one is speaking as an outsider. But I honestly do not think any big leaps will be made until the generation that won the war dies off and younger generations have some years of leadership experience. Today Cuba is rapidly opening to the world. Despite Trump's reversal of Obama's initiatives, massive tourism and travel promote a broad range of ideas about governance and civic responsibility as well as bringing positive and negative influences to the country. Cubans living in the diaspora and Cubans living on the island relate to one another and the influences run in both directions. Pundits outside Cuba like to talk about how these influences are affecting Cuban society, and of course they are. But they often forget that Cubans, after sixty years of revolution, have also changed; and that they possess expectations and attitudes central to the way they see themselves and society.

What is it about the revolutionary project—especially the Latin American experiments so deeply shaped by the Cuban example—that has facilitated or obstructed projects for gender equality and sexuality rights? What discourses, spaces, and policies of the revolution did Cuban women, LGBTQ individuals, and Afro-Cubans use to challenge what they saw as the limits to their full participation in Cuban society?

I believe that the main thing about modern-day Latin American revolutionary projects—all of them inspired and deeply marked by the Cuban Revolution—that has obstructed projects for gender equality and sexuality rights has been a (mis)reading of Marx that assumes that working-class unity trumps all other considerations: women's rights, the combating of racism and other social biases, and certainly the rights of the LGBTQ community. In the face of covert and overt attack by outside forces, unity is certainly important. But it has clearly been used as an excuse by those in power to prevent challenges to that power. What has facilitated projects for gender equality and sexuality rights in all these experiments is obvious: all have included efforts aimed at giving all sectors of society equal opportunities in education, work, healthcare, and so forth. Those important gains, especially in situations of ongoing vulnerability to invasion and military and economic coercion, made it easy to sidestep deeper discussion but also opened up diverse spaces for struggle. In Cuba I remember visiting a nightclub in one of the provinces; it was run by a gay man but open to gay and straight citizens alike. The idea was that if homosexuals and heterosexuals drank and danced together they would get to know one another and barriers would break down. The place was immensely successful in promoting understanding of and respect for gay life among the general population, and soon similar places opened in other cities. Some Latin American revolutionary organizations, such as the Chilean MIR [Movimiento de Izquierda Revolucionaria/Revolutionary Left Movement], the Tupamaros in Uruguay, the early Sandinistas, and the Zapatistas in southern Mexico, went further than others in contemplating women's rights. But these efforts either faded because a male leadership dominated or because the movement itself was defeated.

As for the spaces that Cuban women, Afro-Cubans, and the LGBTQ community are using to challenge the limits on their full social participation, they are many and innovative, ranging from public protest to artistic critique. For those who may not know about it, I want to mention MAGIN, a group of women communicators (journalists, filmmakers, librarians, and anyone whose job entailed communicating with the public). These women got together in the early 1990s, developed a gender analysis of Cuban society, and began holding workshops for women and men. Their work was powerful. I was taking groups of US women to Cuba at the time, and we always spent an evening at the home of one of the MAGIN women, where we took part in rich discussions of gender on the island. Although the MAGIN women tried to interest the FMC in their work, the latter organization couldn't bear what it considered competition. It pressured the Cuban Communist Party to prevent MAGIN from continuing. Some of the women emigrated, but most remained in Cuba where they continue to exert their influence in other ways.

You have returned many times to Cuba since 1980, speaking about your creative and scholarly work, presenting works of translation, and leading delegations of US women and others, all the while collecting new stories about Cuban experiences, especially those of women. How, in your experience, has the revolution continued to shape attitudes and beliefs about women, gender, and sexuality in Cuba over the last three decades?

As you say, I have returned to Cuba often, especially in recent years. In 2018, I was there twice, and I went again in March 2019. I feel a deep connection to the country, its revolution, and to my many friends there. Over the past several years I have written a number of books about Cuba or a particular Cuban, including a large bilingual anthology of eight decades of Cuban poetry and an in-depth study of Cuban internationalism. So, I am also involved in ongoing research. I try to avoid presenting any "snapshot" I get of the country at a specific moment as either "the way things are" or "the way things are going." It's impossible not to observe directions, tendencies. But knowing Cuba as I do, I understand these can shift and change depending on multiple variables. I believe many on the Left as well as the Right, especially those who spend a few weeks or months in Cuba, judge what they see out of context and without sufficient knowledge of Cuban history, culture, and idiosyncrasy. They have frozen a moment in time, the moment they have experienced, and read too much into that moment.

Over the last three decades, progress in terms of women's power-sharing as well as attitudes about gender and sexuality in Cuba have all been frustratingly slow. The revolution's very real struggle to stay afloat—in the face of one economic crisis after another, the dissolution of the socialist bloc, continued hostility from the United States, and the double-edged "solution" which is tourism—has inevitably kept issues such as gender, race, and sexuality on the back burner. I don't think the revolution itself has wanted to promote a conversation about these issues, because that would require a conversation about power. The generation that waged the war and made the revolution still holds power. And until that generation gives way to younger, more adventurous minds, profound change in these areas is going to be difficult. This change has begun, but just barely. The radically egalitarian ideals that brought equal education, equal pay for equal work, and childcare, the improvement in women's lives enshrined in the work of the FMC, the Family Code of 1974, the honoring of heroines who continue to be held up as examples: all this is evident in Cuba. But new ideas about power are not yet on the agenda. Over the past decade, Cuba has also opened to a daily exchange of influences with the outside world, via foreign investment, vastly increased travel, and the internet. Current constitutional debates augur a few changes, but nothing really radical; from what I can see, they will mostly involve incorporating into the laws of the land changes that have already taken place in practice. Yet, having said all this, I am still optimistic. Revolution is not simply a set of decrees, more egalitarian access to education and jobs. Revolution is an idea, the idea that justice is desirable and possible. The legacy of the revolution lives in people in ways that are often difficult to access by the usual social science indicators. We are talking about a people who stood up to the greatest power on earth, a power that is only ninety miles from its shores, fought a war of liberation and won. And not only won but sustained itself—for better or for worse—for six decades. Cubans, and Cuban women in particular, have shown themselves to be extraordinarily brilliant, creative, and resilient. Every time I visit I am surprised.

Elizabeth Quay Hutchison is professor of history and director of the Feminist Research Institute at the University of New Mexico. She is the author of *Labors Appropriate to Their Sex: Gender, Labor, and Politics in Urban Chile, 1900–1930* (2001) and lead editor of *The Chile Reader: History, Culture, Politics* (2015). Her current manuscript, "Workers Like All the Rest of Them," is a study of domestic service relations, legislation, and politics in twentieth-century Chile.

Margaret Randall is a poet, essayist, oral historian, translator, photographer, and social activist. She lived in Latin America for twenty-three years (Mexico, Cuba, and Nicaragua). Randall received the 2017 *Medalla al Mérito Literario* from *Literatura en el Bravo*, Ciudad Juárez, Mexico. A collection of her poems, *Time's Language: Selected Poems (1959–2018)*, was published in 2018. In 2019 she was awarded the "Poet of Two Hemispheres" prize in Quito, Ecuador, Cuba's prestigious Haydée Santamaría medal, and an honorary doctorate in letters from the University of New Mexico. A memoir, *I Never Left Home: Poet, Feminist, Revolutionary*, is forthcoming in spring 2020.

Notes

1. Randall's corpus also includes more than a hundred works of poetry, prose, photography, translation, and anthology. Major retrospectives include Hedeen and Rodríguez Núñez, *Time's Language*; and Randall, *Photographs by Margaret Randall*. Details of Randall's collections can be viewed in finding aids at rmoa.unm.edu/docviewer.php ?docId=nmu1mss663bc.xml and rmoa.unm.edu/docviewer.php?docId=nmu1pict000-663 .xml.
2. Randall, *Cuban Women Now*.
3. Randall, *Women in Cuba* and *Gathering Rage*.
4. Randall, *Inside the Nicaraguan Revolution*, *Sandino's Daughters*, *Christians in the Nicaraguan Revolution*, and *Sandino's Daughters Revisited*.
5. Randall, *Haydeé Santamaría* and *Exporting Revolution*.
6. The new constitution, passed into law in April 2019 subsequent to this interview, did not include marriage equality.

References

Hedeen, Katherine M., and Víctor Rodríguez Núñez, eds. *Time's Language: Selected Poems (1959–2018)*. San Antonio, TX: Wings Press, 2018.

Randall, Margaret. *Christians in the Nicaraguan Revolution*. Vancouver, BC: New Star Books, 1983.

Randall, Margaret. *Cuban Women Now*. Toronto: The Women's Press, 1974.

Randall, Margaret. *Exporting Revolution: Cuba's Global Solidarity*. Durham, NC: Duke University Press, 2017.

Randall, Margaret. *Gathering Rage: The Failure of Twentieth Century Revolutions to Develop a Feminist Agenda*. New York: Monthly Review Press, 1992.

Randall, Margaret. *Haydeé Santamaría, a Cuban Revolutionary: She Led by Transgression*. Durham, NC: Duke University Press, 2015.

Randall, Margaret. *Inside the Nicaraguan Revolution: The Story of Doris Tijerino*. Vancouver, BC: New Star Books, 1978.

Randall, Margaret. *Photographs by Margaret Randall: Image and Content in Differing Cultural Contexts*. Scranton, PA: Everhart Museum, 1988.

Randall, Margaret. *Sandino's Daughters*. Vancouver, BC: New Star Books, 1981.

Randall, Margaret. *Sandino's Daughters Revisited*. New Brunswick, NJ: Rutgers University Press, 1994.

Randall, Margaret. *Women in Cuba: Twenty Years Later*. New York: Smyrna Press, 1980.

"Children of the Revolution"

Generation Gaps in Socialist
and Latin American Cuba: An Interview
with Gregory Randall

Isabella Cosse

Gregory Randall heads an image processing group that includes researchers in France, Spain, and the United States, and he also teaches in the electrical engineering undergraduate program at Universidad de la República in Uruguay. He is also active in university government. Only his intonation reveals he is not a native of Montevideo, the city he considers his home, where he chose to live, work, and raise his children.

Born in New York in 1960, Randall has led a transnational life. His mother, Margaret Randall, was a young writer in the bohemian scene when she decided to become a single mother. From her relationship with the poet Joel Oppenheimer she had Randall, and shortly after, at the height of the Cold War, she took her infant son to Mexico in search of new horizons. Randall spent his early childhood in a comfortable and lively home filled with cultural stimulation. During those years the family expanded, first with Sarah and Ximena, the two daughters Margaret had with the poet Sergio Mondragón, and then with Ana, from Margaret's relationship with Robert Cohen, a young American poet. Life changed dramatically for them after the Tlatelolco student massacre (Mexico, 1968), as repression came knocking on the

Radical History Review
Issue 136 (January 2020)   DOI 10.1215/01636545-7857368
© 2020 by MARHO: The Radical Historians' Organization, Inc.

family's door. Margaret and Robert were persecuted and forced to leave Mexico. They decided to settle in Cuba in 1970, sending the children ahead of them in 1969.

Randall lived in Cuba until the 1980s, when he joined Chile's Revolutionary Left Movement (MIR) and moved to France. There he engaged in political actions to further Chilean resistance efforts and continued his studies at the graduate level. He seldom spoke of his political activism or his life in Cuba until his teenage son convinced him that he needed to tell his story. He invited his mother to write a memoir with him, but they later decided to write separate books. Randall tapped into his family's narrative and confronted his own memories. The result was the book *To Have Been There.*[1] The title reflects the Cuban Revolution's role as epicenter of an era defined by the cultural and political upheaval of the "long 1960s." The book was recently released in Cuba by the publishing house Aldabón.

Randall provides a unique perspective on Cuba, shaped in part by his displaced position in that historical process. Unmoored from national frameworks, his subjectivity is anchored in his social sensitivity. He was part of a generation of children of the revolution. This interview explores that experience.

Isabella Cosse: *What do you remember of the UNAM* [*Universidad Nacional de México*] *student occupation in 1968?*

Gregory Randall: I was seven. I know because it was right before Cuba. My memories are fragmented. I remember that everything was in a state of flux. For me, personally, that included what was going on at home. My father [Sergio Mondragón] had moved out. He lived nearby, but he and my mother had separated. That's the image I retain. When the university student movement erupted, around July [1968], many in their circle got involved because they were intellectuals. My friends' parents all took part in some way. If students took over the university, these artists supported them by writing an open letter or speaking at the university. And naturally we, as their kids, would be there too. I don't remember the poetry readings, but I remember us playing hide-and-seek in the UNAM garden.

Do you have any memories of the repression?

My mother didn't go to the Plaza de las Tres Culturas protest [in the district of Tlatelolco, which was brutally repressed by the government and resulted in hundreds of students killed]. Their group argued over going, with some considering it too dangerous. They knew something was going to happen, so they decided not to go. A friend of my mother's, who was much younger than her, was there. He ended up under a pile of corpses. He got away after night fell and came to our house, where he hid for three days.

Did you know what he had gone through?

We all knew. The day after the repression my mother took us to the plaza and we could see shoes strewn everywhere. We saw them from afar because it was danger-ous. My mother was like that, wanting to see for herself. I remember that same guy took me to the Olympics two weeks later. When you look back, it seems crazy, but that's how things were. I never saw that guy again, but going with him to the Olym-pics was very important to me at the time.

In your book you write about going on a trip with some Canadian hippies who vis-ited your house. Tell me about that.

That was much later. Tlatelolco happened on October 2 [1968]. I think the magazine [*El Corno Emplumado*] stopped coming out around that time. We left for Cuba on July 25, 1969. So there were almost ten months between Tlatelolco and Cuba. We were in hiding for a month before we left. Bob and Alice had been at my house about three weeks when I went on that trip with them. They came into my life in May and we started out in June. I returned a week later, when the police arrested us. That's when it began [the persecution that would lead to exile in Cuba]. That's more or less the timeline. Things were moving very quickly; it was only five months, but it felt like a lifetime. My sister had been born in March. And now that I think of it, considering the nine months of my mom's pregnancy, Robert [Cohen] was already in our lives when Tlatelolco happened. But I don't know why I can't place him then.

What did those months mean to you?

For me and my family there's a before and after Tlatelolco. To a great extent it marked my entire future, to this day. You can say that about anything. But it was because of Tlatelolco that we left for Cuba; because of it I met my wife [Laura Carlevaro, with whom he is still married]. Everything has to do with that. Sometimes, when I think back to that moment, I see a parallelism—with the obvious differences—between the impact that Tlatelolco had on so many people's lives and how the Spanish Civil War influenced the international labor movement. Although both were failed expe-riences, they were great generators of energy and ideas. They mobilized people who went on to mark many generations; they traced the way forward.

How did you end up traveling with Alice and Bob? How were you arrested?

They were traveling across Latin America. I asked my mom if I could join them part of the way and, as usual, she said yes. I wanted to go as far as Panama. My mother agreed to let me go to the Guatemalan border. I was really excited. I had been on the road with them for five days when the hippie commune where we were staying was surrounded by the police. We were immediately taken away in a bus with the win-dows covered, so nobody would see us. We were taken to a police station in Mexico

City where I was held for thirty-six hours. I was the only kid there. Bob and Alice spoke no Spanish and I didn't speak English because my mom had stopped talking to me in English when Sergio moved in with us. I tried to explain to the police that they were friends and not my parents, and asked them to let me call my mother. They eventually put us in a car to the airport. On the way there they stopped at my house. A policewoman got out and knocked on the door. She handed me over to my mother and told her to cut my hair.

How did you feel through all that? What do you think now of your mom giving you permission to go on that trip?

I can still clearly remember those thirty-six hours. When I got home I ran into my room and burst out crying. The next day, Robert took me to get a haircut. What my mother did then, letting me go alone with those hippies, would be unheard of today. But things were different back then. My mother was a bit more extreme in that sense, more than the average person, but she wasn't unique. I don't remember any other kid going on a trip like that, but I'm sure I wasn't the only one. I think many parents in my mother's generation believed in giving their children freedom and letting them think for themselves. If you're fighting for equality in society, you have to fight for equality in the family. That was the idea. Afterward they processed it more theoretically—"the personal as political"—but back then they really tried to live by that, with all the limitations you can imagine. That attempt at equal treatment—which was never such anyway—was important. Free love, for example. In those days, everyone in my house might each be with their other partner. They saw that as being true to their revolutionary ideas.

We can come back to that in a moment. First, I want to ask you about leaving Mexico for Cuba.

It wasn't easy for my mother to leave Mexico without papers. She couldn't leave with us. She finally decided to send us to Cuba, where we would be cared for until they joined us. I was eight and my sisters were all younger than me (Ana was only four months old), so I was in charge. Cuba started out very traumatically, then, although at the time I didn't experience it like that. I experienced it with joy, and fear also. I feared I would not see them again. But at the same time it was an adventure and I had a leading role. . . . The Cubans were great, welcoming us with open arms. They sent us to a summer camp. All of us except Ana, who was a baby and had stomach flu, so the assistant director of the clinic where we had a check-up offered to care for her at home until my mother arrived. We spent the whole summer at the camp and it was spectacular. We were very privileged. We lived with hundreds of refugee kids from other countries. Some had lost their parents; others were missing an arm or a leg. Compared to them, we were much better off. Two and a half months later, our parents arrived. Robert came first and a week later my mother. We were overjoyed.

What changes were there in the family?

Everyday life changed enormously. Mondays through Fridays we were all (except Ana) at boarding school—what they called the "scholarship" system—and on Friday nights we went home. The aim of these scholarships was to shape the "New Man," considered essential for the future of the revolution. Many Cuban kids were on these scholarships, especially kids from the poorest families. I always felt that the Cuban Revolution was especially devoted to children. The slogan "Children are born to be happy" says it all. The scholarships also suited the parents because while the state looked after their children they were free to "make love and Revolution." The Cubans later examined this practice critically and realized that separating ten-year-olds from their families for such long periods was harsh on the children. So they revised the scholarship system and applied it to secondary schools.

Coming as they did from bohemian experiences and with a countercultural take on personal relationships, what were your mother and Robert like in terms of your education?

Some Cuban friends criticized the way my parents raised us. Unlike other parents, my mother never went to see me on Wednesdays at boarding school. Almost all the other parents visited their kids on that day, bringing them cake and things. My mother and Robert gave no importance to such things. At the same time, I felt really close to them and the weekends were very intense and happy times. Ours was a very cultural house and I was given a lot of freedom. I always felt I had a great relationship with my mother and fathers. Since I was away at school, I wasn't very aware of what everyday life was like at home. There were some pretty strange moments. For example, the time a very tall African American man, who was my mother's lover, came to live at our house, with Robert still living there. At the time, I didn't notice it. To me he was just a *compañero* living in our house. I had no idea. But my sister Ana, who lived at home, realized what was happening. Years later, at a family reunion, she said to me, "You didn't know about that?" It wasn't easy for her. I also knew that a neighbor who lived in our building was my father's lover. At that time in their lives, they obviously had that option. But not much later they split up, so maybe it wasn't really an option. They obviously couldn't take it. That went on for a few years, though, and I didn't see it. I didn't think it was strange that they had other relationships.

And what happened among boys and girls your age?

There was a mixture of free love with strong elements of a macho culture. In my sexual awakening—no doubt influenced by Cuban society—I believed that as a young man it was up to me to take the initiative. It was unheard of for a young girl to do it. It had to be me. That was a huge problem for me, because I didn't know how

to act. On the one hand, at these schools there was a formal level, where the scholarship meant the school had a responsibility to watch over us and make sure girls
didn't lose their virginity. If that happened to a girl, her father would raise hell,
because his daughter had been in the school's care. But, at the same time, among
us kids, when it came to sexuality, it was anything goes. And everyone knew it.

What do you remember from that experience?

At different moments during my scholarship days, I encountered various attitudes
from my teachers in that sense. I remember there was a very repressive atmosphere
at times. They did everything they could to stop us from having sex. I was once punished because I was caught holding my girlfriend's hand in the hallway and then
kissing her—and not even on the lips. That was probably at the Lenin School.
Later, at another school, Río Seco II, where there were sixty of us in one bedroom,
I woke up one night to find two students having sex in the bed next to mine. The
principal there was smart enough to realize it was something they couldn't stop, so
he gathered all five hundred of us in the amphitheater and brought in a nurse to
instruct us on the use of condoms. That was 1976. So you can see that those two
attitudes coexisted. One more influenced by Catholic morality, and the more open
attitude of free love. But because the scholarship was a major part of life, with us
living daily at coed school, it was almost impossible to control.

Were these always consensual relations? Was this something you talked about?

During the discussion of the Family Code adopted around that time, it was widely
accepted that raping a girl under sixteen (the legal age in Cuba then) could be pun-
ishable by the death penalty. I don't remember personally knowing any teachers
who were openly involved with students. I do remember many cases of boys with
crushes on teachers. Our teachers were young girls not much older than us. When I
was fourteen I had a teacher who was sixteen. So crushes were inevitable. I think the
teachers restrained themselves out of that almost religious morality [of the revolu-
tion], which dictated a self-imposed discipline that called on them to avoid "bourgeois deviations," like Che [Guevara]. Later, at the Lenin School, I heard about a
thirty-year-old teacher—the assistant principal, I think—who disappeared from
the school one day and it was rumored that he was in jail for having intimate relations
with female students. I don't know. They were probably consensual. But everyone
agreed that he had been rightly jailed.

How did you experience that time of discovery?

The first time I was in bed naked with a woman it was with a very beautiful girl. I fell
in love with her and we started going out. I must have been around sixteen. Her
father had fought alongside Che and had been killed in Bolivia. We went to my

room—I had my own room, so we had privacy—took off our clothes, and got in bed together. It was obvious she wanted to make love. I had never done it before and I didn't have the nerve. Mostly I was afraid I'd get her pregnant. I don't know, maybe I was also afraid I wouldn't be able to perform. But things didn't go beyond kissing and petting, and she was really angry at me because of that. We were together for two months. It eventually split us up. She expected us to have sex, and I was too afraid. She probably thought I was a coward. Looking back now, it seems significant. Another incident comes to mind, which happened earlier, in '75, when I was fifteen or sixteen. In the first trip of the BIJA [Brigada Internacional Juvenil de la Amistad] —a solidarity group formed by two friends from the Communist Youth—we were on a bus for fifteen hours and I was seated next to a girl. We ended up kissing, making out, like kids that age do. But after a while, when we were right in the middle of it, I realized I wasn't interested in her as a girlfriend. It was just a hookup. I felt really embarrassed. I was afraid she thought that meant we were a couple. So I told her I was sorry, but I didn't want her to expect anything more and that I felt I was taking advantage of her. She felt awful. We're still friends to this day, but at that moment she was clearly upset. That gives you an idea of how I was back then. I think it has to do with a sort of internal questioning of sex as a way of using the other. That didn't feel right to me. I didn't want to be in a relationship in which I was using the other, but at the same time I was using her.

How did you combine the New Man paradigm with your family's unconventional approach to relationships?

You have to be careful when you think about that. Views on gender issues have changed dramatically and very rapidly around the world over the past thirty years. My mother is now a lesbian, but back then the prevailing sentiment was naturally homophobic and none of us thought that was all that terrible. My mother was always a bit more tolerant in that sense, but just that, tolerant. When my mother told me she was a lesbian, which was in '85, I was living in France, and to a certain extent it came as a surprise. Right after she told me I thought, "Oh, ok, that makes sense." But it was a surprise. My mother had had many men in her life. And my fathers—Robert, in particular—he was a guy who had many women, a man women found desirable. That whole macho thing was quite naturalized.

Was that also something that happened in your family, which cultivated "free love"?

There too. The family could aspire to free love, but that doesn't take away from the fact that she was a woman and he was a man. Also, at the time, the Cuban Revolution was very homophobic. I think there is a misconception in that sense. People tend to think the Cuban Revolution was more homophobic than the rest of the world. I don't think it was. It was just as homophobic. The difference was that in Cuba there was an authoritarian power—a dictatorship of the proletariat, so to speak—and that left little room for diversity. It's also true that there were major figures in the Cuban Revolution who were homosexuals, such as Alfredo Guevara, a member of the Central Committee and head of the ICAIC [the Cuban Institute of Cinematographic Art and Industry], who was openly gay. Everyone knew he was gay. He went to the theater with his boyfriend. There was an anecdote involving Alfredo Guevara—almost a myth. Apparently he used to argue with Fidel [Castro] when they were students together in the university, and Guevara would win his arguments by shouting, "macho" style. So he was seen as a guy who could go up against the "horse" [as Castro was known] himself, a term that, incidentally, also has a sexual connotation. It's no wonder, then, that it was the ICAIC that defended Silvio Rodríguez and other young musicians when they were persecuted. It has to be said, also, that the Cuban Revolution did allow for certain spaces of freedom. People would say, "Look at Alfredo, he's a homosexual and he doesn't care; that takes some balls." That said, we need to remember that many people were sent to work camps because they were gay. The bureaucrats in charge would say, "This guy is sick and needs to be reeducated." And they suffered enormously.

So your family was not very different?

Exactly. I think we need to demystify that aspect. My family was not all that different from how other families were. For example, 80 percent of Cuban children were going to boarding schools, so they were living collectively five days a week. That reveals that, in that respect, the role of the nuclear family was less important for everyone. Families experienced a general process of transformation. Like I said, sexual activity in the boarding schools was wild. That was all part of the revolution. And not just in schools. Everyone was screwing around in general. We all knew that among our parents everyone was more or less sleeping with everyone else. We were different mostly because we were foreigners, because we could travel and were in contact with certain people and could access cultural assets. But the fact that my parents practiced free love didn't necessarily make them different. At least I didn't perceive it that way. Maybe in a sense it was, but I didn't feel the difference.

What was it like being a young foreigner in Cuba?

We were a bit in the middle. Cubans considered us foreigners—welcomed and esteemed foreigners—but it was always clear that we were foreigners. For example, the [food allocation] booklet foreigners received was a special booklet, and that was a way of saying, "Okay, these people are here in solidarity and we're not going to force them to make the same sacrifices we have to make." It was somewhat condescending. But my mother refused that special booklet and instead we got the standard one for Cubans. Unlike many people, we were given a house. We also had the privilege of being allowed to travel. But, at the same time, because we were foreigners, the logic of that time dictated that they couldn't let us into key places. We couldn't be party members or serve in the military (and you have to remember that there was always the possibility of aggression), although we could join any social organization. But we also had the freedom, the privilege, of discussing issues that were off limits in Cuba. For example, I was able to debate about Trotsky in my group in the Revolutionary Left Movement [MIR]. So, being a foreigner had its pros and cons.

How was your relationship with other Latin American youths?

There were many of us Latin Americans in Cuba and we loved Latin America. We were from many places, but came from a common magma. There was a certain similarity between the revolution that was happening here and there. To us we were all alike; we were friends and went to parties together. When the MIR had the great idea of telling a group of kids to organize, and we were invited to a meeting, it was like hearing the gods calling us. We were all there, not just Chileans, but Mexicans, Brazilians, Argentines. . . . They told us they were forming an MIR youth group and asked if we wanted to participate. It was what we were waiting for: our place in the Latin American revolution. Most of the groups [of the Latin American Left] did not try to harness that energy.

Throughout this interview you've referred to "us." Was there a generational "us"?

Yes, there was a generational "us." That is, there were three generations. The generation of those who had survived, who were around twenty-five. There was our generation, the twelve-year-olds. And then there were the small kids. We were in the middle. The year 1976 was the year of the war in Angola and 1979 was the year of the war in Nicaragua. For my generation, these were "our wars." We all wanted to go to either war and fight like our parents had, like Che had. As a foreigner, I wasn't allowed to receive military training from the Cubans; I couldn't go. I felt a little like I was crippled. It was very frustrating. At that initial moment, people wanted to go. There was a lot of pride. In my book I recall a conversation during my scholarship at Río Seco II [the rural school] that led to an argument about our leaders. There were twenty or thirty of us, and someone was saying "Che and Fidel had balls, they fought like men. Martí was an idiot. He was all talk and the first time he went into battle he got himself killed. We Cubans are machos and we are unbeatable in combat." That discussion evidenced a mixture of *machismo* and racism that was permeating the very ideology of the revolution. For example, they would refer to Africans as "backward, not much better than monkeys, with no sense of nationality, tribesmen." All these people spoke from within the revolution. It's appalling—and

I thought so then—but it happened among working-class people. The kids in that scholarship were students who had been left back. Later, in France, I learned about the human suffering, about the dark side of the war, the relatives who never received the remains of their dead. That was when I was in France. The worst I heard, while I was in Cuba, was about people who had left for two years and came back to find their wife had been with another man. There was something absurdly rigid about that. The leaders said, "If you're a member of the Party you have to be an example, and if you're an example you can't be cuckolded. Because you lose face with your comrades." As soon as the man stepped off the plane, he was told he had to choose between his wife and the party. It was very dramatic.

Your memoir is written from a place of commitment toward that revolutionary past, but at the same time you're very critical. The book was recently published in Cuba. How was it received?

It was released in 2017 by Aldabón. The editor suggested I cut out a bit from the section on Ochoa, to avoid problems. I thought it over a lot, but in the end I agreed. I wanted my memoir to be read in Cuba. When I went to present the book at the Book Fair, the Minister of Culture, Abel Prieto, was there. He's in favor of opening up Cuban culture, and after my talk (I also spoke about the capitalist restoration) he invited me to speak at an internal "cadre" [leader] school for youths. I discussed the book with seventy Cuban intellectuals, which was very interesting. I also presented the book in the school where I studied engineering [Ciudad Universitaria José Antonio Echeverría, CUJAE]. There were some thirty people there, half of whom had read the book. A third were in their sixties and another third were young people. There were some very good discussions, including about Ochoa and leadership. Seeing my memoir published in Cuba, and the reception it's having, is really satisfying for me.

Translated by Laura Pérez Carrara

Isabella Cosse is a researcher at the Consejo Nacional de Investigaciones Científicas y Técnicas (CONICET) and the Universidad de Buenos Aires. She is the author of multiple books, including *Pareja, sexualidad y familia en los años sesenta* (2010), *Estigmas de nacimiento: Peronismo y orden familiar* (2006), and *Mafalda: A Social and Political History of Latin America's Global Comic* (forthcoming). The Spanish version of *Mafalda* received LASA's Iberoamericano Book Award.

Gregory Randall has a PhD from Université Paris XI (Orsay) and is an engineering professor at Universidad de la República in Uruguay.

Notes

The book was first published in Spanish in 2010 by Ediciones Trilce (Montevideo) as *Estar allí entonces: Recuerdos de Cuba 1969–1983*. It was later translated into English by Margaret

Randall under the title *To Have Been There Then: Memoir of Childhood and Youth. Cuba: 1969–1983* (New York: Operating System Press, 2017). For references to Margaret Randall's works, see Elizabeth Hutchinson's interview in this issue.

References

Randall, Gregory. *To Have Been There Then: Memoir of Childhood and Youth. Cuba: 1969–1983*. New York: Operating System Press, 2017.

"A Cuba That Keeps Unsettling"

An Interview with Ailynn Torres Santana
and Diosnara Ortega González

Michelle Chase

Major oral history projects have not been common in revolutionary Cuba. And while there have been several landmark books of oral history—such as Oscar Lewis's four-volume series published in the late 1970s—these were often conducted by foreign, not Cuban, scholars. Furthermore, while oral history projects in Cuba have often included women's voices, they have less often conceptualized gender as a relation of power or been attentive to the nuances of gender inequalities.

For these reasons, the forthcoming book *Mujeres en revolución: Historias de vida de mujeres cubanas* (*Women in Revolution: Life Histories of Cuban Women*), by the young Cuban scholars Ailynn Torres Santana and Diosnara Ortega González, is exceptionally significant. As the authors describe in the interview below, their book explores the life histories of eight Cuban women, drawn from divergent social, racial, and regional backgrounds, both to understand their life experiences on their own terms and to reflect on the portrait of revolutionary Cuba that emerges from those stories. In this conversation they discuss the status of women's history and gender studies in the Cuban academy, the way they conceptualized their project, and the way the public history and memory of the Cuban Revolution have been constructed.

Torres Santana and Ortega González are part of a new generation of Cuban scholars committed to feminist studies, the study of gender relations, and the history

Radical History Review
Issue 136 (January 2020)   DOI 10.1215/01636545-7857380
© 2020 by MARHO: The Radical Historians' Organization, Inc.

and politics of Cuba and of Latin America. Like some other scholars of their generation, they have benefited from recent migratory reforms that facilitate direct enrollment in foreign graduate programs. As a result, although both are strongly rooted in the Cuban academy, they have studied and taught abroad, gaining a strong comparative perspective on Latin American history and politics. Torres Santana completed her PhD in social sciences and history at FLACSO-Ecuador in 2017. She has taught and been a visiting researcher at the Universidad de la Habana, the Universidad de Barcelona, the University of Massachusetts, and Harvard University. She was a researcher at the Instituto Cubano de Investigación Cultural Juan Marinello in Havana until 2019. Ortega González completed her PhD in sociology at the Universidad Alberto Hurtado (Chile) in 2019. She is currently director of the Escuela de Sociología at the Universidad Católica Silva Henríquez in Santiago, Chile, and director of the journal *Temas Sociológicos*.

Michelle Chase: *How did you first become interested in the themes of gender and women's history? How did the idea of the book come about?*

Ailynn Torres Santana and Diosnara Ortega González: It can be hard to identify an exact point when ideas come in or out of one's life. In our case, our interest in gender came about through the process of living as women. That is, by progressively gaining consciousness of what the "social mark" on and beyond the body implies. Our interest in the history of women gradually became feminist. We are not interested in women as a neutral social group vis-à-vis other groups. We are interested in observing, drawing attention to, and denouncing gender inequalities and their connection with other inequalities.

In one's personal life there are moments of rupture, moments that lead to gender consciousness. For each of us that moment has been different. Motherhood, marriage, meeting other women, and joining feminist collectives have revealed the conditions of our existence and have helped us in the process of intellectual and political formation. One doesn't reach feminist consciousness alone. There are always people, especially women, accompanying you. And it continues. It's a space of constant questioning.

A shared interest in social history and Cuban politics brought us together at first, many years ago. Later, in the intellectual, political, and human links between us, we began to formulate questions about why we Cuban women live the way we live, why the things that happen to us happen, and why we occupy the roles we occupy. We came to the conclusion that the totality of the political—in the Marxist sense of "totality"—cannot be understood without [understanding] the specificity of relations of gender, race, etc. And vice versa. This is [an intellectual] process that, once begun, never ends.

In the book's introduction you thank scholars Colette Harris and Elizabeth Dore. What influence did they have?

Elizabeth Dore has and continues to have a very special place in this journey. From her we began to understand that those who research, write, or speak about Cuba "from the outside and in English" do not necessarily know less about the history of the country and its people than those of us who live in the country. From Elizabeth we learned a professional and feminist ethic that shaped us. She taught us, among many things, to listen. In Cuba, that quality can sometimes be very rare. She became interested in our work and has been an ambassador of our goals, and we still don't know why. Through her we met Colette Harris, who is interested in supporting an intellectual project on Cuban women, thus fulfilling a wish that her aunt—Ruth Wallis—left upon her death. So there was a community of women.

We did the research and wrote the book while we were each doing doctorates on other topics. So this was, then, a project conceived among related projects, which were born together.

In the introduction of the book you give a global overview of the way the categories of gender and oral history developed in the United States, Europe, and Latin America. Can you briefly sketch out how the history of women, gender studies, and oral history developed in Cuba? Are courses offered in the university?

Within the history major [at the University of Havana] there is no program or specific course on oral history, although sometimes there are optional courses or conferences on it.

In revolutionary Cuba, the first research project to use oral history was conducted by Oscar Lewis [1968], who was invited by Fidel Castro. Just over a year later, the project was cancelled. Also in the 1960s, Eva Forest undertook a research project, which was posthumously published under the title *Los nuevos cubanos* (*La vida en una Granja del Pueblo*). It's an excellent text. Until the early 2000s no other big oral history project had taken place in Cuba. Then Elizabeth Dore began a new project—which should be published in the near future—called "Cuban Voices," that also faced setbacks along the way. Once published, it will be an extremely valuable work for Cuban studies.

There are other publications based on biographical studies, personal memoirs, or oral histories. For example, Margaret Randall with *La mujer cubana ahora* (*Cuban Women Now: Interviews with Cuban Women*); Daisy Rubiera Castillo with *Reyita: La vida de una mujer negra cubana en el siglo XX*; Eugenia Meyer, *El futuro es nuestro: Ocho cubanas narran sus historias de vida*; Yohanka Valdés Jiménez and Yuliet Cruz Martínez, *50 voces y rostros de líderes campesinas cubanas*; Ana Vera Estrada, *Guajiros del siglo XXI*; Marjorie Moore and Adrianne Hunter, *Siete mujeres y la revolución cubana*; Yuliet Cruz Martínez, *Chaparreras con luz propia*; and also the contributions of the Centro Cultural Pablo de la Torriente Brau, [which publishes books that] reconstruct our history through the use of oral history, among them the anthology *Piezas para armar nuestra memoria* [edited by Nora Franco].[1] Recently the book *Emergiendo del silencio: Mujeres negras en la historia de Cuba* was published, which is a compilation of works by Daisy Rubiera and Olida Hevia.[2] These are not life histories, nor are they undertaken with a strictly biographical method, but they contribute to the understanding of history through women's lives.

Our book forms part of this long-term effort and enriches it with a gender perspective that is rare. Writing about women is not the same as analyzing gender relations. The latter entails delving into inequalities sustained by the sex-gender division in a given society. That is one of the contributions of our work, which also has a general concern with social history and Cuban politics. With respect to the works mentioned above, our book is probably distinguished by contributing to a social historiography that centers the labor of memory from a feminist ethic.

In broad strokes, what do you think your interviews illuminate about the history of revolutionary Cuba?

The research and development of the book entailed a constant tension between individual lives and national processes.

On the one hand, we wanted to access the lives of women for their own value, not as a pretext to examine something "more"—more general or more important—but to [see them] as having their own value: the lives of concrete people, in micro-scale, are important in their specificity and not only for what they can reveal about general processes. As specific stories, they permit the analysis of dimensions and processes not accessible in other ways.

On the other hand, we wanted to "think Cuba": the country that produced these lives and that was produced by them. We were interested, also, in the absent Cuba: the Cuba that these women spoke less about, and which, for that reason, is present as an absence. For example, the Cuba that one remembers and continues to live even if one is no longer physically in the country (as in the case of those who emigrate), or the Cuba of "big politics" even for those whose lives revolve around "small politics."

The stories, and the whole book, demonstrate the tension between those two ideas. The women that appear there bear witness to their own individual realities and also to the history of a nation with its different stages, actors, dilemmas, projects, and paths.

The book also illuminates the tension between a Cuba narrated by others, a lived Cuba, and a hidden Cuba. These three Cubas hinge on the post-1959 process: the book shows how and why what happened after the triumph of the revolution is fragile, discontinuous, and diverse; and it shows how and why that process is some-times inactive and at other times reproduces gender inequalities and intragender inequalities. The book illuminates a diversity of Cubas, and belies any account of homogenization or unanimity. Still, what we are defending in the book is not a "per-spectivist" account; it is not about the perspectives of women. It is about complicat-ing the study of social processes in which women take part, as actors, as subjects, and also as voices that narrate.

The women in the book show us coordinates different from the "classic" ones considered by History with a capital H; they allow us to question daily life, analyze the relations between public and private, politicize amorous relationships, denatu-ralize unpaid labor, etc. They show us another way to tell and produce history, and help understand the relationship between these histories and official histories and mainstream histories of the Cuban Revolution. The book shows that official History—including subaltern male histories—are only pieces of the events and experiences that make Cuba what it is and what it has been.

How did you design the research? For example, how did you identify interviewees and subjects to discuss? What did you learn from the diversity of the interviews?

One of the premises of the research was that women are diverse. What one woman feels depends not only on her gender; she is also conditioned by racial identifications or experiences, by regional or generational identifications, etc. For that reason we decided to integrate different voices and stories—sometimes radically different. The women in the book were, then, selected deliberately. But the voices that you hear in the book are not of women as "types." They are entry points into diverse social groups, but they do not represent them or exhaust them. The book does not map out either Cuban society or Cuban women. It showcases the voices of diverse women, explores their social contexts, and gives us a historical look at Cuba.

In addition, we defined another element in the selection process: we wanted to include "public" women and "anonymous" women. We were concerned with thinking through "the personal is political," but how could we make that manifest in a historical investigation about a concrete country? We tried to respond to that question. For that reason we incisively explored the dimensions of daily life and experience and the politicization—or not—of that experience. We were interested in that as well as in their public presences. We delved into their political participa-tion as well as into their experiences of motherhood, into their public and private voices.

In the first chapter we offer some suggestions for how to read the book. We think they help clarify two things. On the one hand, intragender inequality: inequal-ities that are structured according to gender but also according to class, region, gen-eration, or racialized experiences. And that is very clear in the text. But, on the other hand, the stories in the book very consistently reveal the persistence of specific gender inequalities that are verified across very different women.

What place have women had in the memory or history promoted by the revolution or the Cuban state?

The history of the revolution has been narrated primarily by men, although men were not its only protagonists. Women's voices are rarer in the history constructed from social sciences and in those that appear in traditional "history places" (school textbooks, for example). That reflects men's dominance in academic research and in the institutionalization of the social sciences, and also the limited presence of feminist movements in the country. That does not mean that there is an absence of women historians. In fact, there are many very notable women historians. We are referring to the scarcity of analysis of the roles of women in history (especially in post-1959 history), which is something different.

In Cuba after 1959, the recognition of the presence of women has taken place, a great number of times, through men's voices. Saying so does not deny the growing feminine presence in educational spaces, in political institutions, or in science and technology, or the benefits that accrue to women in the universalization of rights. That is true. It is also true that there is a pattern of masculine power that sees authorizing women's agendas as part of its duties. We recall that Raúl Castro, in the closing ceremony of the last Federation of Cuban Women's Congress [March 2019], said, "The instructions of the Chief Commander [Fidel Castro] have been carried out." It would seem that this is the goal of the only officially recognized women's organization.

Describe the reception of this type of project in Cuban intellectual circles.

Projects in the field of oral history can be viewed with a kind of suspicion or reluctance, or attributed with a lack of rigor. But, as we say in the first chapter of the book, that is only one way—a positivist way—to assess historic research. Certainly, oral history and life stories have been fields of methodological debate, just as social, cultural, or political histories have been. But these criticisms have also generated responses and reevaluation; the debate has been processed. In the Cuban intellectual field it is still a marginal debate. With very few exceptions—among them the space offered by the Instituto Cubano de Investigación Cultural Juan Marinello—[oral history] does not have a lot of presence or reach.

We should remember that, ever since the experience of Oscar Lewis and his project about the life history of Cuban men and women in the difficult year of 1968, there has been a certain fear regarding what work with memory might reveal. Collective memory has a potent power of interpellation with respect to dominant history. It threatens the hegemony of the latter. This was the case with Lewis, as already mentioned, but also with Marel Gladys García's project about the process of insurrection in Matanzas province from 1952 to 1959. We mention these two examples but there are others.

Who do you think will be interested in these memories? What expectations do you have for the book?

This is a book with women's voices that speak to all of society. A book for people interested in social history and Cuban politics. Through women's life trajectories, we try to show Cuba as a whole. At the same time, it is a book for people interested in thinking through inequalities in general and gender inequalities in particular. In the academic field, we hope that the book supports research on memory in Cuba and stimulates gender studies. But we do not want the book to be destined for academic circles only. It is important for us to contribute to the formation of students and to the feminist debate in Cuba.

What intellectual intervention would you like to make with this book?

We took care to avoid "remaking" the stories narrated by women with our own analysis. It is a text where they, the protagonists, speak and . . . sometimes remain silent. It is a book to be heard. That may be the most difficult task: to train ourselves to hear other voices, rhythms, silences. That may be the challenge and mystery of the volume. That is, we are not offering one more version of the facts; we are offering a filter through which to see reality and history. We hope to contribute to a civic and political exercise that is very deteriorated in our political culture: to learn to move forward without binaries, without being guided by a single truth, but knowing that there are no futile relativisms but rather powers at play. We try not to appeal to exclusion as a recourse, nor to unity as a refuge. The book is provocative in that sense. It has been for us.

We hope to contribute to a social historiography that centers the labor of memory from a feminist ethic. We hope to contribute to understanding the relationship between social change and the persistence of inequalities. We hope to illuminate diversities and commonalities. We hope the women in the book, and others, will recognize themselves collectively as an exercise in the formation of political consciousness. But above all we strive to uncover a Cuba that sometimes surprises us, and that sometimes exhausts us with its repetition. A Cuba that nonetheless keeps unsettling.

Translated by Michelle Chase

Michelle Chase is assistant professor of history at Pace University. She is the author of *Revolution within the Revolution: Women and Gender Politics in Cuba, 1952–1962* (2015). Her current research explores the transnational influence of the Cuban Revolution.

Ailynn Torres Santana is a postdoctoral fellow with the Global Dialogue Program of the Rosa Luxemburg Foundation/FLACSO-Ecuador. She is coauthor, with Diosnara Ortega González, of the forthcoming book *Mujeres en revolución: Historias de vida de mujeres cubanas*.

Diosnara Ortega González is director of the Escuela de Sociología at the Universidad Católica Silva Henríquez in Santiago, Chile. She is co-author, with Ailynn Torres Santana, of the forthcoming book *Mujeres en revolución: Historias de vida de mujeres cubanas*.

Notes

1. Randall, *La mujer cubana ahora*; Randall, *Cuban Women Now*; Castillo, *Reyita*; Meyer, *El futuro es nuestro*; Jiménez and Martínez, *50 voces y rostros*; Estrada, *Guajiros del siglo XXI*; Moore and Hunter, *Siete mujeres*; Cruz, *Chaparreras con luz propia*; Franco, *Piezas para armar nuestra memoria*.
2. Rubiera and Hevia, *Emergiendo del silencio*.

References

Castillo, Daisy Rubiera. *Reyita: la vida de una mujer negra cubana en el siglo XX*. Havana: Verde Olivo, 2006.

Cruz Martínez, Yuliet. *Chaparreras con luz propia*. Havana: Publicaciones Acuario, 2012.

Estrada, Ana Vera. *Guajiros del siglo XXI*. Havana: Instituto Cubano de Investigación Cultural Juan Marinello, 2012.

Franco, Nora, ed. *Piezas para armar nuestra memoria*. Havana: Centro Cultural Pablo de la Torriente Brau, 2004.

Jiménez, Yohanka Valdés, and Yuliet Cruz Martínez, *50 voces y rostros de líderes campesinas cubanas*. Havana: Caminos, 2009.

Meyer, Eugenia. *El futuro es nuestro: Ocho cubanas narran sus historias de vida*. Mexico City: Fondo de Cultura Economica, 2007.

Moore, Marjorie, and Adrienne Hunter. *Siete mujeres y la revolución cubana*. Havana: Editorial Ciencias Sociales, 2003.

Randall, Margaret. *Cuban Women Now: Interviews with Cuban Women*. Toronto: Women's Press, 1974.

Randall, Margaret. *La mujer cubana ahora*. Havana: Instituto Cubano del Libro, 1972.

Rubiera, Daisy, and Olida Hevia, eds. *Emergiendo del silencio: Mujeres negras en la historia de Cuba*. Havana: Ciencias Sociales, 2016.

Historicizing Sexuality in the Cuban Revolution

The Spectral "Before"

Jennifer L. Lambe

A 1968 presentation at Cuba's Hospital Psiquiátrico de La Habana had provoked a heated debate over the nature and treatment of homosexuality, one of many such conversations inspired by the Cuban Revolution. As revolutionary officials, prominent intellectuals, and university students unleashed a campaign against sexual and gender nonconformity, mental health professionals mobilized throughout the 1960s to contribute their own professional expertise. Yet they did not always do so in total agreement, as evidenced in the aforementioned 1968 meeting.

According to one attendee, noted child psychiatrist Gerardo Nogueira Rivero, the "primordial fact" of adult homosexuality was the "relation with the mother, the identification with, or the imitation—as the reflexologists call it—of the feminine process." "If you see a complete homosexual," Nogueira Rivero concluded, "what he wants to be is a woman."[1] In rejoinder, a surgeon by the name of Casuso presented a poignant counterexample. Years earlier, he had operated on a young man with a rectal fistula at the Hospital de Príncipe. The patient's attending physicians had inquired whether he would like to undergo the "Christine Jorgensen" operation, in reference to the world's first transgender celebrity. But the young man rejected this conflation of his sexual and gender identities, replying that he did "not want to be a woman," just himself.[2]

Radical History Review
Issue 136 (January 2020)   DOI 10.1215/01636545-7857392
© 2020 by MARHO: The Radical Historians' Organization, Inc.

This exchange provides insight into debates over sexuality in 1960s Cuba, undoubtedly one of the most fraught and coercive sites of revolutionary subject formation. It also speaks to growing psychiatric interest in homosexuality throughout the 1960s, both in dialogue with and in some cases independent from official campaigns of repression. Yet I have long wondered how to understand the reference to Christine Jorgensen and her apparently widespread Cuban recognizability. Namely, how did "Christine Jorgensen" become a seemingly obvious point of reference, not only to this group of physicians, among whom such familiarity might be expected, but also for the young man on whom they wished to perform such a surgery?

As is often the case, a different set of questions and sources brought Jorgensen back to my attention. While I had imagined some popular awareness of a person who in the early 1950s had become an international celebrity, I was surprised to learn that Jorgensen had in fact traveled to Cuba in 1953 and remained part of popular discourse for nearly a decade after. From today's vantage, her trip is barely a blip on the historical radar, easily overlooked amid the escalation of political violence and popular mobilization against Fulgencio Batista's regime. At the time, however, it was the stuff of splashy news, with her blockbuster appearance at the Tropicana nightclub netting her publicity, island admirers, and even a kidnapping attempt, while also generating protest from conservative sectors.

Christine Jorgensen's Cuban experience thus invites reflection on the relationship between "before" and "after" in Cuban history. The past decade has seen the emergence of a vibrant literature on sexuality under the revolution (1959–2019), with historians, literary scholars, anthropologists, and others examining multiple points of revolutionary influence and inflection. Much of this work has been dedicated to the crucial experimental decade of the 1960s, when the state assumed an ever more prominent role in policing sexual behavior and identities,[3] and has followed those trends through their reversal in the 1990s, with the resurrection of foreign tourism and associated sexual economies.[4] Indeed, the fact that it is possible to participate in a dossier dedicated to sixty years of revolutionary sexual and gender transformations points to the continued vibrancy of this field.

It is striking, however, that no such coalescence has emerged around the previous six decades of the Cuban Republic (1902–59). Despite important studies of different moments or topics, we have witnessed few attempts to carve out holistic unity of the kind that has been taken for granted in the revolutionary period or in other Latin American contexts, where scholars have traced the connections among urbanization, immigration, and sexual (sub)cultural formation in the first decades of the twentieth century.[5] This comparative silence begs a pressing question for scholars of sexuality after 1959. How are we to contextualize the revolution's "after" when it comes to sexual mores, desires, and identities if we have not yet fully wrestled with its "before"? What are the analytical costs of sketching our histories of sexuality and gender after 1959 on a mostly unpopulated slate?[6]

The relative absence of historical context in which to place our scholarship, I would propose, has tended to magnify the role of the revolutionary state in determining the shape of sexual cultures after 1959. I make this point not to deny the significant weight of—and coercion attached to—revolutionary measures designed to root out homosexuality and gender subversion. Thanks to historians Abel Sierra Madero, Lillian Guerra, Rachel Hynson, and others, the extent of the state's reach into private identities and desires is increasingly apprehensible, along with the human cost of such efforts. Though the politicization of sexuality was a common Cold War phenomenon across geographical contexts, the determination and ability of revolutionary officials to bring state power to bear on sexual and gender nonconforming individuals was, in turn, extreme.[7]

A state-centric approach to the history of sexuality after 1959 has thus fueled novel insights and important ethical conversations about sexual politics in Cuba's past and present. Nonetheless, as I explore below, it has also set the stage for other modes of inquiry. One of the most pressing areas for future study is how ordinary Cubans processed state measures and discourses related to sexuality.[8] Yet we might also now entertain sketching disjuncture and continuity over the daunting 1959 gap. When it comes to sexuality under revolution, how, quite simply, do we place its "before"? What kinds of longer threads—and even (dis)continuous histories—could we extend across the divide?

Here, I have begun by pointing to Christine Jorgensen's Cuban sojourn as a window onto one such thread: a tantalizing, if oblique, crucible of the myriad forces shaping Cuban sexual cultures on the eve of revolution, from US tourism to medical technology and organized religion. Yet the world's first transgender celebrity might also reorient us to the analytical salience of the prefix *trans-* in thinking across chronological—and paradigmatic—divides. From the vantage point of state campaigns to enforce normativity, the place of sexuality in the revolutionary project may seem distinctly self-contained, even resolutely synchronic in its confinement to a particular place and time. As Susan Stryker, Paisley Currah, and Lisa Jean Moore have argued, however, the hyphen attached to *trans-* highlights the category's "explicit relationality," not only in the "horizontal" movement "between two established gendered spaces" but also in the "vertical" biopolitical register.[9] Through this approach to *trans-* and its presumed accompaniment, *gender*, the authors propose a kind of "dancing" across "temporality" and "spatiality," with a dynamic "movement between territorializing and deterritorializing 'trans-' and its suffixes."[10] Indeed, as C. Riley Snorton suggests, transitivity might encourage us to linger on "impermanence" itself, those pasts "perceived [only] through glimpses and furtive glances, by fictive traces and fugitive moves."[11]

We might thus frame the relationship between the before and after in the history of sexuality in Cuba, per Snorton, as one of "transubstantiation," with historical difference a nodal dimension of political sense making after 1959. Revolutionary "modes of differentiation" not only subjectified gender and sexual nonconforming individuals in new ways; they also rendered revolutionary self-definition contingent on these very processes.[12] Unsurprisingly, revolutionary officials frequently relied on an abridged vision of Cuba's sexual past to mark their difference on this score. One response to such rescripting might be to deconstruct the assumptions on which it rested. Yet we might also move backward: revivifying those pasts that point in no exclusive or even linear direction. In writing the history of sexuality after 1959, it would behoove us not to posit a solitary "before" (the disgraceful past constructed by revolutionary discourse on the same) but rather to imagine dynamic and multidimensional pasts, with movement—between state and individual, male and female, heterosexual and homosexual, black and white, within and beyond Cuba, even before and after—at its very heart.

Sexuality and the Cuban Republic: Toward a Synoptic History

The revolutionary appropriation of history has long inspired a contrarian historiography. Critical accounts, both lay and academic, have taken up diverse points of political contestation, from economics to public health, race, and US relations. In recent years, the historicist response to revolutionary discourse has been increasingly oriented to resurrecting context for post-1959 events, with the past a potent demythologizing vehicle. Such accounts have aimed to draw out the very complexity of republican history when it comes to race, housing, or health, for example.[13] Given the emphasis in newer scholarship on the 1960s politicization of sexuality, it is surprising, then, that sexuality has figured so rarely in those accounts seeking to decenter revolutionary rupture. Why might this be?

Behind historiographical silences, archival lacunae invariably loom. The history of sexuality in Cuba's republic is no exception. In fact, the very limits on state action in this area before 1959 have tended to become a self-fulfilling interpretive prophecy. Because the state and its various organisms did not aggressively stake claims in this area, at least compared to their revolutionary counterparts, for the most part Cuban archives lack for the kinds of sources through which we might track popular encounters and contestation around sexuality. This has in turn forced historians of sexuality in the pre-1959 period to rely mostly on periodical and published sources—a methodological challenge shared, interestingly enough, by historians of the post-1959 context.

It is worth pointing out, however, that this is not unilaterally the case. Bonnie Lucero, for example, draws on Cuban and US archival material to chart battles over racial and gender identities during the final war for independence and US occupation.[14] Tiffany Sippial's work on prostitution in late colonial and early national Cuba straddles both Spanish and US occupation sources.[15] The significance of the 1936 Social Defense Code and 1940 Constitution, which, among other things, sought to extend progressive scientific management to the private domain, in turn left documentary traces, as Sarah Arvey has explored.[16] Archival and periodical sources tracking the intersection between gender, sexuality, health, and medicine have likewise inspired a burgeoning subfield of historical scholarship.[17]

History suggests there may yet be archival treasures to uncover. In my own work, I was at first perplexed and then delighted to have a pile of unfamiliar documents placed on my desk one day at Cuba's Archivo Nacional. The records contained, among other things, police records of *ofensas a la moral* from 1928 to 1930, as the island catapulted toward political and social upheaval and a broad popular movement against dictator Gerardo Machado. Elsewhere, I explore what these records tell us about Havana's shifting sexual culture in these years—especially with regard to male homosexuality, exhibitionism, and voyeurism—and an emergent preoccupation with visibility among scientific experts and the state.[18]

Such documentation will undoubtedly enrich our conversations about the relationship between sexuality and the various configurations of the republican state. Yet we need not await its discovery to begin fleshing out a less state-centric history. The periodical press has been a bountiful source for many studies of sexuality before 1959. A selective bibliography would include the work of Julio César González Pagés and Maikel Colón Pichardo on masculinity, gender, and race;[19] Abel Sierra Madero on the Cuban response to US sexual mores and a press campaign against gender and sexual nonconformists in the late 1920s;[20] Tomás Fernández Robaina and Mayra Beers on prostitution and the urban demimonde;[21] Lizabeth Lotz on the rise of the *chica moderna* and her impact on urban sexual cultures in the 1920s;[22] Karen Morrison on debates over the social health of the Afro-Cuban family;[23] and Víctor Fowler, Emilio Bejel, Abel Sierra Madero, and others on popular, literary, and medical representations of homosexuality.[24] This scholarship has in turn staged rich dialogues with classic and more recent studies of women and feminism in Cuba's republican history, most notably the work of K. Lynn Stoner.[25]

A rich and increasingly diverse body of work on sexuality in the Republican era seems to invite the kind of synoptic gestures that have long been common in studies of race in the same period.[26] How, for example, might we periodize this history, a long-standing preoccupation in a historiography developed under Michel Foucault's shadow?[27] Such an effort might begin by reaching to Cuba's late colonial context, most notably the influence of racial subjugation and slavery on sexual and gender formations.[28] It might then consider the impact of the independence wars on norms around gender, sexuality, race, and the family, and trace how those conversations evolved under US occupation (1899–1902 and 1906–9) and the emergence of new migration patterns to Cuba. The moment following the enactment of

Prohibition in the United States (1920–33) and its impact on Cuba's leisure and tourist culture, especially in Havana, would in turn represent a period worthy of study, along with the emergence of a nationalist response in the 1920s and early 1930s. This period also saw the coalescence of Cuba's organized feminist movement, members of which took up a number of pressing social issues beyond suffrage, from divorce to legal recognition for children. Such activism fed into what represents a major turning point in this history: the 1936 Social Defense Code and related efforts to extend scientific management to individual desires and behaviors, backed by the force of the state. The bird's-eye view might then consider the evolution of Havana's nocturnal landscape under the influence of the US mob, but also what this picture, and its presumed orientation to sexual adventure and license, looks like from the island's rural areas. Finally, we might conclude by looking to work on the mobilization against Fulgencio Batista over the course of the 1950s and the centrality of both women and gendered symbolism therein.[29]

In sketching a holistic history of sexuality in the republic, we would do well to take a cue from the rich literature on racial formations in the same period.[30] Scholars have highlighted the enduring implication of race and racism in high politics, most notably in the 1912 uprising of the Partido Independiente de Color, and in the mobilizations attached to partisan politics in the first two decades of the twentieth century, the founding and trajectory of the Communist Party in the 1920s through the 1950s, and progress toward and political violence attending the Revolution of 1933 and party politics in its aftermath. In the course of narrating racial politics, however, historians have not neglected everyday social patterns as they manifested in black civil society, health and disease, music and culture, labor organization, and much more. As this list would suggest, scholars of the republic have worked from the assumption that constructions of race necessarily intersect with and impinge on other categories of individuation, most especially gender, sexuality, class, and nationality. They have further attended to the transnational pathways that shaped racial formations in Cuba, with the United States representing a particularly salient foil. Above all, however, historians of race in Cuba have highlighted the enduring impact of slavery on racial politics and identities, a context that scholars of gender and sexuality ought to also bear closely in mind.[31]

Compared to Cuba's publicly contested racial past, the historical landscape of sexuality may seem more amorphous, intimate, and impervious to synthesis. Yet companion literatures—on race, other national contexts, but also gender and sexuality after 1959—might help us identify areas of pending inquiry. Cuba's relationship with the United States has already inspired studies of how transnational ties manifested in the realm of gender and sexuality, as in the deployment of gendered tropes in the final independence war from Spain.[32] There is much still to say about this and other transnational vectors, especially those linking migrant laborers to gendered and sexual contexts in the Caribbean, Spain, and elsewhere.[33] On this front, we have yet to see any in-depth study of the relationship of class formations to gender and sexuality in Cuba beyond the implication of class in feminist struggles of the 1920s and 1930s, though Anasa Hicks's work on domestic service from the colonial period through the revolution promises to broach exciting new questions on this front.[34] Indeed, pioneering studies of black women, as well as the coarticulation of race and gender, remain among the few to bridge the 1898 and 1959 divides, exploring ruptures and continuities at the level of both discourse and experience.[35]

Meanwhile, the mobilization of gendered and sexual tropes in high politics has received only cursory treatment, as have other institutions that undoubtedly shaped popular understandings. We still await an examination of how religion—Catholicism, *espiritismo*, Santería, Protestantism—shaped constructions of sexuality at both the popular and institutional level.[36] Finally, the urban/rural divide will undoubtedly be a key fulcrum of future scholarly efforts, as, with so many other things, we have tended to extrapolate from the vantage point of Havana to Cuba writ large. If Reinaldo Arenas's oeuvre is any indication, however, that conflation, when it comes to gender and sexuality, represents a grievous analytical error.[37]

In short, a fully intersectional history of sexuality in Cuba's republican period would take up race, class, gender, and nationality alongside many of the emergent preoccupations of historians of sexuality elsewhere, from geography and space to nationality.[38] It would orient us to the pronouncements of medical experts and prominent intellectuals but without allowing their voices to eclipse those of ordinary Cubans. Following the cue of scholars of race, such a history might also embrace broad analytical frameworks weaving together state, institutional, and social power. Indeed, one of the most valuable contributions Cubanists have made to transnational conversations about race has been to situate such examinations squarely within the trajectory of state formation. In doing so, they have identified race as perhaps the "metalanguage" of modern Cuban history, to echo the classic words of Evelyn Brooks Higginbotham.[39]

Yet in the process, historians of race in Cuba have not lost sight of the reverberations of state action in the lives of ordinary people. These are lives that stretch across our usual chronological roadblocks, giving lie to grand claims about revolutionary rupture. Here, I am reminded of the opening to Alejandro de la Fuente's *A Nation for All* (2001), where he locates these preoccupations in the mouth not of Fidel Castro but rather of a black former maid. "Will my children be maids again?" she wonders upon witnessing the 1993 return of her former employer to a Cuba in the throes of the so-called Special Period.[40] Her concern reminds us that, whatever the claims of state officials, the texture of embodied experience is resolutely palimpsestic—even transitive. And, much as the past lives on in the present, so the present haunts our historical imaginings, infusing expectations and memories alike.

Conclusion: The Historicity of Homophobia

Homophobia is a slippery historical object. Indeed, charting the history of everyday homophobic sentiment is sometimes as difficult as recovering the embodied lives of those subjects against whom it was unleashed. The very newness of the concept and its associated vocabulary is one looming obstacle.[41] But equally challenging is the impoverishment of our genealogical tools of detection. Are all homophobias the same, or does homophobia have a history? Should we presume that moments of moral outrage over homosexuality are evidence of intensified homophobia? Or does such panic lie always latent, merely awaiting a propitious context to reveal itself?[42]

Here, I am reminded of a revealing 1971 roundtable on homosexuality in Cuba sponsored by the Ministry of Public Health, which brought together a series of expert presentations. Havana prosecutor Magaly Cassell offered the most unequivocal statement on the relationship between homosexuality and revolution:

> We can't forget that we're living in a different social context than that one. If you want, we can go back in time to the period before 1959, when different manifestations of homosexualism were visible and I'm sure that all of you here . . . were aware of certain events that became public and which the leadership of the capitalist society, where the homosexual proliferated and developed, did not repudiate, even though that repulsion always appeared in the heart of the people. The people always rejected the homosexual. It was the capitalist regime that fostered the corruption where the homosexual developed . . . today, thanks to our new structures, to a different conception of moral values, the rejection is greater, and felt at all levels of our society: the leadership and the masses.[43]

This notion that homosexuality was a product of capitalism, doomed to wither away under socialist governance, was pervasive in revolutionary pronouncements on the topic, even if medical experts privately expressed hesitancy that such change would come quickly or at all. More striking, however, is Cassell's claim that homophobia, too, predated revolutionary politicization—that "repulsion always appeared in the hearts of the people." By this logic, full-fledged repudiation awaited only the arrival of a new leadership that would actualize preexisting popular sentiment.

Yet Cassell's insistence on long-standing popular rejection was at odds with the assessment of Bartolomé Arce, an endocrinologist participant in the roundtable. Following the expert presentations, an audience member had inquired about the prevalence of homosexuality after ten years of revolution. In response, Arce warned that experts still lacked for the statistical information to provide a scientific response. Even so, he cautioned that all of the denunciatory energy marshaled against gay men and women in the 1960s had led some ordinary Cubans to conclude

that homosexuality was actually on the rise. That assessment—most likely errone-
ous, by Arce's calculation—prompted him, too, to draw on historical arguments:

> It may be true that one sees in certain areas a worrisome number of
> homosexuals, but, on the other hand, before the Revolution, under capitalism,
> people didn't worry too much about homosexuality; that is, their concern
> reached only to their familial contexts, to their children, their closest relatives.
> And since today this has become a broader social concern, perhaps *one is more*
> *affected* by the sight of some homosexuals [quizás uno tenga mayor afectación
> por la visión de algunos homosexuales].[44]

    There is something at once bald but also elusive about the logic of Arce's and
Cassell's claims on history. In order to understand the course of revolutionary politicization, it seems obvious that scholars must also reckon with questions of change
over time: however amorphous our source base, or challenging the ethical and political questions thereby raised. For too long, however, we have skirted the republican
"before" in our discussions of the revolutionary "after," understandably wary of any
scholarly effort that might downplay the virulence of official homophobia after
1959.[45] There is no question that punitive state action decisively shaped the lives
of gender and sexual nonconforming people after 1959. Yet, however damaging its
impact, it was not the only relevant force at play. If Christine Jorgensen's Cuban
travels are any indication, sexual norms after 1959 did not emerge, Athena-like,
from the solitary consciousness of Fidel or Raúl Castro. Nor were they solely dependent on referents drawn from elsewhere in the socialist world.

    As the assessments of Cassells and Arce would suggest, apologists for revolu-
tionary homophobia have relied on a presumed blank canvas against which to craft
their own interpretations of revolutionary difference. In response, scholars should
reject such first principles, especially in the aftermath of Cuba's recent constitutional
reform process, which reinvigorated a decades-old conversation about state action in
the area of sexuality.[46] The history of sexuality after 1959 cannot be narrated without
some conception of its before(s): not only state intervention (or the comparative
absence thereof) but also the sexual desires, identities, and imaginaries of ordinary
Cubans. In returning to these forgotten and silenced stories, we have good reason, as
I have proposed here, to reject the presumption of uniformity. Yet I wonder if we might
also treat the historiographical mobilization around the revolution as a provocation to
write outside, alongside, and beyond this history as well, to imagine new directional-
ities and, indeed, temporalities for the history of sexuality in twentieth-century Cuba.

Jennifer Lambe is associate professor of Latin American and Caribbean history at Brown University. She is the author of *Madhouse: Psychiatry and Politics in Cuban History* (2017) and coeditor
of *The Revolution from Within: Cuba, 1959–1980* (2019).

Notes

I am grateful to Elizabeth Schwall, Michael Bustamante, Owen Parr, Michelle Chase, Isabella Cosse, and the editorial team at *Radical History Review* for their thoughtful comments on this essay.

1. Discussion following Agramonte, "La homosexualidad," 73.
2. Discussion following Agramonte, "La homosexualidad," 74.
3. See Arguelles and Rich, "Homosexuality, Homophobia, and Revolution"; Leiner, *Sexual Politics in Cuba*; Lumsden, *Machos, Maricones, and Gays*; Guerra, "Gender Policing,"; Hamilton, *Sexual Revolutions in Cuba*; Olivares, *Becoming Reinaldo Arenas*; Hynson, "Count, Capture, and Reeducate"; Chase, *Revolution within the Revolution*; Madero, "'El trabajo os hará hombres'"; and Lambe, *Madhouse*, 156–66.
4. Sierra Madero, *Del otro lado del espejo*; González Pagés, *Macho varón masculino*; Kempadoo, *Sun, Sex, and Gold*; Cabezas, *Economies of Desire*; Fernandez, *Revolutionizing Romance*; Allen, *Venceremos?*; Stout, *After Love*.
5. See, among other titles, Green, *Beyond Carnival*; Macías-González, "A Note on Homosexuality"; Irwin, *Mexican Masculinities*; Ben, "Plebeian Masculinity and Sexual Comedy"; Ben, "Male Sexuality"; and Macías-González and Rubenstein, *Masculinity and Sexuality*. For one important, if at times impressionistic, exception, see Mulhare, "Sexual Ideology in Pre-Castro Cuba."
6. On this question, see Zanetti Lecuona, "Medio siglo de historiografía en Cuba."
7. On Cold War sexual politics in the Americas, see Johnson, *The Lavender Scare*; Green, "Who Is the Macho Who Wants to Kill Me?"; Charles, "Communist and Homosexual"; Manzano, *The Age of Youth in Argentina*; Chase, *Revolution within the Revolution*; and Cowan, *Securing Sex*.
8. See, for example, Hamilton, *Sexual Revolutions in Cuba*.
9. Stryker, Currah, and Moore, "Introduction," 11, 13–14.
10. Stryker, Currah, and Moore, "Introduction," 14.
11. Snorton, *Black on Both Sides*, 7.
12. Snorton, *Black on Both Sides*, 6.
13. On this literature, see de la Fuente, "La Ventolera: Ruptures, Persistence and the Historiography of the Cuban Revolution." For examples of this kind of work, see de la Fuente, *A Nation for All*; Horst, "Sleeping on the Ashes"; Urban, "The Sick Republic"; Lambe, *Madhouse*; and Hicks, "Hierarchies at Home."
14. Lucero, *Revolutionary Masculinity and Racial Inequality*.
15. Sippial, *Prostitution, Modernity, and the Making of the Cuban Republic*.
16. Arvey, "Labyrinths of Love"; Arvey, "Making the Immoral Moral"; Arvey, "Sex and the Ordinary Cuban."
17. See, for example, Rodriguez, "'The Dangers That Surround the Child.'"
18. Lambe, "Visible Pleasure and Sex Policing."
19. González Pagés, *Macho varón masculino*; Colón Pichardo, *¿Es fácil ser hombre y difícil ser negro?* Since 2008, González Pagés has spearheaded the Red Iberoamericana y Africana de Masculinidades, an intellectual network dedicated to this topic.
20. Sierra Madero, *Del otro lado del espejo*, 73–157.
21. Fernandez Robaina, *Recuerdos secretos*; Beers, "Murder in San Isidro."
22. Lotz, "Leading the Life of a Modern Girl."
23. Morrison, *Cuba's Racial Crucible*, 160–90.
24. Fowler Calzada, *La maldición*; Bejel, *Gay Cuban Nation*; Sierra Madero, *Del otro lado del espejo*, 138–57. See also Lambe, *Madhouse*, 126–36.

25. For a small sampling of relevant work, see Stoner, *From the House to the Streets*; Stoner and Serrano Pérez, *Cuban and Cuban-American Women*; González Pagés, *En busca de un espacio*; and Brunson, "Constructing Afro-Cuban Womanhood."
26. The definitive study in this regard is de la Fuente, *A Nation for All*.
27. Foucault, *The History of Sexuality, Volume 1*, 115–33.
28. Stolcke, *Marriage, Class, and Colour*; Prados-Torreira, *Mambisas*; Barcia et al., *Mujeres al margen de la historia*; Franklin, *Women and Slavery in Nineteenth-Century Colonial Cuba*; Mena, "Stretching the Limits of Gendered Spaces"; Díaz Martínez, *La peligrosa Habana*; Barcia Zequeira, *La otra familia*; Cowling, *Conceiving Freedom*; Finch, "What Looks Like a Revolution"; Morrison, *Cuba's Racial Crucible*.
29. Chase, *Revolution within the Revolution*; Bayard de Volo, *Women and the Cuban Insurrection*.
30. For an abbreviated survey of relevant work gestured to here and below, see Portuondo Linares, *Los independientes de color*; Helg, *Our Rightful Share*; Brock and Castañeda Fuertes, *Between Race and Empire*; de la Fuente, *A Nation for All*; Bronfman, *Measures of Equality*; Guridy, *Forging Diaspora*; Guridy, "War on the Negro"; Pappademos, *Black Political Activism and the Cuban Republic*; and Horne, *Race to Revolution*.
31. I am grateful to Marial Iglesias Utset for sharing her thoughts on this question on several different occasions.
32. Hoganson, *Fighting for American Manhood*; Sierra Madero, *Del otro lado del espejo*, 53–78.
33. For one potential model in this regard, see Putnam, *Radical Moves*.
34. Hicks, "Hierarchies at Home." On this topic, see also Pérez Sarduy, *Las criadas de La Habana*.
35. Martiatu and Rubiera Castillo, *Afrocubanas*; Morrison, *Cuba's Racial Crucible*; Hevia Lanier and Rubiera Castillo, *Emergiendo del silencio*; Fraunhar, *Mulata Nation*. For an effort to theorize these connections, see Lane, "Smoking Habaneras."
36. For a suggestive account pointing in this direction, see Román, *Governing Spirits*.
37. See, especially, Arenas, *Antes que anochezca*.
38. For a unique snapshot of the state of the field, see the *Notches* blog (notchesblog.com).
39. Higginbotham, "African-American Women's History."
40. De la Fuente, *A Nation for All*, 1.
41. Wickberg, "Homophobia."
42. On some of these challenges, see Sedgwick, *Epistemology of the Closet*.
43. Ministerio de Salud Pública, *Mesa redonda sobre homosexualismo*, 32.
44. Ministerio de Salud Pública, 37 (my emphasis).
45. On the genesis of one such debate, see Arguelles and Rich, "Homosexuality, Homophobia, and Revolution"; Lancaster, "'Comment on Arguelles and Rich's Homosexuality, Homophobia, and Revolution'"; and Sierra Madero, "'Here, Everyone's Got Huevos, Mister!'"
46. For two thoughtful—and divergent—perspectives on this mobilization, see Nuez, "Vivir en gay"; and Madero, "De la homofobia estatal al matrimonio igualitario en Cuba."

References

Agramonte, Edmundo Gutiérrez. "La homosexualidad: Contribución al estudio de su etiología." *Revista del Hospital Psiquiátrico de La Habana* 9, no. 1 (1968): 72–92.

Allen, Jafari S. *Venceremos? The Erotics of Black Self-Making in Cuba*. Durham, NC: Duke University Press, 2011.

Arenas, Reinaldo. *Antes que anochezca*. 3rd ed. Barcelona: Tusquets, 2017.

Arguelles, Lourdes, and B. Ruby Rich. "Homosexuality, Homophobia, and Revolution: Notes toward an Understanding of the Cuban Lesbian and Gay Male Experience, Part I." *Signs* 9, no. 4 (1984): 683–99.

Arvey, Sarah R. "Labyrinths of Love: Sexual Propriety, Family, and Social Reform in the Second Cuban Republic, 1933–1958." PhD diss., University of Michigan, 2007.

Arvey, Sarah R. "Making the Immoral Moral: Consensual Unions and Birth Status in Cuban Law and Everyday Practice, 1940–1958." *Hispanic American Historical Review* 90, no. 4 (2010): 627–59.

Arvey, Sarah R. "Sex and the Ordinary Cuban: Cuban Physicians, Eugenics, and Marital Sexuality in the 1940s and 1950s." *Journal of the History of Sexuality* 21, no. 1 (2012): 93–120.

Barcia Zequeira, María del Carmen, Jorge Ibarra, Yahima Leyva Collazo, and Fernando Carr Parúas. *Mujeres al margen de la historia*. Havana: Editorial de Ciencias Sociales, 2009.

Barcia Zequeira, María del Carmen. *La otra familia: parientes, redes y descendencia de los esclavos en Cuba*. Havana: Editorial Oriente, Instituto Cubano del Libro, 2010.

Bayard de Volo, Lorraine. *Women and the Cuban Insurrection: How Gender Shaped Castro's Victory*. Cambridge, UK: Cambridge University Press, 2018.

Beers, Mayra. "Murder in San Isidro: Crime and Culture during the Second Cuban Republic." *Cuban Studies* 34 (2003): 97–129.

Bejel, Emilio. *Gay Cuban Nation*. Chicago: University of Chicago Press, 2001.

Ben, Pablo. "Male Sexuality, the Popular Classes and the State: Buenos Aires, 1880–1955." PhD diss., University of Chicago, 2009.

Ben, Pablo. "Plebeian Masculinity and Sexual Comedy in Buenos Aires, 1880–1930." *Journal of the History of Sexuality* 16, no. 3 (2007): 436–58.

Brock, Lisa, and Digna Castañeda Fuertes. *Between Race and Empire: African-Americans and Cubans Before the Cuban Revolution*. Philadelphia: Temple University Press, 1998.

Bronfman, Alejandra. *Measures of Equality: Social Science, Citizenship, and Race in Cuba, 1902–1940*. Chapel Hill: University of North Carolina Press, 2004.

Brunson, Takkara Keosha. "Constructing Afro-Cuban Womanhood: Race, Gender, and Citizenship in Republican-Era Cuba, 1902–1958." PhD diss., University of Texas, 2011.

Cabezas, Amalia L. *Economies of Desire: Sex and Tourism in Cuba and the Dominican Republic*. Philadelphia: Temple University Press, 2009.

Charles, Douglas M. "Communist and Homosexual: The FBI, Harry Hay, and the Secret Side of the Lavender Scare, 1943–1961." *American Communist History* 11, no. 1 (2012): 101–24.

Chase, Michelle. *Revolution within the Revolution: Women and Gender Politics in Cuba, 1952–1962*. Chapel Hill: University of North Carolina Press, 2015.

Colón Pichardo, Maikel. *¿Es fácil ser hombre y difícil ser negro? masculinidad y estereotipos raciales en Cuba (1898–1912)*. Havana: Casa Editora Abril, 2015.

Cowan, Benjamin A. *Securing Sex: Morality and Repression in the Making of Cold War Brazil*. Chapel Hill: University of North Carolina Press, 2016.

Cowling, Camillia. *Conceiving Freedom: Women of Color, Gender, and the Abolition of Slavery in Havana and Rio De Janeiro*. Chapel Hill: University of North Carolina Press, 2013.

De la Fuente, Alejandro. *A Nation for All: Race, Inequality, and Politics in Twentieth-Century Cuba*. Chapel Hill: University of North Carolina Press, 2001.

Díaz Martínez, Yolanda. *La peligrosa Habana: violencia y criminalidad a finales del siglo XIX*. Havana: Editorial de Ciencias Sociales, 2005.

Fernandez, Nadine T. *Revolutionizing Romance: Interracial Couples in Contemporary Cuba.* New Brunswick, NJ: Rutgers University Press, 2010.

Fernandez Robaina, Tomas. *Recuerdos secretos de dos mujeres publicas.* Havana: Editorial Letras Cubanas, 1983.

Finch, Aisha. "'What Looks Like a Revolution': Enslaved Women and the Gendered Terrain of Slave Insurgencies in Cuba, 1843–1844." *Journal of Women's History* 26, no. 1 (2014): 112–34.

Foucault, Michel. *The History of Sexuality, Volume 1: An Introduction*, translated by Robert Hurley. New York: Vintage Books, 1990.

Fowler Calzada, Víctor. *La maldición: Una historia del placer como conquista.* Havana: Editorial Letras Cubanas, 1998.

Franklin, Sarah L. *Women and Slavery in Nineteenth-Century Colonial Cuba.* Rochester: University of Rochester Press, 2012.

Fraunhar, Alison. *Mulata Nation: Visualizing Race and Gender in Cuba.* Jackson: University Press of Mississippi, 2018.

Fuente, Alejandro de la. "La Ventolera: Ruptures, Persistence and the Historiography of the Cuban Revolution." In *The Revolution from Within: Cuba, 1959–1980*, edited by Michael Bustamante and Jennifer L. Lambe. Durham, NC: Duke University Press, 2019.

González Pagés, Julio César. *En busca de un espacio: Historia de mujeres en Cuba.* Havana: Ediciones de Ciencias Sociales, 2005.

González Pagés, Julio César. *Macho, varón, masculino: Estudios de masculinidades en Cuba.* Havana: Editorial de la Mujer, 2010.

Green, James N. *Beyond Carnival: Male Homosexuality in Twentieth-Century Brazil.* Chicago: University of Chicago Press, 1999.

Green, James N. "'Who Is the Macho Who Wants to Kill Me?' Male Homosexuality, Revolutionary Masculinity, and the Brazilian Armed Struggle of the 1960s and 1970s." *Hispanic American Historical Review* 92, no. 3 (2012): 437–69.

Guerra, Lillian. "Gender Policing, Homosexuality and the New Patriarchy of the Cuban Revolution, 1965–70." *Social History* 35, no. 3 (2010): 268–89.

Guridy, Frank Andre. *Forging Diaspora: Afro-Cubans and African Americans in a World of Empire and Jim Crow.* Chapel Hill: University of North Carolina Press, 2010.

Guridy, Frank Andre. "'War on the Negro': Race and the Revolution of 1933." *Cuban Studies*, no. 40 (2010): 49–73.

Hamilton, Carrie. *Sexual Revolutions in Cuba: Passion, Politics, and Memory.* Envisioning Cuba. Chapel Hill: University of North Carolina Press, 2012.

Helg, Aline. *Our Rightful Share: The Afro-Cuban Struggle for Equality, 1886–1912.* Chapel Hill: University of North Carolina Press, 1995.

Hevia Lanier, Oilda, and Daisy Rubiera Castillo, eds. *Emergiendo del silencio. Mujeres negras en la historia de Cuba.* Havana: Editorial de Ciencias Sociales, 2016.

Hicks, Anasa. "Hierarchies at Home: A History of Domestic Service in Cuba from Abolition to Revolution." PhD diss., New York University, 2017.

Higginbotham, Evelyn Brooks. "African-American Women's History and the Metalanguage of Race." *Signs* 17, no. 2 (1992): 251–74.

Hoganson, Kristin L. *Fighting for American Manhood: How Gender Politics Provoked the Spanish-American and Philippine-American Wars.* New Haven: Yale University Press, 1998.

Horne, Gerald. *Race to Revolution: The United States and Cuba during Slavery and Jim Crow.* New York: Monthly Review Press, 2014.

Horst, Jesse. "Sleeping on the Ashes: Slum Clearance in Havana in an Age of Revolution, 1930–1965." PhD diss., University of Pittsburgh, 2016.

Hynson, Rachel. "'Count, Capture, and Reeducate': The Campaign to Rehabilitate Cuba's Female Sex Workers, 1959–1966." *Journal of the History of Sexuality* 24, no. 1 (2015): 125–53.

Irwin, Robert McKee. *Mexican Masculinities*. Minneapolis: University of Minnesota Press, 2003.

Johnson, David K. *The Lavender Scare: The Cold War Persecution of Gays and Lesbians in the Federal Government*. Chicago: University of Chicago Press, 2010.

Kempadoo, Kamala. *Sun, Sex, and Gold: Tourism and Sex Work in the Caribbean*. Lanham, MD: Rowman & Littlefield Publishers, 1999.

Lambe, Jennifer L. *Madhouse: Psychiatry and Politics in Cuban History*. Chapel Hill: University of North Carolina Press, 2017.

Lambe, Jennifer L. "Visible Pleasure and Sex Policing: State, Science, and Desire in Twentieth-Century Cuba." In *Psychoanalysis in the Barrios: Race, Class, and the Unconscious*, edited by Patricia Gherovici and Christopher Christian, 121–42. Oxon and New York: Routledge, 2019.

Lancaster, Roger N. "Comment on Arguelles and Rich's 'Homosexuality, Homophobia, and Revolution: Notes toward an Understanding of the Cuban Lesbian and Gay Male Experience, Part II.'" *Signs* 12, no. 1 (1986): 188–92.

Lane, Jill. "Smoking Habaneras, or A Cuban Struggle with Racial Demons." *Social Text* 28, no. 3 (2010): 11–37.

Leiner, Marvin. *Sexual Politics in Cuba: Machismo, Homosexuality, and AIDS*. Boulder, CO: Westview Press, 1994.

Lotz, Lizabeth M. "Leading the Life of a Modern Girl: Representations of Womanhood in Cuban Popular Culture." PhD diss., University of North Carolina, 2010.

Lucero, Bonnie A. *Revolutionary Masculinity and Racial Inequality: Gendering War and Politics in Cuba*. Albuquerque: University of New Mexico Press, 2018.

Lumsden, Ian. *Machos, Maricones and Gays: Cuba and Homosexuality*. Philadelphia: Temple University Press, 2010.

Macías-González, Víctor M., and Anne Rubenstein, eds. *Masculinity and Sexuality in Modern Mexico*. Albuquerque: University of New Mexico Press, 2012.

Macías-González, Víctor Manuel. "A Note on Homosexuality in Porfirian and Postrevolutionary Northern Mexico." *Journal of the Southwest* 43, no. 4 (2001): 543–48.

Manzano, Valeria. *The Age of Youth in Argentina: Culture, Politics, and Sexuality from Perón to Videla*. Chapel Hill: University of North Carolina Press, 2014.

Martiatu, Inés María, and Daisy Rubiera Castillo, eds. *Afrocubanas: Historia, pensamiento y prácticas culturales*. Havana: Editorial de Ciencias Sociales, 2011.

Mena, Luz. "Stretching the Limits of Gendered Spaces: Black and Mulatto Women in 1830s Havana." *Cuban Studies* 36, no. 1 (2005): 87–104.

Ministerio de Salud Pública. *Mesa redonda sobre homosexualismo*. Havana: Ministerio de Salud Publica, Hospital Psiquiatrico de la Habana, 1972.

Morrison, Karen Y. *Cuba's Racial Crucible: The Sexual Economy of Social Identities, 1750–2000*. Bloomington: Indiana University Press, 2015.

Mulhare, Mirta de la Torre. "Sexual Ideology in Pre-Castro Cuba: A Cultural Analysis." PhD diss., University of Pittsburgh, 1969.

Nuez, Iván de la. "Vivir en gay, en género, en disidencia." *El País*. July 24, 2018, sec. Cultura. elpais.com/cultura/2018/07/23/actualidad/1532373738_394636.html.

Olivares, Jorge. *Becoming Reinaldo Arenas: Family, Sexuality, and the Cuban Revolution.* Durham, NC: Duke University Press, 2013.

Pappademos, Melina. *Black Political Activism and the Cuban Republic.* Chapel Hill: University of North Carolina Press, 2014.

Pérez Sarduy, Pedro. *Las criadas de La Habana.* Havana: Ediciones Extramuros, 2014.

Portuondo Linares, Serafín. *Los independientes de color. Historia del Partido Independiente de Color.* Havana: Editorial Libros Selecta, 1950.

Prados-Torreira, Teresa. *Mambisas: Rebel Women in Nineteenth-Century Cuba.* Gainesville: University Press of Florida, 2005.

Putnam, Lara. *Radical Moves: Caribbean Migrants and the Politics of Race in the Jazz Age.* Chapel Hill: University of North Carolina Press, 2013.

Rich, B. Ruby, and Lourdes Arguelles. "Homosexuality, Homophobia, and Revolution: Notes toward an Understanding of the Cuban Lesbian and Gay Male Experience, Part II." *Signs* 11, no. 1 (1985): 120–36.

Rodríguez, Daniel A. "'The Dangers That Surround the Child': Gender, Science, and Infant Mortality in Postindependence Havana." *Cuban Studies* 45 (2017): 297–318.

Román, Reinaldo. *Governing Spirits: Religion, Miracles, and Spectacles in Cuba and Puerto Rico, 1898–1956.* Chapel Hill: University of North Carolina Press, 2009.

Sedgwick, Eve Kosofsky. *Epistemology of the Closet.* 2nd ed. Berkeley: University of California Press, 2008.

Sierra Madero, Abel. "De la homofobia estatal al matrimonio igualitario en Cuba." Letras Libres, August 2, 2018. www.letraslibres.com/espana-mexico/politica/la-homofobia-estatal -al-matrimonio-igualitario-en-cuba.

Sierra Madero, Abel. *Del otro lado del espejo: la sexualidad en la construcción de la nación cubana.* Havana: Fondo Editorial Casa de las Américas : Delegación de Cultura de la Diputación de Córdoba: Centro Cultural de la Delegación del 27 de la Diputación de Malaga, 2006.

Sierra Madero, Abel. "'El trabajo os hará hombres': Masculinización nacional, trabajo forzado y control social en Cuba durante los años sesenta." *Cuban Studies* 44, no. 1 (2016): 309–49.

Sierra Madero, Abel. "'Here, Everyone's Got Huevos, Mister!' Nationalism, Sexuality, and Collective Violence in Cuba during the Mariel Exodus." In *The Revolution from Within: Cuba, 1959–1980,* edited by Michael Bustamante and Jennifer L. Lambe. Durham, NC: Duke University Press, 2019.

Sippial, Tiffany A. *Prostitution, Modernity, and the Making of the Cuban Republic, 1840–1920.* Chapel Hill: University of North Carolina Press, 2013.

Snorton, C. Riley. *Black on Both Sides: A Racial History of Trans Identity.* Minneapolis: University of Minnesota Press, 2017.

Stolcke, Verena. *Marriage, Class and Colour in Nineteenth-Century Cuba: A Study of Racial Attitudes and Sexual Values in a Slave Society.* Cambridge: Cambridge University Press, 1974.

Stoner, K. Lynn, and Luís Hipólito Serrano Pérez, eds. *Cuban and Cuban-American Women: An Annotated Bibliography.* Wilmington, DE: Scholarly Resources, 2000.

Stoner, Kathryn Lynn. *From the House to the Streets: The Cuban Woman's Movement for Legal Reform, 1898–1940.* Durham, NC: Duke University Press, 1991.

Stout, Noelle M. *After Love: Queer Intimacy and Erotic Economies in Post-Soviet Cuba.* Durham, NC: Duke University Press, 2014.

Stryker, Susan, Paisley Currah, and Lisa Jean Moore. "Introduction: Trans-, Trans, or Transgender?" *Women's Studies Quarterly* 36, no. 3 (2008): 11–22.

Urban, Kelly. "The Sick Republic: Tuberculosis, Public Health, and Politics in Cuba, 1925–1965." PhD diss., University of Pittsburgh, 2017.

Wickberg, Daniel. "Homophobia: On the Cultural History of an Idea." *Critical Inquiry* 27, no. 1 (2000): 42–57.

Zanetti Lecuona, Oscar. "Medio siglo de historiografía en Cuba: la impronta de la revolución." *Cuban Studies* 40 (2010): 74–103.